Soldiers, War, Knowledge and Citizenship:
German-American Essays on Civil-Military Relations

Donald Abenheim and Carolyn Halladay

Soldiers, War, Knowledge and Citizenship: German-American Essays on Civil-Military Relations

Donald Abenheim
and
Carolyn Halladay

2017

Carola Hartmann Miles-Verlag

Bibliografische Information der Deutschen Nationalbibliothek
Die Deutsche Nationalbibliothek verzeichnet diese Publikation in der Deutschen Nationalbibliografie; detaillierte bibliografische Daten sind im Internet über www.dnb.de abrufbar.

© 2017 Carola Hartmann Miles-Verlag
www.miles-verlag.jimdo.com
email: miles-verlag@t-online.de

Herstellung: BOD – Books on Demand, Norderstedt

Printed in Germany

ISBN 978-3-945861-63-9

Table of Contents

Foreword

"The historian should be a partner to the soldier in the attempt better to understand culture as a featured of present-day military service. To do so, however, such historians must also be experts in the culture of soldiers." With these words, the authors rightly remind us in their introduction that an historian who writes on war should also have expertise in the culture of the soldiers.

The authors of this book combined, however, have more than fifty-five years of expertise in the field of history as well as in the culture of the soldiers. Donald Abenheim was strongly influenced by the military historian Charles Burdick at San Jose State University where he pursued his M.A. At Stanford University, the late Gordon A. Craig and Peter Paret, internationally respected historians, who had researched and published widely in military history and strategy encouraged Abenheim to write his dissertation on the search for tradition of the West German armed forces. Abenheim's book *Reforging the Iron Cross* was soon translated into German and it remains today the most important publication in the field. In Germany, Abenheim is a highly respected scholar, well known in and to the entire Bundeswehr. He served as a curator at the *Presidio*, the famous former military installation of the U.S. Army in San Francisco and as a civilian liaison officer of the U.S. Army to the German Armed Forces. Since 1985 he has taught at the Naval Postgraduate School (NPS) at Monterey where he has an ongoing relationship with the Bundeswehr, the Austrian Bundesheer and the Swiss armed forces among allied and partner forces. Realizing much earlier than others the importance of civil-military relations, the Associate Professor for National Security Affairs founded in 1993 the Center for Civil-Military Relations at the NPS. Having taught American soldiers and also soldiers from allied forces for so many years Abenheim is truly an expert in the culture of soldiers.

The same can be said about Carolyn Halladay. She finished her studies of Modern European History with an M.A. and a Ph.D. at the

University of California, Santa Cruz with a study of popular culture in the German Democratic Republic, completed in no small part thanks to a Fulbright fellowship. At Stanford University she added an M.A. in International Policy Studies and a Juris Doctor. She taught history and international relations at Pennsylvania State University, Erie, and The George Washington University, in Washington, D.C. Her government service has included working as an historian at the U.S. Department of State, as a federal tax prosecutor in the U.S. Department of Justice in addition to legal assignments in the offices of general counsel at the U.S. Departments of Defense and Transportation. Halladay is senior lecturer at the Department of National Security Affairs at the Naval Postgraduate School (NPS) and teaches in the Center for Civil-Military Relations and the Center for Homeland Defense as well as in the homeland security and European curricula in National Security Affairs Department.

As can be expected by specialists of such academic experience, the chapters of this book treat a variety of interesting and fascinating subjects. Theses comprise such themes as the citizen in uniform as a military professional; the role of tradition in armed forces; the cycles of Navy Strategy; conscription and political culture; and the importance of education and the need for cultural competency in military service.

Of course the inter-cultural competency, which is needed so much by todays soldiers deployed on missions all over the world, can be fostered by many academic disciplines. But historians can and should do their fair share in this task. Different from authors like Frederick Kagan or Ralph Peters, who are posing like historians but in reality are promoting legends and myths, Abenheim and Halladay are warning us against the tendency of terrible simplifiers, trying to polarize analysis. They bravely point at the institutional failure not to engage political, social, cultural and economic realities of nations in conflict like Iraq or Afghanistan.

The study and knowledge of history forms an important component of the education of an officer which should not be finished after Officer School and Military Academy, but should be in reality a lifelong process. Only then one might be able to answer the questions of the past and shatter the vice grip of myths and legends. Abenheim and Halladay indeed link the history of conflict, military institutions, and soldiers to greater historical and contemporary developments in politics, culture, economy, and society. The book therefore really offers much more than a look at a pretty gallery of ancestors or a trendy catalog of lessons learned.

Reiner Pommerin

(Prof Emeritus Dr. Reiner Pommerin taught Modern and Contemporary History at different German Universities. He was German Kennedy Fellow at Harvard University; German Visiting Professor at St. Antony's College at Oxford University and holding the German Fulbright Distinguished Chair at Vanderbilt University. Pommerin is Colonel (Res) of the German Air Force and served 20 years as Chairman of the Advisory Board for Civic Education and Leadership of the German Minister of Defense).

1. Inter-Cultural Expertise: Soldiers and Historians

The historian should be a partner to the soldier in the attempt better to understand culture as a feature of present-day military service.[1] To do so, however, such historians must also be experts in the culture of soldiers—a different kind of inter-cultural expertise that must underlie any serious effort to bring the nuances of cultural study and understanding to the practice of soldiering.

The study of the past faces notable limits in the higher aspects of security, defense, and war that inhere in the culture of soldiers as well as the regard (or rather disregard) for the past in post-modern society, especially in the United States. These professional limits and the challenges to what one might call an understanding of inter-cultural expertise at the strategic level form the subject for this inquiry. The question at hand also has implications for democratic civil-military relations, a subject that remains germane without interruption. What follows contains a distillate of some 40 years' experience in this matter as historians in university think tanks, U.S. and European places of advanced study and the U.S. and allied governments.

This chapter offers: a.) a brief introduction to the role of historical study in intercultural expertise in the record of the U.S. and German armed forces; b.) a reflection on the historian's calling and the habits of the mind and character that strike me as central to expertise about one's own culture and the cultures of others; c.) a warning of the danger that arises when, as now, the history of war is falsely

---

[1] This chapter is based on a presentation on democratic civil-military relations and cultural protection given at the Austrian Armed Forces National Defense Academy in November 2007. A revised version was published as Donald Abenheim, "Inter-kulturelle Kompetenz: Soldaten und Historiker," in Dieter Kollmer ed., *"Vom Einsatz her Denken!" : Bedeutung und Nutzen von Militärgeschichte zu Beginn des 21 Jahrhunderts* (Potsdam: Zentrum für Militärgeschichte und Sozialwissenschaften der Bundeswehr [ZMSBw], 2013) pp. 61–72. For further reading on the history of war in contemporary Germany and the evolution of its historiography, see: Thomas Kuehne et al., eds. *Was ist Militaergeschichte?* (Paderborn/Munich: Schoeningh, 2000); Rolf Dieter Mueller, *Militärgeschichte* (Cologne/Weimar: Böhlau, 2009).

conceived and, thus deformed, becomes a weapon in what in the United States are called "culture wars." The ensuing polarization of U.S. domestic politics obscures and eschews inter-cultural expertise, to say nothing of the harm it does to the effective making of strategy more generally. In other words, the loudest tones in the current debate disserve all varieties of inter-cultural expertise.

Two Bad Examples

At the outset stand two polemical examples of the limits of history and inter-cultural expertise in the form of two U.S. figures who make generalizations about the military past of central Europe and the connections of this past to the present. These tendentious pronouncements betray to me, at least, a deficient degree of inter-cultural expertise. The first is contained in a 25 October 2007 opinion article in the *New York Times*— also in the *International Herald Tribune*[2]—by Roger Cohen. In it, he pits the existing burden-sharing calls in the North Atlantic Treaty Organization (NATO) from the Dutch, British, and Australians against the so-called national caveats and limitations for the International Security Assistance Force (ISAF) and especially for a greater German (and French and Spanish) combat role against the Taliban in the southeast of Afghanistan, and he comes up with a peculiar wish: Remember the Wehrmacht?

It was a formidable fighting force. The modern German Army, the Bundeswehr is also very effective. Thing is, it is reluctant to fight or even to place itself in danger. Given history, that may seem just fine. The U.S. helped to frame the institutions of today's Germany precisely to guarantee peace over war. But in AFG, where 3200 German troops serve in a hard-pressed NATO force, a touch of "Bundesmacht" would be welcome.[3]

---

[2] The *International Herald Tribune* became the *International New York Times* on 14 October 2013.

[3] Roger Cohen, "Time for the Bundesmacht," *New York Times,* 25 October 2007, http://www.nytimes.com/2007/10/25/opinion/25cohen.html .

A similar flourish of inadequate inter-cultural expertise about the past comes from movieland. Since the summer of this year [2007], one has the strange case of Tom Cruise's discovery of Claus Schenk von Stauffenberg.[4] Such is part of the general recent Hollywood romance with the new Berlin, but also what I believe to have been a deliberate attempt by Scientologists to target the German armed forces for ideological reasons.[5] The German Ministry of Defense (MOD) initially turned down this man's request (rightfully, I might add) to film in the former headquarters of the Ersatzheer, in the Bendlerblock, next to the present-day German MOD.

Here, cinematic popular culture of a kind collides with the central European culture of soldiers to form a gross disservice to the serious business of soldiering versus the Tinseltown make-believe version of the soldier in the Third Reich joined with the agit-prop of L. Ron Hubbard's kook army (with its rather different uniforms).

These examples call into question whether leading figures in U.S. elite political culture (i.e. opinion editors of the *The New York Times*) or American popular culture are fundamentally capable of a serious appreciation of the history of central Europe, its culture or more properly its political and strategic cultures. This question is germane to the matter of the cultures of the Middle East and Southwest Asia, for if my charges (student-officers who must embody and advance the U.S. military's intellectual and scholarly aspect) are incapable of understanding the politics, society, and culture of Europe, then the prospects for the more immediately urgent assignments are doubly problematic.

In this connection, I do not want to fall into the trap of expatriate snobbery on foreign territory, in that I mock my ill-informed

---

[4] "Valkyrie," directed by Bryan Singer (Metro Goldwyn Meyer [domestic U.S.] and 20th Century Fox [international]: 2008).

[5] The author was a witness to repeated attempts by scientology linked figures to gain information on senior Bunesdwehr officers in the 1980s while he served with USAREUR. Also see for Cruise's altercation with the Bundeswehr in the production of the film: http://www.spielfilm.de/news/7949/bundeswehr-erteilt-tom-cruise-drehverbot .

countrymen in front of you. Such a thing is too facile, and does nothing to resolve the festering problem. On the contrary, I appeal to the high standards given to me by my European teachers in my long struggle to understand the role of culture in politics in modern times and the culture of soldiers—that is, in my own attempt to become an inter-cultural expert.

The U.S. Experience in Short, 1940 to Now

For this veteran historian in public service and military educator, the post-2004 call for inter-cultural expertise in military operations[6] also can provoke a shrug of exhaustion amid the protracted campaigns in Iraq and Afghanistan, where the persistence of inter-cultural in-expertise continues to complicate the discourse and, thus, the prospects for sustainable resolutions.

This fatigue becomes even more profound when one considers the record since the 1950s as concerns the role of the sciences, the humanities, and the arts in the higher aspects of war, the making of strategy and the soldierly profession in the United States. From the eclipse, in the first atomic clouds of the 1940s, of such traditional figures in the cultural pantheon of soldiers as Henri de Jomini, Alfred Thayer Mahan, and Billy Mitchell, to the rise of the military manager as business school graduate and the nuclear scientist and the systems analyst as arbiters of war and peace, the mid-century strategic debate sought to replace the archaic notions of soldiering before The Bomb with newer ideas more suited to a strategic environment that had to be without precedent, granted the pure mega-tonnage at stake. That is, war could wrongly be said to be a union of physics, management theory, and economics.

This triumvirate predominated until the late 1960s, when the advent of Mao's protracted war unsettled the whole arrangement. The discomfiture of the military manager/defense manger and economist in the Vietnam debacle then saw the revival of the historian as

---

[6] Paula Holmes-Eber, *Culture in Conflict: Irregular Warfare, Culture Policy, and the Marine Corps* (Stanford, CA: Stanford University Press, 2014).

partner to the strategist in the return of strategic idealism in the mid-1970s, evident in the reform of curriculum in the U.S. Naval War College with the addition of the humanities, as well as in the so-called Clausewitz renaissance associated with the re-invention of doctrine (FM100-5) in the U.S. Army of the late 1970s and early 1980s.[7]

The success in combat in the 1990–1991 Gulf War led to an over-optimistic return to the management sciences as the source of all strategic wisdom, though this time, the emphasis fell less on "whiz kids" ca. 1961 than on computer and communications wizardry of our rising digital age. Now, the nuclear strategist found himself con-signed to the dustbin of defense-intellectual fashion, as the so-called revolution in military affairs (RMA) declared the atom-splitters to be old-fashioned and, worse, wholly irrelevant to strategic situation that only the Nintendo-fluent generations could adequately grasp. [8] A great deal of nonsense based loosely on the past—or a misreading of it[9]—accumulated around this idea until the summer of 2003, when the campaign in Iraq stumbled into the insurgency.

Since then, the failure of this stillborn revolution in the fight against the Jihadists—and the disgrace of the RMA's proponents in the bloody back streets of Baghdad and in the mountains of Afghani-stan—has been startling to some, but entirely expected by others more at home in the history of war and in the roles of society and culture in warfare. And now the humanities and social sciences have once again achieved a kind of boom phase in the protraction of the

---

[7] See Donald Abenheim, "Geschichtserziehung, Traditionspflege, 'lessons learned', historische Bildung in den US Streitkraeften unter dem Aspekt der neueren Kriege" in Joerg Echternkampf et al eds. *Perspektiven der Militaergeschichte: Raum, Gewalt, und Representation in historischer Forschung und Bildung* (Oldenbourg: Munich, 2010), pp. 343ff.

[8] See MacGregor Knox and Williamson Murray *The Dynamics of Military Revolution, 1300-2050* (Cambridge and London: Cambridge University Press, 2001).

[9] See, for example, the US Department of Defense press release from the year 2000 on "full spectrum dominance," at
http://archive.defense.gov/news/newsarticle.aspx?id=45289

anti-jihadist U.S.-led military campaigns that began at the end of the year 2001 and have been escalated again a decade and a half later. Indeed, one sees the rise of the anthropologist-at-arms as the partner to the counterinsurgency specialist and the nation-builder.

The Past versus History

This development marks a kind of throwback to the late 19th century as exemplified in the British experience in the empire of the late 19th and early 20th centuries—consider here such luminaries as T.E. Lawrence and Getrude Bell.[10] I do not wish to reflect on them as a model, *per se*, because I am a historian of central Europe, not of Edwardian Britain nor of its elites in universities and in the colonial armed forces. But reflection on their lives in the context of their time might aid us better to understand their circumstances of service, and, as a result, our own, as well. That is, the political, social, and intellectual world that produced Lawrence and Bell has little in common with the experience of my U.S. student officers, and hence has limited utility in the 21st century.

Such is the case, in part, because the brains of the U.S. forces are oriented toward goals other than an understanding of culture and society in organized violence. In contrast to the armies of most European nations, the U.S. forces have an enormous historical establishment—or what one might call a historical capability—that has vast offerings in training, education, and defense management somehow connected to the analysis, interpretation, and rendering into the realm of the symbolic of the past, described by others as history. Do look at the websites of the service centers for military history, especially that of the United States Army, the service that plainly has the most well developed program in this area.[11]

---

[10] Douglas Porch, *Counterinsurgency* (Cambridge and London: Cambridge University Press, 2013).
[11] See the U.S. Army Center of Military History (CMH) website at: http://www.history.army.mil/ .

The overall impression even to me as a veteran of this system is astonishing, especially in comparison, say, with Germany and Austria in terms of size. But the number of personnel as well as the variety of their activities should not be the final determinant of the question before us. Quantity and quality remain two different categories. To what intellectual end within the goals of policy within a democracy does this effort successfully operate, and by what means?

In the U.S. case, those expert in the past are principally engaged in the application or exploitation of the past for the formation of operational doctrine as well as for the maintenance of soldierly tradition, i.e. *Sinnstiftung*. I call this activity *die Verwertung der Vergangenheit*. It entails a didactic application of the past on a huge scale and on a technocratic basis, in which the idea of culture, in a central European sense, has played scarcely any role at all.[12]

Consider in this connection the job description of the U.S. Army Chief of Military History, who "is responsible for ensuring the appropriate use of military history in the teaching of strategy, tactics, logistics, and administration" and whose "mission includes the requirement that military leaders at all levels be aware of the value of history in advancing military profession."[13] To put the matter another

---

[12] See, for example, the U.S. Army CMH mission statement at: http://www.history.army.mil/about.html .

[13] U.S. Army Center of Military History, *Strategic Plan 2007–2011* (Washington DC: HQ, Department of the Army, 2007) pp. 2–4. The 2017 mission statement includes:

- To improve our business processes and create a superior history and museum structure to meet the demands of a globally engaged Army in the twenty-first century.
- To align the Center with Army knowledge management initiatives by leveraging twenty-first-century best practices and technology to transform our culture and historical information into an asset that has relevance to the Army.
- To reaffirm the invaluable and indisputable value of the Army Historical Program to the Army and the nation.
- To achieve greater effectiveness, enhance credibility, and expand the influence of the Army historical community.

way: the institutional exploitation of the past for didactic purposes—often described as military history and disseminated as the inevitable "lessons learned"—serves the formation of pertinent systems of military doctrine and the cataloging of lessons of war on the operational or tactical levels.[14]

This practice has a glorious past that speaks to the culture of soldiers in my country. It also speaks to the limitations of this time-honored approach to the past for intercultural expertise. The experts do not even ask the necessary questions of their subject or their material to achieve inter-cultural insights. Inter-cultural inquiry seldom enters into the basic analytical calculus.

Cohen's statement about the Wehrmacht in comparison to the Bundeswehr reflects this phenomenon. The admiration in the Anglo-Saxon world for the German soldier of the early 20th century inevitably fails to grasp the political and social context, that is, the central European culture of the soldier.[15]

This problematic heritage stands in contrast to the metaphysics of Carl von Clausewitz and, in my opinion, more reflects the pseudoscientific approach of Henri de Jomini and his many acolytes as it endures into the present in endless systems of formalistic schemas of war.[16] This peculiar instrumentalization of the past began with the foundation of West Point in 1802 on the basis of a French school of applied military engineering and continued through to the foundation of the U.S. Naval War College in 1890, of the U.S. Army War

---

- To provide a highly motivated and loyal workforce that has superior professional capabilities and skills.

Source: https://history.army.mil/banner_images/focus/CP-61/dalessandro_cp-61.html

[14] Abenheim, "Geschichtserziehung," p. 345. See also Brian Linn, *The Echo of Battle: The American Way of War* (Cambridge, MA: Harvard University Press, 2007).

[15] Donald Abenheim, " 50 Jahre Offiziersausbildung der Bundeswehr aus internationaler Sicht" in Eckart Opitz, ed. *50 Jahre Bundeswehr-50 Jahre Offiziersausbildung* (Hamburg: Temmen, 2007) pp. 92–106.

[16] John Shy, "Jomini," in Peter Paret ed. *Makers of Modern Strategy from Machiavelli to the Nuclear Age* (Princeton, Princeton UP, 1986) pp. 143-185.

College in 1901, and of the Industrial College of the U.S. Army in 1924[17]—all institutions that accord pride of place to applied sciences or subjects that can be dressed as such.

The U.S.-sponsored recycling of German general staff officers from the prison camp to NATO's entryway in the late 1940s was guided by a similar practical concern. The "lessons learned" by Wehrmacht general staff officers were abstracted in American minds from their political and social context and made into universal principles applicable in 1950s NATO, Europe, or other fronts in the Cold War.[18]

RMA and the Dead End of Dogma

In the 1990s, this process—that is, the construction of ideal types based on so-called lessons from history—took a turn into the extreme amid the "revolution in military affairs," originally a Soviet idea popularized by the U.S. Department of Defense Office of Net Assessment led by Andrew Marshall, one of the original group at RAND in Santa Monica in the 1950s. The ensuing application of the legacy of railroads and rifles, and of armored vehicles and radios, to contemporary conflict had its origins in the middle and late 1970s. This false dogma of technological progress as the dominant force of warfare represented a wrong-headed attempt to generalize about the role of technology in conflict, while seeking a kind of new paradigm for combat that would have the same persuasiveness as nuclear deterrence doctrine of the 1950s and 1960s.[19]

---

[17] Carol Reardon, *Soldiers and Scholars: The U.S. Army and the Uses of Military History* (Lawrence, KS: University Press of Kansas, 1990).
[18] Christian Greiner, "'Operational History (German) Section' and 'Naval Historical Team,'" Deutsches militärstrategisches Denken in Dienst der amerikanischen Streitkräfte von 1945-1950" in MGFA eds. *Militärgeschichte: Probleme-Thesen-Wege* (Munich: Oldenbourg, 1982) pp. 409–435. The published versions of the "Foreign Military Studies," prepared by captive Wehrmacht officers in U.S. service in the years after 1945, were widely found in U.S. Army Europe Headquarters and subordinate echelons as late as the 1980s. These works were still in print as of 1990s.
[19] Knox and Murray *Military Revolution*.

This idea also embodied an attempt to uphold the strategic idealism of the late 19th and early 20th century in the face of rapid political, social, and economic change at the end of the 20th century. This dubious ideal then and now embodied a compact, self-referential doctrine of the elite control over machine warfare and later over digitalized combat that sought to canalize or otherwise control the uncontrollable escalatory forces of imperialism, integral nationalism, technology, racism, anger, and hatred as factors of actual warfare.[20] Such an idea and its application in practice also wished away or sought to make only incidental the question of culture and society in warfare, especially the culture and society of likely opponents once the Soviet Union collapsed.

The failure of this dogma and its proponents (symbolized by the downfall of Donald Rumsfeld[21]) in the face of irregular warfare as well as the respective traditions of organized violence in Middle Eastern and southwest Asian societies requires a full institutional and scholarly interpretation that has yet to unfold. But surely the technocratic system of lessons learned and best practices amid the selective exploitation of the past as an adjunct to management sciences has turned up a great big dud. Such a system is poorly suited to produce inter-culture expertise even if, in the years after 2005, the attempt began to remedy this problem amid the counter-insurgency doctrine put forward by General David Petraeus while in command of U.S. Army Training and Doctrine Command.[22]

---

[20] See Donald Abenheim and Carolyn Halladay, "Clausewitz: Primordial Violence, Hatred and Enmity," starting on p. 117 of this volume.
[21] Sheryl Gay Stolberg and Jim Rutenberg, "Rumsfeld Resigns as Defense Secretary After Big Election Gains for Democrats," *New York Times*, 8 November 2006, available at:
http://www.nytimes.com/2006/11/08/us/politics/09BUSHCND.html
[22] Porch, *Counterinsurgency*.

The German Experience as Contrast

Lest my critique above strike you as too negative or defeatist, the example of Oberst i.G. Hans-Meier Welcker,[23] the first chief of the Military History Office (Militärgeschichtliches Forschungsamt der Bundeswehr or MGFA) in the year 1957 until 1964, opens a different and more suggestive perspective as concerns inter-cultural expertise and the culture of soldiers. Whereas in the wake of the Cruise movie and Berlin tourism, Stauffenberg's name may yet become a household word in various locales, even in the Bundeswehr, Meier-Welcker is scarcely known save to those of us professionally associated with the Militärgeschichtliches Forschungsamt der Bundeswehr/Zentrum fuer Militärgeschichte und Sozialwissenschaften der Bundeswehr or in the education and training establishment of the Bundeswehr. Nonetheless, his legacy offers us a way forward to inter-cultural expertise that can contribute to the harmony between democracy and the professional soldier.

Of primary importance to us here is the manner in which Meier-Welcker, a veteran of the Reichswehr and a general staff officer in the Wehrmacht (as well a colleague of Stauffenberg), contributed to the eradication of the Nazi abuse of scholarship and to the democratic consolidation of West German democracy in the 1950s and the 1960s by the integration of the German soldier into the spirit and letter of the German Basic Law. He did so in an attempt to answer the question of what and whether a soldier and historian could learn from history in the wake of the experience of arms and the state from 1918 until 1945.[24]

His question formed but part of what presently came to be known as *Innere Führung*, in which civic education forms a significant

---

[23] Martin Rink, "Hans Meier-Welcker – Soldat und Wissenschaftler," *Militärgeschichte* 2/2007, p. 31; Hans Meier-Welcker, *Aufzeichnungen eines Generalstabsoffiziers 1939–1942* Vol. XXVI in *Einzelschriften zur militärischen Geschichte des Zweiten Weltkrieges* (Freiburg im Breisgau: Rombach, 1982).

[24] Echternkamp et al., eds. *Perspektiven der Militärgeschichte*, pp. 41ff. Hans Meier Welcker, *Soldat und Geschichte: Aufsätze* (Boppard: Boldt, 1976) pp. 11–25.

part of this unifying ideal of constitutional imperatives and enlightened principles of leadership, command and morale. [25] *Innere Führung* relies, in part, on *historische Bildung*, a process for which no comparable activity exists in the U.S. forces. *Historische Bildung* forms a component of the *Bildung* (education) of an officer or a soldier amid a life-long process. One seeks to answer the questions of the past, even the very recent past, and to shatter the vice grip of myths and legends. One does so with an ideologically neutral, scholarly reading of primary sources that adheres to the standards of academic research at the highest level. [26]

Historische Bildung also keeps in mind that past events unfolded as a consequence of cultural, political, social, economic, technical, legal, and religious factors. As a result, the history of conflict, military institutions, and soldiers becomes linked to greater historical and contemporary developments in politics, culture, economy, and society. [27] Thus *historische Bildung* represents something very different from a catalog of lessons learned or a gallery of ancestors.

This aspect of the soldier scholar in *Innere Führung* broke abruptly with past custom and tradition. Before 1945, the use of history-at-arms in the Prussian/German experience had been, in the first instance, to provide the dynastic elites with their claim to political and social privileges of the old regime. [28]

---

[25] Donald Abenheim *Reforging the Iron Cross: The Search for Military Tradition,* 3d. ed. (Princeton, NJ: Princeton University Press, 2014) See also Frank Nägler, *Der gewollte Soldat und Sein Wandel* (Munich: Oldenbourg, 2010). BMVg, eds. Zentrale Dienstvorschrift 10/1 *Innere Führung: Selbstverständnius und Führungskultur der Bundeswehr* (Bonn: BMVg, 2008).

[26] Hans Meier-Welcker, "Über die Kriegsgeschichte als Wissenschaft und Lehre," *Wehrwissenschaftliche Rundschau,* V 1955, pp. 1-8; *idem.* "Entwicklung und Stand der Kriegsgeschichte als Wissenschaft," *Wehrwissenschaftliche Rundschau* IV 1956, pp. 1–10.

[27] Hans Hubertus Mack, "Historische Bildung in der Bundeswehr" in *Militärgeschichte* 2/2007 pp. 4–7.

[28] Abenheim, *Reforging the Iron Cross.*

In the second instance, it furnished the military managerial elite of the late 19th and early 20th centuries with their claim to professional expertise in the art and science of war during the age of the machine and mass politics.[29] To be precise, the interpretation of the history of war in the late 19th century lay in the hands of the Prussian-German general staff, whose emphasis on lessons learned as well as the formation of a compact, self-referential doctrine has been handed down to the U.S. armed forces of this day.[30]

Finally, the history of war, super-charged with the experience of the front fighter as well as integral nationalism and racism, became a means to instill a totalitarian, militarist ethos in the citizens of greater Germany.[31]

After receiving a doctorate at Tübingen in 1952, Meier-Welcker joined Ulrich de Maizière, one of the fathers of *Innere Führung*, in the Amt Blank in Bonn, the forerunner of the Ministry of Defense. The two had been educated together as general staff officers in 1937–1939. Meier-Welcker led the small history section in the Ermekeilkaserne in what eventually became the Ministry of Defense in Bonn. He became head of the new MGFA in Langenau near Ulm in 1957 and built, in the years until his retirement in 1964 in Freiburg in Breisgau, an intellectual bridge to the life of the mind according to the standards of universities in the Federal Republic of Germany and beyond.

Meier-Welcker had the following to say about the value of history in the culture of soldiers, and his ideas reveal a path to greater

---

[29] Hajo Holborn, "The Prusso-German School: Moltke and the Rise of the General Staff," in Paret ed., *Makers of Modern Strategy* (Princeton, NJ: Princeton University Press, 1986), pp. 281-295; Gerhard P. Gross, *Mythos und Wirklichkeit. Die Geschichte des operativen Denkens im deutschen Heer von Moltke d. Ä. bis Heusinger* (Paderborn: Schoeningh, 2012).

[30] U.S. Department of the Army, *Field Manual FM 100-5* (Leavenworth, Kansas: U.S. Army TRADOC, 1986).

[31] Rolf Dieter Mueller and Karl Volkmann, *Die Wehrmacht: Mythos und Wirklichkeit* (Munich: Oldenbourg, 1999).

inter-cultural expertise through the study of the past that adheres to high scholarly standards:

Our skepticism as concerns the educational possibilities via the study of history does not concern history itself, but rather concerns ourselves. It may be that history no longer can cause enthusiasm in us, that is, according to Goethe, the best that it can give us. If it can be said to have any value for education, ... then such can only exist when it compels human beings to face themselves; to remind them of their potential and their limits, as well as to show them in their entanglement and dependency, but also to show them in their freedom. Where is such more possible than in the history of war? Surely one must reach the essence of the past events. *Das Denken im Ganzen bleibt immer das Gegenstück zum Handeln im einzelnen.*[32]

Surely if there exists a single idea before us that speaks to the contribution of the historian to inter-cultural expertise, it is this last sentence, which draws its inspiration from the world of German classicism. The message and meaning here further is wholly alien to the technocratic, lessons learned catalog mindset that characterizes—and limits—historical and inter-cultural understanding today.

In my own experience as a promoter of inter-cultural expertise in the U.S. forces, I have found a general institutionalized resistance to conceive of matters in the sense of the whole, in favor of an overemphasis on tactics and technology as well as on the strategic buzzword fad of the moment and the hierarchical miniutiae of endless military reorganization, all at the expense of inter-cultural expertise.[33]

The accomplishment of Meier-Welcker and the men and women who have followed him in the last half-century has been to establish a standard of intellectual excellence in historical research and education in the Bundeswehr in the face of some fairly major obsta-

---

[32] Cited in Mack, "Historische Bildung," p. 5.

[33] The most fluent critique of this tendency remains Bernard Brodie, *Strategy in the Missile Age* . (Princeton, NJ: Princeton University Press, 1959). Also see the 2017 mission statement of the US Army Center of Military History.

cles. This approach connects the historian in military service to German professional soldiers; it has also built a path to the scholarly world and facilitated the democratic integration of armed forces in a united Europe and beyond. Such labor has unfolded with adequate bureaucratic resources and with some controversy, especially about the perennial question of the Wehrmacht in National Socialism.

To be sure, a younger generation of editorial writers and even younger screen idols know far too little of this issue, nor are they likely to learn. Meier-Welcker is a worthy heir to Hans Delbrück, Carl von Clausewitz, and Gerhard von Scharnhorst in the manner in which the intellectual rigor of these men and their sense of the whole are exemplary for inter-cultural expertise in the 21st century.

Put another way, if one embraces the best that historical scholarship has to offer as regards the link between war in the past to society, culture, economy, and politics, then one has made a step in the direction of education for inter-cultural expertise—the hegemony of management or physical sciences notwithstanding—to an understanding of the nature of war in theory and practice, and to the role of culture in these issues. Historians who follow Meier-Welcker's example can well be partners of the soldier in the quest for inter-cultural expertise.

Conclusion: Beware the Terrible Simplifiers

The story above points to an even greater question in my own country as concerns the culture of soldiers and their ability to deal with the ongoing and aimless conflict that is really quite traditional in character, 11 September 2001 and so called "new wars," notwithstanding.[34] This question has profound implications for how the culture of soldiers is perverted by the institutional failure to engage the political, social, cultural, and economic realities of such nations as Iraq and Afghanistan or, since 2014, of Russia or Ukraine and various

---

[34] On the so-called new wars, see, for example, Martin van Creveld, *The Transformation of War* (New York: Free Press, 1991); Herfried Münkler, *Die neuen Kriege* (Reinbek: Rowohlt, 2002).

central and eastern European nations, as well, for instance in the Baltic democracies.

However, one can pose this question to the cases of Mexico, North Africa, central Europe, Japan, Korea, Vietnam, and elsewhere in the past record of the U.S. soldier. I warn here especially against the tendency of certain journalistic terrible simplifiers and pied pipers to polarize analysis on these issues of politics, war, and culture especially via the weaponization of the record of war in the past and its relationship to democratic society and politics.

The absence of a pluralistic foundation in society and government for the writing of history about contemporary conflict and the military past opens the gates to the seizure of soldierly honor and the martial tradition by figures who have no interest in our agenda here. Hence my reproach of Cruise for trying to put on the carmine-red collar patches stained with blood of a man like Stauffenberg.

This episode reflects a more generalized and worrisome trend, a larger tendency in the public mind of western democracies in crisis in which make-believe and reality merge with disastrous effects. Certain writers about the past and present intend a kind domestic political Cold War in the United States and elsewhere as part of what is called the long war against jihadism as well as in the face of post-2013 Russian political manipulation of the collective will to defense of NATO nations combined with the postmodern electronic warfare linked with the limited use of armed forces. These men reflect the union of political and psychological forces in what Clausewitz so well described as the nature of war to seek its absolute form.

The abuse or overuse of the catalog of lessons learned can degrade into the formation of legend and myth for partisan political purposes at the expense of democracy and military effectiveness on a constitutional basis. The German experience in the years 1890 until 1920 is duplicating itself in my country, at least as visible in the pathetic speech of the year 2007 by General Ricardo Sanchez to a meeting of military reporters, whom this man blamed for the misfortunes in Iraq.[35] That is, the neo-MacArthurian legends of "never again" digs deeper the domestic political trenches in U.S. partisan terrain, where the search is on for the guilty of all stripes.[36]

The history of the so-called long war is presently being written, in part, by such men as Victor Davis Hanson,[37] Frederick Kagan,[38] and Ralph Peters[39] in a manner that is incompatible with democratic civil-military relations. These men promote legends and myths especially with a tendentious interpretation of war in antiquity and a hypertrophy of nostalgia for the Second World War.

All of this says more about political culture in the United States than about the political culture, culture at arms, and society of our opponents. These legends and myths, written by figures who pose as historians—but who are really partisan political figures, propagandists, and journalists—direct their anger and hatred against domestic political foes and the U.S. constitution and the American ideal of the citizen in uniform. The legends they promote are a result, in part, of the intellectual shortcomings and weaknesses of an official exploitation of the past of poor academic quality in which the otherwise central bond between imperatives of soldiering and the duties of citizenship is damaged in civil-military relations.

The integration of soldiers and defense civilians into multinational defense organizations and combat and post conflict operations in their variety requires intercultural expertise on a large scale. The example of central Europeans in the past 50 years (or at least to

---

[35] Ricardo S. Sanchez, "Military Reporters and Editors Forum Luncheon Address," delivered 12 October 2007 in Arlington, VA; audio and transcript available at: http://americanrhetoric.com/speeches/wariniraq/ricardosanchezmilitaryreportersf orum.htm

[36] On MacArthur and the "never again" school, see Donald Abenheim, "NATO: War, Generals, and Critics in 1999," in Abenheim, *Soldier and Politics Transformed* (Berlin: Miles-Verlag, 2007), pp. 51–78, esp. pp. 53 and 58.

[37] See, for example, Victor Davis Hanson, *The Savior Generals* (New York: Bloomsbury Press, 2013).

[38] See, for example, Frederick Kagan, *Finding the Target: The Transformation of American Military Policy* (New York: Encounter Books, 2006).

[39] See, for example, Ralph Peters, *Endless War* (New York: Stackpole Books, 2011).

about 2013) somehow to have robbed nationalism-at-arms of its capacity to cause total war reflects the success of inter-cultural expertise of a kind of European cosmopolitanism that requires a redoubled defense in the year 2017 in the face of its enemies across the globe. This virtue must be extended beyond the narrow frontiers of what was once called the Article VI area of the North Atlantic Treaty.

Inter-cultural expertise can thus be seen, despite the shortfalls of such startling ignorance as that of Cohen and Cruise, as being part of Article II of the North Atlantic Treaty, that is the famous Canadian clause on the promotion of democracy as a core aspect of the Washington Treaty. Inter-cultural expertise in the hands of soldiers can also be the means, within the limits of the task, to extend values of security, peace, and freedom to areas that have traditionally been devoid of it or are at risk of discarding these virtues amid the trials of democracy, economy, and culture in the 21st century.

Such inter-cultural expertise can also be fostered by many academic disciplines in aid of security and defense education for reform of government and military service. The historian can and should do his or her fair share in this task, while we all should turn our backs on propaganda masquerading as soldierly virtue in time of waxing political polarization and incipient generalized political violence for totalitarian goals in 21st-century guise.

I.   *Innere Führung* and Tradition

2. Professional Soldiers and Citizens in Uniform: Some Thoughts on *Innere Führung* from a Transatlantic Perspective[*]

Innere Führung should remain the professional code of all German soldiers especially at a time of upheaval in the German nation, on the European continent, and beyond. The record of leadership, command, morale, ethics, and obedience among the soldiers of the Western alliance since 11 September 2001, has become ensnarled in various civil-military interpretations of how soldiers have managed irregular warfare and counterinsurgency campaigns now and in the past. This debate gives rise to the well-meaning, if frequently facile, arguments by some who, in the face of jihadist violence and "hybrid war," would junk *Innere Führung* as a nostalgic absurdity. Instead, the times call for more, not less, *Innere Führung*, adapted and modernized to continue the German legacy of soldiers in democracy among young combat veterans unsure of their place in state and society in the wake of their experience of irregular warfare in Afghanistan and elsewhere.

For anyone familiar with the history of the Bundeswehr and its almost forgotten origins, the story of *Innere Führung* comprises the accounts of its critics and the misunderstandings that either consciously or unconsciously surround this ideal of soldierly professionalism in the Federal Republic of Germany (FRG). These core principles of command, obedience, and ethics rightly emphasize the remarkable trinity of political purpose, constitutional essentials, and soldierly command and discipline in the blast of fighting, anger, and hatred native to war and political violence in its variety.

---

[*] Originally published as Donald Abenheim and Carolyn Halladay, "Berufssoldaten und Staatsbürger in Uniform," in Zentrum für ethische Bildung in den Streitkräften, eds., *Ethik und Militär: Kontroversen der Militaerethik und Sicherheitskultur* 1 (February 2016), available at
http://www.ethikundmilitaer.de/en/themenueberblick/20161-innere-fuehrung/abenheim-halladay-berufssoldaten-und-staatsbuerger-in-uniform-die-innere-fuehrung-aus-transatlantischer-perspektive/

The Citizen in Uniform and the Military Professional—A German-American Comparison, Why Bother?

German military professionalism forms a unique case in its civil-military aspect as well as its ethical refinement that can be better understood by comparison to other nations and across the history of the Bundeswehr itself. The German institutions at arms of command, obedience, and morale have evolved from the trinity of the people, the government, and the army, itself; they are poorly served by tendentious polemics, military romanticism, and cultural pessimism.

Although German and American soldiers no longer serve together in the depth and breadth of the Cold War, this professional bond endures, albeit in altered form, despite the vogue of anti-Americanism prevailing on German talk shows and in Alternative für Deutschland (AfD) campaign umbrage. It has been present in NATO Stabilization Force (SFOR) and ISAF campaigns and is undergoing a revival with NATO's Article V response on the eastern border of the alliance with the rapid reaction NATO Very High Readiness Joint Task Force (VJTF). Today the chief of staff at the U.S. Army Europe in Wiesbaden is a senior German officer, while the very best German officers still attend training and education in the professional military education of the U.S. armed forces.

Constitution, Militia, and the Regulars

The story of the soldiers in America and the ideals of command have long existed between the constitutional pole of the militia man-at-arms (and now also woman-at-arms), on the one hand, and the regular soldier as heir to the European dynastic tradition of arms, on the other. Since the rise of the all-volunteer force in the early 1970s, the latter ideal of the professional has predominated in the self-image of the American soldier and the practice of command. This doctrine of the professional soldier has also become internalized in American society, while the heritage of the citizen soldier as a product of conscription has faded in its attraction without this widely shared rite of citizenship, service, and obedience.

The American birthright of the citizen-at-arms owes much to the heritage of medieval England, where the impact of the wars of religion and the Enlightenment transformed this institution within a national army and also led the authors of the Constitution of the United States to embrace it. In this respect, the militia—that is, to-day's National Guard—has long formed the heart of the U.S. military. Since the American Civil War, it has been subject to much greater federal control than in its earlier iterations. The tradition of the citizen-at-arms—and an American version of the citizen in uniform—is, in this sense, the original American ideal of the soldier.

The competing model—of an elite corps of soldierly professionals—was founded in the U.S. Military Academy in the 19th century and remained in line with the growth of the military during the 20th century in the age of total war. This now-legendary place was originally patterned after the model of an early 19th-century French military school for applied military engineering and siege warfare. An ample dose of management science was then added to this foundation in the 20th century. The professionalization, specialization, and self-differentiation of the U.S. military began, and the tension between the citizen soldier and the military professional that describes these divergent developments thus arose.

Duty, Honor, Country

Nowhere is this professional ideal of "Duty, Honor, Country" better codified than in Samuel Huntington's still widely cited volume of the mid-20th century, *The Soldier and the State*. Based on how West Point imagines itself as the thin gray line between order and anarchy, the volume contains an interpretation of the ethos of the professional soldier in a democracy with Prussian overtones. Most significantly, the core of U.S. soldierly professionalism resides in exemplary conservative social and political values. The regular American soldier should embrace a strictly neutral posture toward partisan politics and arm himself or herself against the weakening influences of pluralist society.

The soldier, in turn, demands of civilian political authority that the cabinet and the legislative provide specialized military forces with a kind of depoliticized professional dominion. This arena of the professional soldier should be untrammeled by too many civilians and their ceaseless disorder, so as to preclude the politicization of the soldier, as the well as to prevent the pollution of this realm by hedonism, materialism, and pacifism.

Although this formulation is 60 years old, it more than coincides with aspects of the contemporary debate in Germany about how, in the view of critics, *Innere Führung* has gone *kaputt* while German soldiers have defended the nation on the Hindu-Kush.

Contemporary Conflict and the Idea of the "Stab in the Back"

Irregular warfare as waged by Western democracies in distant lands, nonetheless, harbors an inherent danger for which *Innere Führung*, as the core of a soldierly code, offers an excellent defense against the danger of the blowback when the distant battle field comes home to the detriment of society and the constitution in the face of domestic turmoil, as well as the rise of fringe political movements hostile to the fundamentals of German politics and society as they have existed in peace and security for decades.

All too common, particularly among disgruntled ex-soldiers and nervous civilians, is the civil-military syndrome in which internal conflict, radical ideology, and lack of an obvious front line deeply burden conventions of military action, even when such action concerns security building in the face of variously hostile local populations. The "stab in the back" myth has been the response to this phenomenon in such democracies as France, Great Britain, and the United States. It also has a particularly—and particularly unfortunate— role in Germany's early and embattled mass politics in the age of total war.

The "stab in the back" has no place in today's German military. *Innere Führung*, with its emphasis on the primacy of constitutionally validated statecraft, a code of command, and obedience anchored in constitutional norms, shows its enduring strength in just this circumstance.

At the same time, even the most peace-minded society must react with a disciplined measure of understanding and support for the soldier's need for the sense that their service is not demonized for domestic political advantage or simply ignored in the pursuit of profit or pleasure. Slogans about civil society and a superior German moral political culture are so easily voiced, but they may not dominate the public discussion to the exclusion of any gradations of debate or otherwise exacerbate the tendency of soldiers to see themselves as ignored and shunted aside for the glories of lifestyle and ecological excellence.

Drones, Computers, Anger, and Hatred in Warfare

Has the need to defend democracy with soldiers grounded in duties and rights of the Western democracies become any less urgent in the face of special warfare irregulars without collar patches amid a barrage of digital chaos and psychological operations of special refinement? Have the principles of an army in a democracy been eradicated by those blood-thirsty men and women with their black flag of death who want nothing else but to destroy the rule of law and replace it with an orgy of pseudo-religious violence? Can the ballistic progress of weapons from crossbow to H-bomb and now to unmanned aerial vehicles (UAVs)/drones and the digital grand slam of Stuxnet eclipse the human element in war altogether?

How will this process eclipse and/or eradicate the essentials of human genius, character, intellect, and discipline in the soldier? These imponderables of machines and society confront German and American soldiers, and how they answer these questions also derives from a shared experience of ideas, government, military institutions, weapons, and combat.

Weapons in their variety are always tools wielded by human beings. The human element remains constant and dominant. Men- and women-at-arms will always be compelled to grapple with the actual forces of real war described by Clausewitz chance, political purpose, and the combination of anger and hatred in the use of force on a limited or unlimited scale to some coherent end. Through the forces of acceleration and compression, the digital age has augmented the dynamic of anger and hatred in human affairs in a manner that should cause anyone interested in the ideals of the soldier to pause and respond with great care.

As Carl Schmitt noted with a frightening brilliance in an earlier crisis that warns our epoch, technology cannot erase or neutralize conflicts that are inherent to society and politics. The reality of artificially intelligent machines in combat hardly upends war as a political process or that genius and friction remain features of war that should adhere to some coherent, limited political goal.

The *fata morgana* of science-fiction combat only waged by computers, without the need for a conventional army, cannot mask the incontrovertible fact that the contemporary transformation of irredentist and revanchist warfare as well as the revival or paramilitary formations in Europe itself are changing the face of organized violence in ways poorly apprehended by technology-first partisans in the self-image of soldiers. One response, as visible in the revival of total defense doctrines, is an armed citizenry in northern Europe, and the realization that the lack of a mobilization base on the traditional pattern in Western armies, to include that of the United States, constitutes a significant problem of escalation dominance in the snarling maw of great-power conflict. What are the implications of this startling and unforeseen process as concerns the ideal of the citizen in uniform and the role of men and women with arms in contemporary conflict?

Innere Führung is not Outdated

All these things in their dizzying variety argue for the revitalization of *Innere Führung* as an ideal and practice of the integration of the soldier into democracy at home and in the Euro-Atlantic world. This requirement is especially urgent as a variety of new foes of this order have embarked on a violent and persuasive campaign to junk the post-1945 system in Europe and beyond with catastrophic consequences. We in the United States would do well to emulate many of the principles of *Innere Führung* in the ongoing life of the U.S. soldier, whether a professional or a citizen one. As part of *Innere Führung*, the education of officers and soldiers as well as defense civilians remains an imperative not only for the requirements of professional excellence, but for effective democratic civil-military relations in the higher aspects of conflict and defense institutions. Ignorance forms no basis to make the kind of subtle comparison of the respective record of the soldier, command, and society in allied nations as attempted in this essay.

The critics of *Innere Führung* in this writer's country as well as among NATO and European Union (EU) allies, who see this institution of integration, command, obedience, and morale as either irrelevant or outdated, are making an old mistake from the 1950s and 1960s that has lost none of its harmful nature in the present century. Those who hold in their hands the levers and pullies of security and defense must answer this old error with clarity—and refute it, not the least because Germany's role in the 21st century assigns special meaning to the nature of power in all its facets, even in a nation that celebrates the primacy of civil power.

Members of society cannot blindly neglect this requirement and hope to keep enjoying healthy and peaceful civil-military relations. This society has the most to gain from "rediscovering" *Innere Führung*—and the most to lose from failing to understand its enduring relevance to Germany, both today and tomorrow.

3. German Soldierly Tradition in the 21st Century: The View of an Outsider*

German soldiers of today can be proud of their service far from home, not the least because their profession stands anchored in a valid soldierly heritage with its foundations in German democracy in a united Europe. Despite skepticism in public about the Afghan NATO/ISAF operation, the imperative for the limited use of force to the ends of policy in 21st-century conflict adds legitimacy to what now is called *"Eine Armee im Einsatz."* With this new prominence, how does the heritage of the Bundeswehr—in particular, the historical exemplars of values, ethics, the symbols, the lineage and honors of this *Parlamentsarmee*—appear to friends, allies, or even enemies?

In this writer's four decades of experience, most NATO allies fail to grasp the spirit and essence of the institutions of command and the soldierly ethos of the Bundeswehr, which means they fail to comprehend the military tradition of the Bundeswehr. In its least helpful form, this misunderstanding of the German soldier and the German past gives rise to screeds against the citizen in uniform in favor of a cult of the warrior, as exists in allied armies. The seductive simplicity of such mis-reasoning, as well as the lacunae in self-knowledge that sustain it, must not overtake the healthy discourse about and among German soldiers, particularly at this moment, when their example gives the lie to the false dichotomy between "soldier" and "democracy."

For young German citizens in uniform—who, fresh from their baptism of fire in Afghanistan or Kosovo, have as much right to celebrate their profession and tradition in its ethical, symbolic and historical dimension as do their Danish, Dutch, Polish, Spanish, French, British, and U.S. fellows—soldierly culture confronts pre-

---

* Originally published as Donald Abenheim, "Deutsche Militärtraditionen im 21. Jahrhundert: Der Blick von aussen nach innen," in Eberhard Birk et al., eds. *Tradition für die Bundeswehr: Neue Aspekte einer alten Debatte* (Berlin: Miles-Verlag, 2012) pp. 79–88.

sent-day conflict in all its dimensions of political and social change as these forces shape the lives of soldiers and military institutions. On the one hand, this interaction is nothing surprising. That is, the passage from a Europe of dynasties to a revolutionary Europe occupied Scharnhorst, Clausewitz, and the Prussian reformers two hundred years ago. Further epochal shifts comprised the rise of machine warfare and the modern, mass politics and culture, as well as the nuclear age and its impact on the military organization and the soldier's calling within state and society.

On the other hand, the ideals of the German soldier in their historical legacy strain to accommodate the far-reaching organizational change in the brains and limbs of the German military, the abolition of conscription—a real break with tradition that is roundly underappreciated among even Germany's closest allies—and the strategic reorientation of the mission of the Bundeswehr toward security-building operations in international organizations, to include combat. In addition, the political upheaval in Europe as a result of the world financial crisis, notably the reappearance of extreme right-wing violence, suggests ways that the heritage of the army can become a political weapon for civilians in a cause that can only harm the code of the soldier.

As such, a new generation of German soldiers must reexamine their historical legacy as a feature of their professional code amid the changing face of war, political upheaval in a united Europe, retrenchment in the Atlantic alliance, the suspension of conscription, as well as the maelstrom in society of the medium-is-the-message dilution of traditional symbols and values. Such a reassessment of military tradition cannot be entrusted by the German nation to an advertising agency, to management consultants, to those suffused with a Taylorite view of the military profession, or to those who reside solely in social networks. This appraisal should be undertaken by enlightened civilians and educated, trained, and experienced soldiers who can live up to yet another tradition of the Bundeswehr: the role of the combat soldier in the life of the higher affairs of the army and its place in society, who nonetheless manifests a remarkable degree of advanced education as part of citizenship. He or, today, she can assist in the selection of values, symbols, and traditions for the pantheon of the German armed forces within the frame of the Basic Law. He or she should be aided, in turn, by former soldiers in the civilian professions as well as by citizens who have crafted the valid heritage of the Bundeswehr, as well as those corners of German society where citizens have a vital interest in the inner structure of the Bundeswehr and its durability in the future.

Such a review of the durable features of a valid soldierly heritage should, in the first instance, manifest an adequate degree of historical empathy for earlier phases in the history of the inner structure of the Bundeswehr in order to understand the choices of policy about reform and tradition in what is now a very remote time of an untested democracy and its new army in the shadow of defeat in total war. It most especially must include those Germans not treated in the traditions decree of 1982, not the least because the *Armee der Einheit* in its maturity has created a new model army that persons of this writer's generation would have poorly predicted in the year 1991, to say nothing of 1981.

For the German soldier of the intermediate past (say, 1980), the normalcy of a martial tradition embedded within democracy and constitutional values (rather than in an estate or caste) was hardly a given in German political life. The tradition of the soldier as a thing of politics has provoked controversy in state, society, and the military itself, especially in the 1970s and 1980s, to say nothing of the foundation of the Bundeswehr in the 1950s and 1960s. This issue has endured not the least because, before 1933, the cult of soldierly tradition represented a bastion of caste privilege, hostile or at best indifferent to pluralism in state and society, while from 1933 to 1945 the cult of tradition with the swastika formed a weapon of National Socialist propaganda that perverted soldierly ethics.

The answer in the wake of defeat of those civilians and soldiers who refashioned military professionalism in West Germany has been *Innere Führung*—the core tradition of the Bundeswehr. (One should also recall, that, in the former East Germany with its Nationale Volksarmee (NVA), the communists fashioned a competing image of German soldierly virtue in the army of the socialist type, by deployment of conflicting heroes who were made to leer at each other in the propaganda war across the inner German border, while nevertheless sharing some of the pantheon with the class enemy.) As *Innere Führung* became established as the practice of democratic integration, military reform and modern leadership and command—amid some bloody domestic fights in the first two decades of the Bundeswehr—the question of the soldier's heritage became conflicted with contrary, retrograde attitudes about the military profession in society and within the army itself. As dramatic as all of this sounds in looking back, the process worked out in a manner that few would have thought possible in the early 1980s when the still-valid ministerial policy document on military tradition came into existence.

The birth of *Innere Führung* in the 1950s had Scandinavian, Prussian, north German, Lutheran as well as Catholic origins, which interoperate with some friction with the inner structures of the armies of the western allies—especially that of the United States—a phenomenon too complex to be analyzed in this short essay. This fact of limited interoperability of tradition, however, should never lead to the abandonment of *Innere Führung* either as a tradition or as the guiding principle of soldierly ethos, command, and morale. Change for change's sake, as offered by management consultants in uniform, poses a major threat to the maintenance of this tradition at a critical moment in the development of the Bundeswehr.

The fate of the German solider in the state since 1989 underscores this imperative, especially in view of the need to honor the citizen in uniform in national unity. The professionalism at arms of the German soldier in this national trial on both sides of the inner-German border, foreseen by all too few, relied, in part, on *Innere Führung*. This code better enabled the soldiers of the Bundeswehr, who went to the new states, to undertake the peaceful resolution of the German-German struggle by civilians and by soldiers without bloodshed—an event witnessed by this author at the time. This peaceful demobilization of the soldiers of the former NVA and the establishment of the Bundeswehr in the east with new citizens in uniform in the years 1989–1995 or so signifies an exemplary case of defense institution building and soldierly professionalism. It also marked the beginning of the enlargement of NATO, and an aspect even of the enlargement of the European Union.

This chapter has the radiance to be a feature of a 21st-century military tradition in Germany and beyond. Indeed, in those nations where the army lives in more of a caste or elite posture, set aside from pluralist society, the adjustment to what in NATO is called the comprehensive concept—that is, the limited use of military organizations in civil-military union with other civil branches of government—can function better because of the record of the German soldier in a democracy, and in an alliance.

Missions of security building since the mid-1990s, first in ex-Yugoslavia and later in Afghanistan, represent a small revolution in the record of the German soldier. These operations have involved not only peacekeeping in the traditional sense as performed in the years until 1989, but peace-enforcement with combat—a necessary step despite all taboos in German political culture and domestic politics about the hatefulness of war and the dubious value of military service. While the combat operations particularly in Afghanistan drew the greatest criticism at home, especially after the escalation of fighting in the year 2009, the adaptation of German soldiers in peace support and security-building operations since the early 1990s eventuated, also, in part, because of *Innere Führung*. The robust integration of the soldier in state and society has been a benefit and no liability to the effectiveness of the Bundeswehr in the Balkans and Afghanistan.

To be sure, the parameters of the Afghan NATO/ISAF operation as concern the limits of the use of force, domestic politics, and alliance cohesion are troubling to strategic idealists as well as to those who suggest that continental European nations should shoulder a greater part of the NATO burden. However, strategy in an alliance never simply conforms to textbooks in war colleges, while the sharing of the burden among the armed forces of democracies remains always a thing of controversy and inflated rhetoric. What is worthy of tradition, however, is how a new generation of German soldiers, many of whom are from Saxony, Saxony-Anhalt, Brandenburg, Mecklenburg-Vorpommern, and Thuringia, have accepted the burdens and sacrifice of such service under fire and not. They do so in the face of a society that no longer accords soldiers the devotion and affection as in former times. This truth is made more problematic by the suspension of conscription, which may yet undermine the political fundamentals and professional ideals of the German soldier, if soldiers and citizens abandon the central feature of what is called the Bundeswehr's own traditions—the citizen in uniform.

The criticism of the year 2014 from certain young Bundeswehr combat veterans that *Innere Führung* cannot apply to the operational conditions in the Afghan mountains beset by Taliban gunmen because German society fails to honor its soldiers confuses cause and effect. This critique fails to recognize the skewed character of civil-military relations in western democracies amid extended counter jihadist operations on a broad front that generally have failed to balance fairly the burdens of combat and service in the present.

This German soldierly heritage levied against that of, say, the UK, of France, or the United States highlights the differences in political and strategic culture that go well beyond the years 1914–1918 or 1933–1945. Ideals of command and obedience in these nations are, in a word, more traditional, less enlightened, and less innovative than in Germany. British and French soldiers also stand at a greater distance to the respective political cultures of their nations and nourish ideals of citizenship that diverge from the German tradition. British and French soldiers, nonetheless, exist within well-grounded democractic statecraft and can honor their history, symbols, and tradition with fewer contradictions, perhaps, than can a German soldier. British and French uniforms are more colorful and recall the past with less self-consciousness than is the case in Germany. A new generation, with no direct memory of the world of the 1950s and the wreckage of war, will have to square the circle of these differences of soldierly heritage between Germany and its Anglo-Saxon and its western European neighbors who maintain an intact heritage of the soldier on constabulary and imperial service in overseas colonies. While one easily speaks of a common European tradition of the soldier—a desirable thing, to be sure—the reconciliation of particularism should avoid fundamental harm to the historical accomplishments of German military professionalism in a democracy. The renationalization of politics in western and central Europe poses an additional burden against which the integrating core of *Innere Führung* provides a brake on integral nationalist extremes in the ranks of soldiers.

In view of the original, how-to-fight and psychological warfare basis of *Innere Führung* in it the 1950s, let a word of warning sound in the present amid what is perhaps too glibly called the greatest reform of the Bundeswehr since its creation in the years 2010 and 2011 (i.e. the phase-out of conscription, a broad reorganization of the command echelons, the rise of a professional force, as well as a reduction of the "tail"—base structure, training base and headquarters—in favor of the "tooth," or forces in the field, and a reform of the ministry) makers of policy cannot chuck out the constitutional and ethical fundamentals of soldierly existence like so much old factory equipment in the midst of a modernization based on management school methods. That is, too many in this writer's experience believe that the *Armee in Einsatz* should break with the ideal of the *Staatsbürger in Uniform* in an attempt to orient all military life to deployment, i.e. *"von Einsatz her...."*

One gets the impression that the need to fulfill a list of operational and tactical requirements set in the narrowest confines, with a smaller budget and reduced force structure, should eradicate not only the democratic heritage of the German soldier, but much of the very best of German military thought and experience assembled over two centuries. *Innere Führung* must remain the core of the maintenance of tradition the Bundeswehr, especially in view of the security and military operations since the 11 September 2001, where allied forces have shown deficits in their code of leadership, command, obedience, and morale in combat and post-conflict missions. The headlines of reform in 2010 and 2011—yet another budget driven reduction in force, are now overtaken by geopolitical events of drama and shock in the wake of the Crimean annexation in early 2014. The prospect since 2014–2015 that the Bundeswehr will reverse its 25-year shrinkage in force and its general orientation away from the defense of continental Europe back to what from 1955 until 1990 have been its core missions enables a revival and reinforcement of *Innere Führung* under the banner of alliance and national defense. The demands for the use of German soldiers at home for a constabulary role in the face of jihadist terror incidents in the years 2015–2017 makes the maintenance of *Innere Führung* equally urgent and necessary as a goal of German civil-military relations and the requirements of able leadership and management of the German soldier by the German parliament.

In conclusion, few outside of Germany understand the evolution and character of the soldier's valid heritage. The collective biography of educated soldiers and civilians who crafted this tradition out of a mountain of rubble in the 1950s remains mostly unknown, despite contemporary instances of the need to rebuild armies in the wake of conflict in a new state. This fact represents an opportunity for a younger generation to redouble their effort to maintain and develop the leadership principles of the German forces in a wider multinational context.

The formation of a common European soldierly tradition requires in the present education and training to remove these deficits in perception beyond Germany's borders, a need made more problematic by budget cuts and the reduction in the size of military forces as a result of the financial crisis. The record of the German soldier in the wake of World War II and the end of the Cold War signifies the effectiveness of military professionalism in its adaptation to the needs of pluralism, including most especially the need to integrate soldiers and civilians formerly of the opponent side into one's own ranks. In the view of this outsider, who nonetheless has spent more than 40 years in close proximity to German soldiers, this tradition of integration has arisen because of the genius of *Innere Führung* as the heart of this valid heritage.

4. Tradition für den Einsatz?
Gedanken eines amerikanischen Militärhistorikers zu Bildung, Ausbildung und Erziehung in den Streitkräften*

Die vergangene sowie die gegenwärtige Traditionsdebatte in der Bundeswehr und in der Bundesrepublik Deutschland verkörpert viel mehr als eine bloße Auseinandersetzung über das Erbe vergangener deutscher Kampfflieger in der Gegenwart oder über den geeigneten Platz für militärisches Zeremoniell im 21. Jahrhundert. Dieses „viel mehr" zielt auf die Bedeutung des (Staats-)Bürgers in Uniform und dessen Erbe im 21. Jahrhundert. Ein Jahrhundert, dessen Kennzeichen—das kann schon jetzt prognostiziert werden—eine Vielzahl von Krisen darstellen wird.

Ich will Ihnen in den nächsten 30 bis 40 Minuten diesen Komplex präsentieren, um sodann mit Ihnen in einen freimütigen Gedankenaustausch zu treten.

Dem Inspekteur der Luftwaffe und den Kollegen an der Offizierschule der Luftwaffe bin ich sehr dankbar für die Einladung hier in diesem hohen Kreise. Als Außenseiter, aber auch Freund der Bundeswehr und der deutschen Luftwaffe fühle ich mich tief geehrt, eine Einladung zu dieser Tagung bekommen zu haben.

Zur Begrifflichkeit der Richtlinien zur Traditionspflege von 1982

Mein Anliegen hier liegt nicht darin, soldatische Tradition radikal neu zu definieren oder Ihnen ein magisches „lean sigma six"

---

* Presentation, Chief of Staff of the German Luftwaffe Commander's Conference on education at Offizierschule der Luftwaffe, Wildbad Kreuth, February 2009. Thanks to LTC Dr. Peter Popp and LTC Michael Lux of the German Air Force for their kind assistance with this translation.

51

Mittel in die Hand zu geben, das diese Frage für Sie endgültig beantwortet und aus Ihrer beruflichen Welt wegpustet.

Sie müssen und sie wollen als Soldaten Verantwortung tragen. Sie sollen im Einklang mit der Verfassung, dem Grundgesetz, handeln. Und sie besitzen auf nationaler Ebene das Vertrauen des Parlaments und auf internationaler Ebene das Vertrauen der Partner in EU und NATO.

Da dem so ist, müssen Sie sich der erhabenen Pflicht stellen, über das Wesen des Staatsbürgers in Uniform, gerade auch in historischer Dimension, nachzudenken.

Die Definition des Begriffes „Tradition" im 1982er Erlass—„Tradition ist die Überlieferung von Werten und Normen"—ist selbsterklärend und bedarf eigentlich als solcher keiner eigenen Erwähnung. Doch der Haken kommt mit dem zweiten Satz des Erlasses, nämlich dass die Tradition sich „in einer wertorientierten Auseinandersetzung mit der Vergangenheit" bilde. Auf Englisch: „that's the hard part!"

Denn welche Rolle spielen Sie als Vorgesetzte und ich als Wissenschaftler im Dienste des Staates in dieser „wertorientierten Auseinandersetzung mit der Vergangenheit?"

Der 1982er-Traditionserlass führt aus, dass „die Pflichten des Soldaten (...) unserer Zeit sittlichen Rang durch die Bindung an das Grundgesetz" erlangen. Der Maßstab der symbolischen Bedeutung unseres Dienstes ist also eindeutig festgelegt: Es geht nicht um Werte an sich, sondern um deren Verbindung, deren Rückkoppelung, ja deren Rückbezug auf die im und durch das Grundgesetz definierte freiheitlich-demokratische Grundordnung.

Die soldatische Tugend der Tapferkeit darf durchaus weiterhin als klassischer, als „ewiger" soldatischer Wert aufgefasst werden. Doch von entscheidender Qualität für die Tapferkeit ist das „Warum" und „Wofür". Tapferkeit muss sich an der Zielrichtung und an der Motivation soldatischen Handelns messen lassen.

Der 1982er Traditionserlass ist gefasst im Sinne des mitdenkenden Gehorsams und dem Mut zur Entscheidung. Er atmet den

Geist der offenen Gesellschaft. Dem Soldaten und insbesondere dem Vorgesetzten, also Ihnen, kommt damit die Aufgabe zu:
• diesen Freiraum zu begreifen und
• Differenzierungsvermögen in nicht abstrakter Form an den Tag zu legen.

Meine Verpflichtung als Wissenschaftler besteht darin:
• Sie zu sensibilisieren, und
• Ihnen in Anbetracht einer nicht einfachen historischen Sachlage wie auch der Notwendigkeit der Entscheidung, die nun einmal mit dem Status des Offiziers und auch Unteroffiziers verbunden ist, zur Seite zu stehen.

Im Sinne dieser Sensibilisierung gleich provokant gefragt: Haben uns Geschichte und Tradition, die Wirklichkeit und die Idealbilder der deutschen Demokratie uns heute überhaupt noch etwas zu sagen? Denn die Geschichte geht bekanntlich weiter und die heutige strategische Lage stellt sich ja ganz anders dar als die im Jahre 1982, d.h. am Ende der Regierung unter Helmut Schmidt, deren letzter Handlungsakt ja die „Richtlinien zur Traditionspflege" waren.

Ich meine „JA". In einer Einsatzarmee stellen gerade Geschichte und Tradition, d.h. die Auseinandersetzung um die Werte, die Idealbilder und die Wirklichkeit des Soldatentums, besondere Herausforderungen für den Soldaten nicht minder für den Historiker dar. Denn es geht um wertorientiertes Handeln!

Freilich darf unter dieser ideellen wie auch materiellen Vorgabe die Geschichte nicht zur bloßen Keule oder zum Fundus, zur Asservatenkammer, für vermeintliche Rechtfertigungen verkommen. Beispiele, die dann letztlich doch nicht sehr viel zur Lösung des Problems beitragen, finden sich in der deutschen Vergangenheit, nicht minder in der amerikanischen Gegenwart zu Hauf.

Wenn die Definition von „Tradition" im 1982er Erlass sich noch einfach darstellt, so bildet dagegen die Unterscheidung zwischen

„Geschichte" und „Tradition" eine Hauptschwierigkeit der wertge-
bundenen Auseinandersetzung mit der Vergangenheit auf Grundlage
des deutschen Grundgesetzes. Beachten Sie bitte, dass das Grundgesetz kein bestimmtes Geschichtsbild zwingend vorgibt. Es ist die
Verfassung in einer und für eine offene Gesellschaft. Darüber hinaus
machen die meisten unserer Mitmenschen, gleich ob im militärischen
oder im zivilen Umfeld, leichtfertig keinen Unterschied zwischen
diesen beiden Begriffen.

In meinem Land ist während der letzten neun Jahre dieses
Problem mit den begrifflich zwei Aspekten der Vergangenheit be-
sonders virulent gewesen. Darauf möchte ich am Ende in analytischer
Hinsicht näher eingehen.

Meine Damen und Herren, ich weiß, dass Sie Praktiker sind.
Es kann hier auch nicht meine Aufgabe sein, eine kompakte philoso-
phische Abhandlung zur Geschichtstheorie zu liefern. Doch ich muss
ansprechen, dass völlig unbefangen in der zivilen wie militärischen
Öffentlichkeit und in der Truppe „Geschichte" und „Tradition" mit-
einander vermengt und verwechselt werden.

Ich provoziere weiter: Die drei Traditionssäulen der Bundeswehr, die übrigens im Traditionserlass von 1982 nicht explizit aufge-
führt sind, betonen den Wert der Bundeswehrgeschichte als eine
Quelle der Überlieferung.

Doch wie kann ausgerechnet diese Geschichte eine soldati-
sche Tradition begründen in einem Zeitalter wachsender politischer
Gewalt mit quasi religiöser Fundierung, wenn die Geschichte der
Bundeswehr im Zeitraum zwischen 1955 und 1990 gekennzeichnet
wurde durch das in sämtlichen Strategien des Nordatlantischen
Bündnisses getragene Prinzip der Abschreckung unter der Parole
„Der Friede als Ernstfall?"

Salopp formuliert: jetzt aber haben wir die „Bundeswehr im
Einsatz"; es muss und es wird gekämpft; die Feuertaufe steht unmit-
telbar bevor. Wäre es da nicht besser, man griffe in die Rüstkammer,
die die deutsche Militärgeschichte des 20. Jahrhunderts prall gefüllt

bietet, und reaktiviere den deutschen Soldatentypus des Ersten, noch besser des Zweiten Weltkrieges?

Ich will Ihnen erklären, worin die Implikationen dieses Lösungsansatzes liegen, auf dass Sie sich nicht darin verheddern.

Bei unserer Suche nach wertvollen soldatischen Traditionen angesichts der verschiedenartigen Aufträge sowie der „roles and missions", die die deutsche Bundeswehr heute als Armee im Einsatz hat, muss man sich davor hüten, in die „Traditionsfalle" zu tappen, indem man zum Beispiel gewisse gefallene Kampfflieger vergangener Epochen nur als Inbegriff der latenten oder expliziten demokratiefeindlichen Gesinnung in der Bundeswehr versteht.

Solch Argwohn gegenüber „brauner Gesinnung" bei den Soldaten mag im Jahre 1956 vielleicht eine Berechtigung gehabt haben. Heute wirkt er anachronistisch und aufgesetzt. Die Bundeswehr war und ist eine erfolgreiche Armee in der und für die Demokratie.

Wenn man in diese Falle dennoch tappt, so wird der Blick darauf verstellt, dass die Debatte über die gültige Tradition von denen mitunter ge- und missbraucht wird, die als lautstarke Interessengruppen auftretend die Traditionsdebatte innenpolitisch instrumentalisieren, um zu dokumentieren, dass sie der Bundeswehr samt der Verteidigungspolitik dieses Landes, der EU und der NATO verneinend gegenüberstehen.

Bei manchen Wortführern in dieser Debatte findet man Argumentationsmuster alter Provenienz neu aufgeputzt, die sowohl sehr extrem als auch zugleich unhistorisch sind.

Solche extremen Positionen erschweren uns den Auftrag sehr. Man darf aber auch nicht vergangene Erfahrungen militärischen Könnens und soldatischen Tuns einfach als Bedienungsanweisungen oder als Werkzeugkasten für die Gegenwart sorglos wieder- oder weiterverwenden, ohne den politischen, strategischen und sogar kulturellen Kontext dieser damaligen Ereignisse und Persönlichkeiten zu erwähnen und darüber zu reflektieren.

Das heißt, unser Nachdenken über Beschaffenheit und Charakter des gültigen Erbes benötigt fundierte Kenntnisse der Geschichte über einen langen Zeitraum, länger als die viel diskutierten Ereignisse des 20. Jahrhunderts—seien es die „zwölf Jahre des Dritten Reiches", seien es die Jahre des mehr oder minder frostigen Kalten Krieges mit seinen zuweilen sehr heißen „highlights".

Dieses Reflektieren über lange historische Zeiträume steht konträr zur Kurzfristigkeit und Kurzatmigkeit politischen und militärpolitischen Handelns. Auf die Bundeswehr gemünzt: die Fähigkeit zu dieser Zeitanalyse eröffnet dem immer am Prinzip der Verantwortung zu orientierenden militärischen Handeln neue Horizonte.

Damit erschließt sich erst der Sinn historisch-politischer Bildung in der Bundeswehr als Komponente der Inneren Führung. Nur wer weiß, woher er kommt, der weiß, wohin er geht. Die Vermittlung dessen ist Aufgabe des Historikers insbesondere in der Lehre und—nicht minder—ist auch Aufgabe des gebildeten Offiziers.

Als einer der von außen auf ihr Land blickt, versage ich mir nicht, einen heiklen Punkt hier gleich direkt anzusprechen—gleich, ob es vielleicht hart klingt oder gegen gewisse Anstandsregeln hierzulande verstößt. Eine gefestigte Demokratie wie sie im Deutschland des Jahres 2009 existiert, muss sich selber sowie ihren Soldaten erlauben, die Notwendigkeit des Kampfes und des Opferns im Gefecht so zu ehren, wie es in den demokratischen Nachbarländern der Fall ist, ohne dass dabei die geringste Sorge darüber besteht, die Demokratie könne daran Schaden nehmen oder zerbrechen.

Die Briten, die Franzosen, die Holländer, die Italiener und die Polen ehren ihre Soldaten mit ihren Traditionen, ihrem Brauchtum und ihrem Zeremoniell. Und es sollte auch hier in Deutschland mit der notwendigen Anwendung von „common sense" möglich sein, die Notwendigkeit des Kampfes und des Opferns im Gefecht so zu ehren wie es in den demokratischen Nachbarländern der Fall ist, ohne dass dort die geringste Sorge um die Demokratie besteht.

Historiker sind Analytiker und Interpretatoren der Zeiten

Der Traditionserlass von 1982 stellt hierbei einen brauchbaren Wegweiser dar, indem er den überragenden Stellenwert politisch-historischer Bildung erkennt und „fordert, den Gesamtbestand der deutschen Geschichte in die Betrachtung einzubeziehen und nichts auszuklammern", sowie unmissverständlich klar macht, dass „ein Unrechtsregime wie das Dritte Reich Tradition nicht begründen kann".

Und so begreife ich in der Auseinandersetzung um die Ethik und die Wertgebundenheit des Soldaten meine Rolle als Historiker als Träger der Verantwortung. Dieses Selbstverständnis und dieses Postulat beschäftigen mich als Amerikaner sehr seit dem 11. September 2001.

Die Entgrenzung des Krieges, die im Kalten Krieg für überholt geglaubte Koppelung von Religion und politischer Gewalt, die schwindende Trennung zwischen innerer und äußerer Sicherheit im Dienst des Soldaten, die Bereitschaft, im Namen des Soldaten mit Lockerungen des Rechtsstaates Folter in Uniform zu dulden, stellen allesamt große Herausforderungen dar. Ich bin davon überzeugt, dass zu deren Meisterung geisteswissenschaftliches Format entscheidend beitragen kann.

Der Historiker im Gefüge der Streitkräfte (so wie ich meinen Auftrag betrachte) darf nicht nur der Mahner, der ewige Neinsager und die Kassandra spielen, sondern muss sich als Partner des gebildeten Offiziers in der Erziehung und Bildung seiner oder ihrer Soldaten und Soldatinnen verstehen.

Diese Forderung heißt nicht, dass ich meine eigenen ethischen und beruflichen Werte als Historiker vulgär preisgebe, wie es so mancher Geschichtsdeuter, Publizist oder gar Propagandist vor allen Dingen aus einem bestimmten politischen Lager in meinem Lande getan haben. Es sind die Persönlichkeiten, die Ihnen bekannt sein dürften. Robert Kagan zählt zu dieser Kategorie.

Um auf Deutschland zurückzukommen: Wenn von einem berühmten Jagdflieger in Verbindung mit dem Begriff der „Bundeswehr im Einsatz" gesprochen wird, so bildet dies zwangsläufig Bestandteil fortwährender Debatten über die Rolle der Soldaten in der Demokratie sowie die politische Zweckmäßigkeit militärischer Institutionen in der deutschen, europäischen und Atlantischen Sicherheits- und Verteidigungspolitik.

Die Kontroverse über militärische Tradition geht demnach erheblich weiter als es auf den ersten Blick der Fall scheint.

Es bleibt nicht bei bloßen Traditionsfragen Es geht um Grundorientierungen, die in Konkurrenz zueinanderstehen und sich im Extremfall ausschließen können.

Die Kontroverse über historische Vorbilder und Nichtvorbilder bildet selbst schon eine Tradition. Sie gehört zur dritten Traditionssäule, dargestellt durch die Geschichte der Bundeswehr. Sie verkörpert einen Teil der Geistes- und Mentalitätsgeschichte der Bundeswehr, d.h. von verschiedenen, zum Teil kontroversen Vorstellungen vom Staatsbürger in Uniform und einer Armee in der Demokratie.

Diese mentale Dimension, diese Geistesgeschichte des Soldaten ist nicht etwas Lästiges. Ganz im Gegenteil, sie verkörpert ein im besten Sinne des Wortes teures Gut, einen Wert an sich, auf den Sie mit Recht stolz sein können.

Warum gelange ich zu diesem für Sie vielleicht überraschenden Urteil?

Wie Sie wissen, lehre ich an der Naval Postgraduate School in Kalifornien.

Seit etwa acht Jahren befindet sich mein Land im Krieg, und Kriegseinsätze prägen meine Studenten und Studentinnen. Täglich bin ich—die ausländischen scholars tun ein Übriges—mit der Notwendigkeit konfrontiert, historisches Wissen im Sinne des gebildeten Offiziers im besten Sinne weiterzureichen und zu interpretieren.

Ich muss Komplexes erklären, und dies vor dem Hintergrund einer emotionalen Dimension, die Rückwirkungen auf das politische und gesellschaftliche Selbstverständnis des Soldaten hat.

Junge Leute, deren Uniform versehen ist mit einer sehr schweren kleinen Ordensspange voller Dekorationen, gestehen mir in stillen Momenten ein, dass sie „burned out" seien.

In dieser Lage gewinnt für diese jungen Leute die Devise, „Bildung habe einen Wert an sich" eine sehr spezifische Bededutung. Wenn es heute mehr denn je bei der Gestaltung unserer Sicherheits- und Verteidigungspolitik um Orientierung geht, so durch den Wert historischer und politischer Bildung.

Heute ist in den USA der Leitwert des gebildeten Offiziers im klassischen mitteleuropäischen Sinne wichtiger denn je, was nicht ausschließt, dass ich in meiner Funktion jetzt und in Zukunft nicht der Verpflichtung enthoben bin, die Bedeutung der soldatischen Ethik und die Rolle der Geisteswissenschaften selbst auf der taktischen Ebene geduldig und sorgfältig zu erklären.

Die Kontinuität alter Debatten— Traditionsdebatte im Staatlichen und internationalen Kontext

In meinem Lande nimmt man vielen Aufgaben gegenüber noch immer eine unhistorische Haltung jenseits der Historie ein, ohne dass Clausewitz' heute mehr denn je gültige Forderung nach der Analyse der Chronologie, den Ursachen und Folgen dieser sowie die Gesamtwertung der Geschehnisse überhaupt berücksichtigt, geschweige denn überhaupt nur ansatzweise erwogen wird.

Im Gegenteil, man formuliert gleich eine Liste von „lessons learned," die alles andere als historisch sind oder man zieht gleich die „Parallelen" mit vermeintlich ähnlichen Ereignissen in der Vergangenheit, ohne dabei wirklich historisch zu denken: Geschichte verkommt dabei unter Ignorieren der unabdingbaren Reflexion zum Steinbruch. Militärwissenschaft zur bloßen Zitatologie.

In Deutschland hingegen kam die Kontroverse um das gültige Erbe und die Benennung von Truppeneinheiten oder Kasernen der Jahre 1998 bis 2005 nicht von Ungefähr oder aus heiterem Himmel.

Diese Kontroverse bildete nur eine neue Episode einer alten Auseinandersetzung, deren Charakter ich noch kurz skizzieren möchte.

Entscheidend ist, dass dieser „simple" Tatbestand bei manchem in Vergessenheit geraten war. Ich will eine Reaktivierung des

Gedächtnisses versuchen, indem ich das Stichwort „Cold War compromise" hier in die Runde werfe. Es beschreibt den zivil-militärischen Kompromiss der Gründungsväter der Bundesrepublik hinsichtlich eines demokratiekompatiblen und der Verteidigungssituation der alten Bundesrepublik und des Nordatlantischen Bündnisses entsprechenden Soldatenbildes, das auch die Gefühlslage der den wiederbewaffneten Deutschen ja verständlicherweise mitunter anfangs weiterhin skeptisch gegenüberstehenden Nachbarn in Rechnung stellen musste, wenn die junge Bundesrepublik Vertrauen erringen wollte.

Schließlich waren seit 1945 erst gut zehn Jahre vergangen, und Deutsche trugen ohne vorherigen biologischen Austausch schon wieder Militärklamotten und die „Braut des Soldaten".

Man muss gerade im Schatten der Ereignisse vor etwa vier Jahren, die besonders die deutsche Luftwaffe betrafen, die wichtigen Linien der Kontinuität dieser alten Debatte seit der Bewaffnungsphase der Bundesrepublik Deutschland bis hin in die Gegenwart herausheben. Diese Geschichte des Ringens um gültige Werte soldatischen Selbstverständnisses hat besonders für deutsche Streitkräfte eine entscheidende Bedeutung.

Sie haben auch zu tun mit der Rolle der Bundeswehr bei „security building" und „postwar reconstruction". Wie diese „postwar reconstruction" im inneren Gefüge der Bundeswehr in den 1950er und 1960er Jahren sich entfaltete, bleibt für unser Thema von entscheidender Bedeutung.

Die Debatte um den historischen Charakter des soldatischen Erbes angesichts eines gewandelten Bildes der politischen Gewalt ist sogar ein notwendiges Merkmal einer demokratischen politischen Kultur in Deutschland.

Ich unterstreiche, dass Deutschland damit einen Vorbildcharakter für Europa und andere Länder bekommt. Das heißt, die Traditionsdebatten sind nicht dysfunktional.

Die Karikatur dieser politischen und strategischen Kultur, wie die von Robert Kagan im Jahre 2002 von pazifistischen Europäern und martialistischen US-Amerikanern, bildet ein entstellendes Zerrbild der Wirklichkeit. Kagan liegt falsch.

Die deutsche politische Kultur mit dem Staatsbürger in Uniform im Gefüge des Grundgesetzes ist eine große Errungenschaft der Bundesrepublik Deutschland sowie der Bundeswehr im sechsten Jahrzehnt ihres Bestehens.

Man sollte immer im Auge behalten, dass „es auch anders hätte kommen können" – und zwar mit schlimmen Folgen.

Wie würde denn der 60. Jahrestag der Bundesrepublik begangen werden, wenn die Skeptiker der Bundeswehr im Jahre 1956 Recht gehabt hätten und die Bundeswehr sich als Staat im Staate entwickelt hätte?

Ganz so abwegig ist diese kontrafaktische Frage nicht. Wenn schon die Erfahrung des deutschen Soldaten in der ersten Hälfte des 20. Jahrhunderts flapsige Vergleiche mit anderen Ländern oder Geschichtsepochen verhindert oder dieses sich sogar verbietet, muss man als Historiker —als Partner des Soldaten—diese Debatte über brauchbare Traditionen in historischen Kontext stellen, und den Wandel des Traditionsverständnisses in ihren Bezug zur deutschen Innenpolitik, zum internationalen Staatensystem sowie zum Charakter der politischen Gewalt in den letzten 60 Jahren mit mehr Sorgfalt interpretieren als es besonders in meinem Lande üblich ist.

In den USA geht man mit der Geschichte des Krieges, mit dem Erbe des Soldaten im politischen Umfelde, sowie mit den spezifischen Begebenheiten des Wandels im Zeitalter der sogenannten asymmetrischen Kriege, Terrorismus, und Globalisierung ziemlich unhistorisch und propagandistisch um.

Als Außenseiter, der freilich dennoch mit ziemlich langer Erfahrung nicht nur mit der deutschen Bundeswehr, sondern mit den Streitkräften der NATO-Länder sowie der PfP-Staaten und sogar außer-europäischen Nationen (einschließlich der Vereinigten Staaten) gesammelt hat, möchte ich zunächst hier einen biographisch vergleichenden Ansatz verwenden, um die Tradition der Bundeswehr im Einsatz zu diskutieren.

Innere Führung und Tradition—
Persönlichkeiten im Geflecht des strategischen Wandels

Wie Sie bemerkt haben, bildet den Schwerpunkt meiner Ausführungen die historische und politische Verbindung zwischen der Inneren Führung der Bundeswehr und dem Ringen in den Reihen der Soldaten und in der vorerst nur westdeutschen Gesellschaft über die politisch brauchbaren Traditionen einer Armee in der Demokratie im Schatten der deutschen Katastrophe.

Mit dem Beginn der Inneren Führung in den Jahren 1950 bis 1953 (bevor es überhaupt die Bundeswehr mit diesem Namen eigentlich gab) ist die Auseinandersetzung über ein gültiges Erbe des deutschen Soldaten in die Wiege der neuen Armee gelegt.

Für unsere jungen Offiziere ist diese Welt schwer nachvollziehbar, aber sie bleibt wichtig, weil die Zeitgenossen von der geistigen Frische und Vitalität vorbildlich waren.

Diese lange und heftige Debatte über die Bedeutung der Inneren Führung war unzertrennlich mit der Bestimmung der sogenannten „Vergangenheitspolitik" bzw. „Traditionspolitik" in der Ära von Adenauer bis Kohl im Kalten Kriege verbunden. Dabei war die Integration des Soldaten in die junge westdeutsche Demokratie im Sinne des Bürgers in Uniform anstatt des militärischen Standes im 19. Jahrhundert oder des Seecktschen 100.000-Mann-Heeres oder des nationalsozialistischen „Volksheeres" namens Wehrmacht oder sogar des Musters einer Armee sozialistischen Typs (NVA und Warschauer Pakt) der entscheidende, aber auch sehr kontroverse Schritt in den 1950er und 1960er Jahren.

Dieser Schritt erscheint uns heute in einem anderen, klareren Lichte als es im Oktober 1989 der Fall war, also kurz vor Erscheinen meines Buches über „Bundeswehr und Tradition" in der so genannten roten Schriftenreihe des Militärgeschichtlichen Forschungsamtes.

Für unsere militärischen Vorgänger wie auch für viele (Alt-) Bundesbürger, die diese wertorientierte Auseinandersetzung über soldatische Werte im Zeitraum von etwa 1955 bis 1985 verfolgten, war diese Kontroverse gekennzeichnet durch die Kurzformel einer militärischen Dialektik in menschlicher Form: die Reformer—d.h. die Verfechter der Inneren Führung in Uniform, im Parlament und in der politischen Kultur im Allgemeinen—gegen die Traditionalisten, die Skeptiker oder Gegner der Inneren Führung, die Wertkonservativen in Uniform und die Vernunftdemokraten unter den Soldaten sowie ihre Fürsprecher in der Gesellschaft.

Die Diskussion um die soldatische Tradition in den entscheidenden Phasen bis zum 1982er Traditionserlass wurde immer mit dieser dialektischen Begrifflichkeit umschrieben. Ob diese Dialektik die ganze Wirklichkeit dieser zivil-militärischen Reform zum Ausdruck brachte, dessen bin ich nicht ganz überzeugt.

Doch Sie dürfen mit Recht erwarten, dass ich als Historiker dies zu beschreiben versuche.

In diesem geradezu epischen Drama mit dem Titel „Reformer gegen Traditionalisten" ragten zwei Hauptpersönlichkeiten immer wieder mit eben diesen zwei dialektischen Positionen bei der Truppe und in der Öffentlichkeit heraus: Wolf Graf von Baudissin und Heinz Karst. Obwohl beide Personen entscheidend an der Konzeption und der Durchführung des Staatsbürger in Uniform-Reformkonzepts in den Jahren 1951 bis 1961 mitgearbeitet und gewirkt haben, entwickelten sich zwischen ihnen in der zweiten Hälfte der 1950er Jahre, als die Bundeswehrplanung in der Vorlaufphase mit der strategischen Wirklichkeit der Zeit zusammenprallte, bedeutende Meinungsverschiedenheiten zur Reform sowie persönliche Rivalitäten zu einer öffentlichen Fehde. Der Begriff der Tradition war immer Gegenstand dieser persönlichen, institutionellen und gesellschaftlichen Auseinandersetzung. Dieses Verhältnis zwischen den beiden Männern und deren Wirkung bei der Truppe und im Staate hatte viele Facetten, die uns auch heute wichtig sind.

Graf Baudissin wurde bekannt für seine funktionalistische, ethische Auslegung der Inneren Führung gründend auf mit zum besten zählenden preußischen Erbe, dem Pietismus, aber auch beseelt vom besten Geiste des Infanterie-Regiments „von Neun" in Potsdam sowie der Märtyrer des 20. Juli. Seit den Tagen im Eifelkloster Himmerod im Herbst 1950, wurde er Vertreter einer Armee ohne Pathos, eingebettet nicht nur im neuen demokratischen Staat, sondern auch in der bundesdeutschen Gesellschaft im Wandel der Westbindung und der Abkehr vom deutschen Sonderweg.

Heinz Karst dagegen, der im Jahre 1952 ins Amt Blank in der Bonner Ermekeilstraße kam, wurde eher bekannt als wortstarker und truppennaher Verfechter eines traditionellen militärischen Standes selbst in der jungen Bundesrepublik. Nach ihm sollte der Soldat als Fels in der Brandung einer immer mehr pluralistischen Gesellschaft der Bundesrepublik Deutschland der damaligen Großen Koalition stehen. Wohlgemerkt: eine Haltung die sich kaum vom Amerikaner Samuel Huntingtons zur damaligen Zeit unterschied oder abwich von den Positionen vieler britischer und französischer Offiziere in der NATO zu etwa gleicher Zeit.

Für viele Beobachter der Bundeswehr in den späten 1960er und frühen 1970er Jahren war diese Dialektik immer einfacher beschrieben: Graf Baudissin mit seiner eher skeptischen Haltung zur Tradition (besonders dem Traditionskult der Reichswehr und der Wehrmacht) sei sozusagen ein roter Edelmann ohne nötige Ostfronterfahrung, der immer linker wurde bis er als Professor in Hamburg berufen wurde. Karst, der Vordenker der konservativen Richtung in der Bundeswehr, war hingegen bereit, vielleicht etwas zu viel von der vergangenen Traditionspflege wiedereinzuführen, bis Verteidigungsminister Helmut Schmidt und er sich im Jahr 1970 auf keine einheitliche Linie in der Erziehung und Ausbildung des Heeres einigen konnten und Karst in Ruhestand gegangen ist.

Beide Persönlichkeiten aber verkörperten den „Cold War compromise" im inneren Gefüge der neuen Bundeswehr: den ehemaligen Soldaten der Wehrmacht wurde die Möglichkeit eingeräumt, mit dem Eid auf das westdeutsche Grundgesetz weiter zu dienen, und zugleich die eigenen taktisch-operativen Erfahrungen insbesondere von der Ostfront nicht zu vergessen. Mehr noch und ganz im Gegenteil: sie unter der NATO-Flagge weiterzuentwickeln. Konventionelle und atomare Elemente bildeten dabei ein durchaus widersprüchliches Amalgam. Bis in die 1960er Jahre hinein blieb die ganze Wahrheit der

Kriegführung im Zeichen des Rasse- und Vernichtungskrieges gegen die Sowjetunion mit den hier nur zu nennenden Stichworten „Kommissarbefehl" und „Generalplan Ost" unausgesprochen.

Hier nun kommt der entscheidende Punkt: die Auseinandersetzung sowohl zwischen diesen beiden Männern als auch zwischen den sogenannten Reformern und Traditionalisten hatte eindeutig eine Verbindung zur strategischen Gesamtlage der damaligen Zeit (MC 14/2 & MC 48 bis MC 14/3 also „massive retaliation" bis „flexible response"), die entscheidend war in der Geschichte der Bundeswehr, genauso wie heute das Zusammenspiel von nationalen Interessen, der Staatskunst und der Bündnisstrategie unsere Welt beherrscht.

Die Wertung der soldatischen Tradition in den Werken dieser beiden Männer war nicht allein die Frage des Erbes der Wehrmacht im Nationalsozialismus in der Bundeswehr, obwohl diese Frage nicht in geringster Weise heruntergespielt werden darf.

Denn die Frage der Tradition war und ist die Fortsetzung oder die Erweiterung der strategischen Gegenwart mit symbolischen und historischen Mitteln in der demokratischen politischen und strategischen Kultur. Das heißt auf den Punkt gebracht: die wertorientierte Auseinandersetzung über das Bild der soldatischen Tradition muss zwangsläufig mit gegenwärtigen Strategiedebatten verbunden werden.

In Rückschau auf die Schriften Baudissins und Karsts von den 1950er bis in die 1970er Jahre hinein wird klar und deutlich, in welch enger Verbindung Traditionsverständnis und strategisches bzw. taktisch-operatives Denken zueinander stehen.

Karst blieb immer ein Vertreter des klassischen preußisch-deutschen operativen Denkens der Landkriegführung—und das selbst im Thermo-Nuklearzeitalter.

Graf Baudissin hingegen wurde in den frühen 1960er Jahren ein Interpret der nuklearen Abschreckung. In diesem Szenario wären klassische Kampfhandlungen alten Stils sehr problematisch, ja fast unwahrscheinlich-absurd gewesen.

Ich empfehle in diesem Zusammenhang ausdrücklich die neuesten Publikationen des MGFA zur Strategie der NATO und zur Bundeswehr. Sie geben guten Aufschluss über die strategische Problematik im Umfeld der beiden Persönlichkeiten.

Bei den beiden Symbolfiguren und prominenten Protagonisten im Traditionsdisput ist der Bezug zur strategischen Debatte im Wandel von der Nuklearstrategie der „massive retaliation" hin zur Strategie der „flexible response" immer gegeben.

In der letzten Phase seines Lebens wurde Graf Baudissin ja auch bekannt für seine Schriften zu strategischen Gegenwartsfragen, die er auf Grund sowohl seiner NATO-Erfahrung als auch seiner Tätigkeit bei der sicherheitspolitischen Forschung im universitären Bereich analysierte.

Angesichts der sowjetischen Hochrüstung in den 1970ern und zu Beginn der 1980er Jahre blieb die strategische Notwendigkeit der Aufrechterhaltung der „flexible response" unabdingbar. Und dies hinwiederum ist ein Beleg für das enge Geflecht zwischen der Bundeswehr-Traditionsdebatte und den damals wie auch heute aktuellen strategischen Entwicklungen.

Auch hierfür ein historisches Beispiel: In den Jahren 1976 bis 1977 entbrannte nicht von ungefähr die Kontroverse über den Besuch des Eichenlaubträgers und des die innere Ordnung der Bundesrepublik aus rechter Perspektive verneinenden ehemaligen Kampffliegers Hans-Ulrich Rudel beim Immelmann-Geschwader in Bremgarten. Just zur selben Zeit begann eine neue Kontroverse über die künftige Nuklearrüstung der NATO. Sie ging einher mit dem Ausklang der Anfang der 1970er vorherrschenden Entspannungseuphorie.

Genau zu diesem Zeitpunkt fing auch der „cold-war compromise" der 1950er und 1960er Jahre an, im soldatischen Selbstverständnis der Bundeswehr zu erodieren.

Natürlich: dies alles liegt inzwischen schon etwas zurück. Doch die Geschichte wiederholt sich mitunter trotz anderer Gesamtkonstellation. Zweifelsohne liegt auch heute eine Neuformation in strategischen Dingen vor. Und so gesehen sind die Rückwirkungen auf das Traditionsverständnis der Bundeswehr geradezu zwangsläufig. Der Bundeswehr, die eine Einsatzarmee sein will und soll, bleibt gar nichts anderes übrig, als eine Traditionsdebatte zu führen. Gleichgültig, ob es politisch-militärische Entscheidungsträger wollen oder nicht wollen.

Die Umbenennung des Jagdgeschwaders 74 erfolgte unter dem Primat der Innenpolitik. Die Diktion des einschlägigen Parlamentsbeschlusses von April 1998 beweist es nur zu gut.

Getreu der These vom Primat der Außenpolitik—um mit Leopold von Ranke, dem Vater der Geschichtswissenschaft als akademische Disziplin, zu sprechen—bildet dessen ungeachtet die Suche nach dem gültigen Erbe schlechthin den Gradmesser für die Einbettung der Armee in den demokratischen Staat und die Verinnerlichung von dessen Außen- und Sicherheitspolitik seitens des Militärs.

Es will dabei bedacht sein, dass mittlerweile eine viel kritischere Sicht auf staatliche Institutionen angesichts der Auseinandersetzung mit dem Nationalsozialismus gegeben ist. Dies hat Rückwirkungen auf die Denkweise hinsichtlich der Inhalte und der Gültigkeit der deutschen soldatischen Tradition. Die Geschichte ist über die Gründungsphase der Bundesrepublik Deutschland und die Aufstellungsphase der Bundeswehr hinweggegangen.

Halten wir fest: Die rasante Abfolge weltgeschichtlicher Veränderungen seit November 1989 und September 2001 haben der scheinbar betagten Debatte über die Tradition, die Symbole, das Brauchtum und das Bild des Soldaten in der Demokratie neue Bedeutung gegeben. Mehr noch: eine neue Prägung einer alten Form. Dies erfolgte gerade im Hinblick auf die begrenzte Anwendung der politisch legitimierten Gewalt angesichts der weitreichenden ideologischen Zielsetzung eines Weltanschauungskrieges.

Weil diese soldatische institutionelle Traditionsdebatte ein Gradmesser deutscher zivil-militärischer Beziehungen ist, müssen wir uns am Ende noch mit den gegenwärtigen Folgen dieser Debatte auseinandersetzen. Es geht um das Prinzip „Verantwortung". Wir haben die Folgen gerade in der Frage der historischen Dimension des soldatischen Selbstverständnisses zu bedenken.

Das Zeitalter der Bundeswehr als Einsatzarmee, soll heißen, die—in griffigem Englisch formuliert—„roles and missions of federal armed forces in security building, post war reconstruction and counter terrorism" haben aus meiner Sicht der Dinge der bereits selbst schon Tradition gewordenen Debatte über den buchstäblich zum Symbol gewordenen Charakter des deutschen Soldaten neue Schubkraft gegeben: sowohl in der politischen Kultur Deutschlands als auch weit über Europa hinaus!

Doch was für eine Bedeutung hat das Feld mit den Markierungen ‚Einsatz', ‚Transformation' und ‚Tradition' für die Deutsche Luftwaffe?

Die Auseinandersetzung mit dem Begriff ‚Tradition' führt einen am Schluss immer auf die Institution des Staatsbürgers in Uniform zurück, und dieser verkörpert beileibe kein Überbleibsel einer leblosen, weil fern und mit dem Jahr 1989/90 abgeschlossenen Epoche.

Die lebendige Tradition des Staatsbürgers in Uniform muss im 21. Jahrhundert erhalten bleiben, weil die Alternativen einfach nicht akzeptabel sind.

Das Geschöpf der Inneren Führung und die Schaffung der Institution des ‚Staatsbürgers in Uniform' sind nicht einseitig deutsch. Sie orientieren sich an klassischen sowie in jüngerer Vergangenheit liegenden nordeuropäischen, schweizerischen und sogar US-amerikanischen Beispielen. Sie sind demnach Teil der transatlantischen Kultur im Sinne der Aufklärung und des Rechtsstaates.

Beide Komponenten sind virulent und damit Teil der Gegenwart. Sie wirken herausfordernd gerade im Gefolge der NATO Osterweiterung. Weil sie provokant sind, werden sie konsequenterweise auch vehement angefeindet. Jetzt und in Zukunft!. Doch dies geschieht gänzlich unverdientermaßen.

Sowohl die wertorientierte Auseinandersetzung mit der Geschichte Deutschlands als auch der heftige Disput bei den Nachbarn

Deutschlands über die ‚Innere Führung' als bedeutende Errungenschaft deutschen strategischen Denkens und politischer Militärkultur liefern Ihnen eine Antwort auf die Frage nach der Relevanz soldatischer Tradition für eine Armee im Einsatz.

Das sollte Sie nicht frustrieren. Erst recht nicht deshalb, weil die zu gebenden Antworten schwierig sind. Ermuntern und ermutigen sollte Sie vielmehr, dass der Prozess der Auseinandersetzung in sich völlig stimmig ist.

Sie haben sicher bemerkt, dass ich ganz mit Vorbedacht nicht die Ereignisse zwischen 1998 und 2005 in Bezug auf die Umbenennung des Mölders-Geschwaders akribisch aufgelistet und danach analysiert habe.

Diese Aufgabe wird von Klügeren andernorts als in Monterey viel besser geleistet. Ich will an dieser Stelle nur auf den Vortrag meines verehrten Kollegen Prof. Dr. Reiner Pommerin verweisen, den er vor der Clausewitz-Gesellschaft Mitte August 2007 in Hamburg an der Führungsakademie der Bundeswehr gehalten hat.

Sehr frei nach Goethes Faust: „allwissend bin ich i.S. Mölders nicht, doch mir ist als Mitglied der Clausewitzgesellschaft „manches wohl bewusst". Mir geht es hier darum, diese Ereignisse in einen erhellenden Kontext zu stellen. Ich bin der festen Überzeugung, dass dieser von anderen bislang nicht genügend gewürdigt worden ist.

Mein Anliegen war es, Ihnen einen Weg aufzuzeigen, damit Sie weder gleich am Anfang noch etwas später in die Traditionsfalle tappen unter dem schlagkräftigen Motto „Basta! —Schluss jetzt!"

Mauern Sie nicht, igeln Sie sich nicht ein und blockieren Sie sich selbst nicht gegenüber der Geschichte, indem Sie sich—weil es scheinbar so einfach ist— an Henry Ford orientieren, der im übrigen Hitler und Mussolini sehr aufgeschlossen gegenüberstand. Ford war ein schrecklicher Vereinfacher, indem er in Schlichtheit des Denkens propagierte „History is bunk!"

Bleiben Sie gerade in geographischer Hinsicht authentisch und plappern Sie nicht das nach, was mancherorts gerade auch ‚überm großen Teich' propagiert wird.

Ich kann Ihnen auf Grund meiner 35jährigen Karriere als Historiker für Soldaten und als im soldatischen wie im universitären Umfeld Tätiger die nachfolgende dreifache Erkenntnis eindringlich versichern. Nicht nur dies, ich möchte lauthals ausrufen:

1. Bad history makes bad policy.
2. No history makes even worse policy.
3. The past in the hands of demagogues signifies a complete disaster, especially for soldiers.

Die Forderung des Traditionserlasses von 1982 nach einer wertorientierten Auseinandersetzung ist immer zugleich auch eine Frage der soldatischen Verantwortung vor unseren Soldaten und Soldatinnen, also vor den Staatsbürgern in Uniform.

Und dafür tragen wir ja eine besondere Verantwortung.

Diese Auseinandersetzung bildet keine Last, sie ist eben nicht dysfunktional, sondern verkörpert eine Stärke durch die Pflichten Ihres Amtes dem Soldatentum in der Demokratie gegenüber.

Als senior officers of the German armed forces haben Sie aber mit dieser Verpflichtung zugleich auch die Mittel in der Hand, die andere andernorts nicht haben.

Glauben Sie mir bitte, ich weiß, wovon ich rede, wenn ich mich hier auf meine Nation innerhalb der letzten acht Jahre beziehe.

Dem unbedarften Anfänger oder dem Aussenseiter im Sinne desjenigen, der von außen die Sache betrachtet, muss die Traditionsfrage wie ein Minenfeld, gespickt mit Tretminen in Form lauter kleiner Hakenkreuze oder Fratzen mit Hitler-Bärtchen vorkommen. Wie überwindet man vermintes Gelände? Nun, indem man Minenfelder entweder umgeht oder sie mit technischen Tricks unschädlich macht.

Die Wirklichkeit ist hier dagegen viel komplexer: Die Traditionsdebatte ist nämlich geprägt durch viele Ebenen:

• Sie ist beileibe nicht nur eine geistige Auseinandersetzung über den Inhalt eines gültigen Erbes des Soldaten.

- Sie ist nicht minder eine Art von ‚Stellvertreterkrieg' über den Widerstreit, den der Historiker Gerhard Ritter einmal in die Polarität fasste: ‚Staatskunst und Kriegshandwerk'.
- Dies wiederum ist nicht nur ein innenpolitisches Problem, zu erfassen mit der Befürchtung, das Militärische werde gesellschaftlich akzeptiert und Staat und Gesellschaft würden in den Militarismus entgleiten.
- Nein, es geht auch um die Frage, ob und inwieweit Macht in der internationalen Politik militärisch bestimmt ist oder bestimmt sein darf.

Das Symbolische in Form der Frage nach der richtigen Tradition und das Handfest-Konkrete in Form der Frage nach der richtigen Strategie zur Verteidigung dieses Ihres Landes bilden gleichsam ein Amalgam. Das heißt, es liegt eine untrennbare Verwobenheit vor. Es gibt sehr wohl eine Verzahnung

- zwischen den teilweise bereits vermeintlich historischen Kapiteln öffentlicher Debatten über den Soldaten, soldatische Symbolik und Tradition einerseits,
- und der Zielrichtung der Außen, Sicherheits- und Verteidigungspolitik dieser Ihrer Nation andererseits.

Wie gesagt: Das ist alles andere als etwas Neues: diese Tatsache datiert bereits in die Anfänge der 1950er Jahre.

Gerade unter der ministeriellen Vorgabe, dass „Deutschland am Hindukusch verteidigt" werde, nimmt es sich nicht Wunder, dass sich Kritiker der Bundeswehr gerade an soldatischen Symbolen festhaken und Traditionen anzweifeln. Sehen Sie es bitte gelassen: dies sind Mittel und Mechanismen in der demokratischen Auseinandersetzung um Krieg und Frieden.

Schließlich und endlich: Einsatz ist weitaus mehr als das Gefecht.

Bekanntlich sehen viele in meinem Lande den Begriff ‚Einsatz' als „kinetic effects", d.h. als Kampfhandlungen, konzentriert auf die ballistische Wirkung von Waffen, Geschossen, und Sprengköpfen auf die feindlichen Ziele.

Wie Sie wissen, rührt dieser unglückliche Versuch der Wortfindung, Interpretation und Definition aus dem Munde zeitgenössischer minderbemittelter strategischer Denker:

- einerseits aus der Geschichte des Festungswesens,

- andererseits—das klingt moderner und sensibilisiert Sie als Angehörige der Luftwaffe vielleicht stärker!— den Doktrinen über den Luftkrieg.

Sie zeugt aber auch von der Auslegung des Begriffs des Krieges im Sinne einer naturwissenschaftlichen theoretischen Tradition.

Interessanterweise hat letztere Sicht der Dinge in diesem Ihrem Lande heute weniger Anhänger als in meiner Nation.

Bitte beachten Sie eingehend: Der ‚Staatsbürger in Uniform' (mit seiner ‚lästigen' Traditionsdebatte zwischen den Positionen eines Wolf Graf von Baudissin und eines Heinz Karst in der mittlerweile fernen Vergangenheit der ‚alten Bundesrepublik') verkörpert nicht die Schwäche einer „unsoldatischen" Puderzuckerarmee von einem fernen Stern der Liebe und totalen Harmonie bar jeglicher irdischer Realität. Diesen Quatsch können nur Dummköpfe verzapfen, die selbst weit ab von der Realität angesiedelt sind.

Das Gegenteil ist der Fall: Der „Staatsbürger in form" und ein damit stimmiges Traditionsverständnis ermög-lichen es einer Armee im Einsatz, die „roles and missions" wirklich anzupacken sowie strategisch und operativ besser zu bewältigen. Gerade dort, wo hochtechnisierte Waffen allein aufgrund von „kinetic effects" angesichts der wuchernden Zunahme organisierter politischer Gewalt in Glaubenskriegen versagen müssen und versagen werden!

Bekanntlich gibt es in meiner Nation und den US-Streitkräften keine Innere Führung. Seit 1973 haben wir auch eine Freiwilligenarmee, die aber seit 2002 überfordert und noch dazu— so meine persönliche Meinung— missbraucht worden ist.

Diese Tatsache ist geschichtlich leicht belegbar. Seit Anfang der 1970er Jahre haben wir uns vom Ideal des Staatsbürgers in Uniform konsequent entfernt, und dies ist uns in den letzten acht Jahren, in denen die USA Krieg führten, sehr teuer zu stehen gekommen.

Die Verbindung zwischen der Demokratie und ihren Soldaten muss immer erhalten bleiben. Sie kann nicht durch „burden shifting" von Verantwortungslosen an Verantwortungsträger abgewälzt werden: dieses ‚Schwarze-Peter-Spiel' zwischen feinen ungedienten Herren in den „think tanks" unserer Hauptstadt Washington D.C., dem Militärapparat, den Berufssoldaten, den Reservisten, auch Söldnern à la Blackwater, sowie Politclans einerseits und dem US-amerikanischen Steuerzahler andererseits.

Die wertorientierte Auseinandersetzung mit der Vergangenheit, die Sie in Deutschland heute führen und—seien Sie sich sicher!—auch noch morgen werden führen müssen, stellt eben diese schwierige Verbindung zwischen der Demokratie und dem Soldaten her. Sie ist Komponente der Inneren Führung und repräsentiert damit im Kern das gültige Erbe des deutschen Soldaten.

5. Bundeswehr, Tradition, and Right-Wing Extremism[*]

Where we meet today symbolized in an earlier age not only a place, but also a tradition of Prussian virtues described as the spirit of Potsdam. Today, all of these terms—"tradition," "Prussian virtues," and even "spirit of Potsdam"—elicit controversy wrought in and of the past, to wit, the late Wilhelmine era, the Weimar Republic, and especially the year 1933. On 21 March of that year, the unknown corporal of the world war and the aging field marshal, now President of the First Republic, joined hands in the Garrison Church above the crypt of the Hohenzollern kings in the founding of the Third Reich. These two men took the march past on the Breite Straße of SA and SS together with the Reichswehr regiments, the beginning of a parade of military and paramilitary might that finally stumbled to an end 12 years later in the bunker near the Voßstraße and Wilhlemstraße in Berlin.

Yet the "spirit of Potsdam," in its more original sense of the 18th century, has also signified the unity of state and intellect as in the court of Frederick II and the writings of Voltaire, the achievements of progressive policy in the state-building, and the integration of various religiously persecuted and surplus populations, as well as tolerance of faiths of remarkable and admirable kind. The spirit of Potsdam in the century past also included the noteworthy figures associated with the military resistance to Hitler in the years thereafter, culminating in the 20 July 1944 assassination plot. These men and women stand among the ancestors and historical exemplars honored by the Bundeswehr of the Federal Republic of Germany.

The founders of the Bundeswehr, themselves, also partook of the spirit of Potsdam in its best sense for the political culture of the Federal Republic of Germany and should form a source of profes-

---

[*] Presentation at Militärgeschichtliches Forschungsamt, Potsdam, Auschwitz Liberation Day ceremonies, January 2011.

sional pride and self-confidence. Part of this project entails the mastery of these competing meanings within a democratic civic and ethical ideal of leadership, command, education, and training, an ongoing process itself. And part of "mastery" here means understanding the negative, as well as the positive, associations of such ideas as the spirit of Potsdam or tradition. This undertaking requires study and critical engagement—and more than a little courage in the face of difficult and disputed subject matter.

At the heart of the controversy circumscribed by these historical contradictions has been the cult of tradition in modern German history and how it became a political weapon and a cultural pathology, especially in the lives of soldiers as well as in the character of military institutions in German state and society. The examples I have cited here—that is, the tensions between the soldier's legacy and the history of state, society, and culture—contain the promise and contradictions of not only soldierly tradition, but also the use or, perhaps, application of modern history to the political foundations of contemporary political institutions. This problem of a valid heritage and a usable past always becomes acute in a period crisis in democratic statecraft, as in the present.

For very good historical reasons Germans reflect on the role and value of tradition among soldiers, especially within such key institutions as the armed forces of the Federal Republic, the European Union and, dare I say, NATO. At the same time, though, the reality in both the past and the present is that the term "tradition," when applied by irresponsible persons of the radical right here and elsewhere possessed of discredited ideologies of blood, soil, race, empire, and militarism, manifests the use of the past as a weapon to wretched political ends that have nothing in common with the clauses of the German Basic Law, of the constitutional documents of the European Union, and even the Washington Treaty as it has evolved since 1949—that is, the bases of contemporary German democracy.

Let me be clear at the outset, further, that this generalization about the radical right and the misuse of the legacy of the soldier applies to those who would undermine and pervert the constitutional, political, and social order of the German constitution in their attempt to restore the Reich—and/or a *Führerstaat*—based on racial supremacy, especially with the re-creation of an enemy race or class. This distinction is important, as I do not mean to place all political conservatives or everyone who celebrates soldierly honor perhaps more than the average citizen in this country in the same category as the odious extremists. Such a gross mis-characterization brings no clarity to the complex issues at hand—and, in fact, does no honor to the tradition of educated discourse that sustains any democracy and its institutions.

For this reason, I have been asked by my colleagues in the MGFA to speak to you about some aspects of the Bundeswehr, its soldierly tradition in a pluralistic state and society, and right-wing radicalism in the present. My project hangs on the meaning in the wider sense of our theme especially based on the political and strategic change in central Europe of the last 20 years. Here I am concerned not so much with the ideal definition of the term "military tradition" as a thing in itself, nor the well-known abuses of this idea that continue to lend the term a certain negative charge especially among skeptics and critics of this institution on the left and the right.

I certainly will not recapitulate for you the manifest vices of the radical right wing—fascist, national-socialist, or brown esoteric— that is all too luridly present on the internet, in this country, in Germany's neighbors, and even in my native country, for that matter. Instead, I mean to examine the tradition of the modern German soldier particularly in connection with the word "integration," that is, to seize on the word of the season and speculate about it as means of examining the tradition of the German, European, and NATO soldiers, sailors, and airmen and -women in the year 2011.

The Shadow of the Swastika

The shadow of the swastika looms over the heritage of the German soldier. To be sure, the source of this swastika today is not to be found in the heart and brains of the German armed forces. Rather, it emanates from the brown cloud that has formed more thickly in central Europe and beyond, as a continuity of politics and society, among the fraction of citizens still seized of discredited ideas from the era 1933–1945. Thus, the issue bears more on civil society, political culture, and the ideas there about the role of the armed forces in the past and present—a topic that never goes out of fashion for reasons I want to examine here.

A generation ago, at the end of his public life, Wolf Graf von Baudissin said that the problem of tradition was the traditional problem of the Bundeswehr. That is, when one cites the tradition of the soldier or its leading ideals, practices, and symbols, one quickly finds among skeptics and critics the idée fixe that the armed forces have long formed an undemocratic, or Nazi or neo-Nazi fifth column, biding its time until it can erupt again into a distracted German state and society. This critique typically continues that those men and women who opt to join the military are closet Nazis or at least nascent totalitarians. Either way, in this simplistic disparaging view, the maintenance of military tradition infects disoriented young people with Nazi ideas through the implicit or explicit glorification of the Wehrmacht that is taken to form the ineluctable inclination of all such military "tradition." The maintenance of traditional soldierly symbols, customs, regalia, and militaria is a sure sign of this perfidious longing for a resurrection of a totalitarian empire.

This shadow of the swastika, as it were, perhaps represents more about the political, social, and historical worldview of its proponents in our society and culture than it does about life in the armed forces here today. The valid heritage of the German soldier naturally does not begin and end with the Wehrmacht in National Socialism, nor with the propaganda view of the heritage of the German soldier as offered by Goebbels and others in the era of total war. Rather German soldiers and civilians, with much effort and reflection over more than 50 years, have fashioned a valid heritage of armies that symbolizes not only well-founded concepts of leadership, morale, discipline, and obedience, but the effective integration of the soldier into a pluralist, democratic state and society, as well as into a united Euro-Atlantic world.

And yet, the shadow persists in the face of perpetual conflict, economic crisis, and social dislocations. Indeed, this shadow seems darker the farther one is away from Germany and the less one knows about the Bundeswehr (as opposed to ripping yarns about World War II in those countries where the memory of the war bulks large in national self-image—for example in the UK and my country. In these cases, the stylized caricature of the more or less Prussian German soldier is far more important than any historical understanding of the actual record of the German military in a democratic state and the success of defense institution building here across the decades. For one example, YouTube and the Worldwide Web more generally have some curiously brown and field-grey corners, in which right-wing extremists here and elsewhere have recycled and fetishized such Third Reich propaganda films as the Riefenstahl documentaries and the Deutsche Wochenschau newsreels.

The preponderance of the contributors of such material with a neo-Nazi worldview is neither German nor old enough to have experienced the war or its immediate aftermath. Though they respond to the shadow of National Socialism and of the corruption of military professionalism in the 20th century, they cannot be said to represent—or even really understand—the "tradition" they claim to celebrate for reasons that, in fact, have nothing to do with the actual spirit and real life of this army in this nation. Their presence, however, requires us to examine why and how the Bundeswehr has been so successful at shattering this stereotype, particularly in its search for a valid heritage.

The Bridge of Values

The substantive discussion of the valid legacy of today's German and European soldier underscores the core principles of the political culture of this great nation and this fine army—and serves to remind those in the European Union and NATO of their real calling to uphold values in the face of the reality of power. In fact, I would characterize this search for a usable past based on the German Basic Law as the light that banishes this brown shadow. What do I mean?

I refer to the manner in which this civil-military search for a valid soldierly tradition within the framework of democratic statecraft has engaged conflicting political groups in German society as a whole, as opposed to the dogmas of a cult in which a caste, power elite, political party, or dominant class has marginalized or disenfranchised other social groups while imposing a monolithic and self-serving "tradition," often with a willful distortion of historical truth. "Tradition" cannot become the buzzword for a political or social group that seeks to delimit and thereby control its position in pluralistic Germany and Europe, especially with self-serving myths and legends that include an image of the enemy population. In other words, the measure of a valid heritage is the capacity of the tradition of the soldier to act as a means of integration in state and society and even in the international system of states while upholding the necessary principles of professional excellence at arms in the face of the rigors of military service, including combat. Soldiers in Germany are entitled to a tradition, as it were, that helps to instill the necessary soldierly self-confidence and esprit de corps, as well as honor, as in Britain, France, Poland, and the Czech Republic. To do so, such soldiers need the cooperation of civil society, even if this cooperation might also come along with criticism by civilians of aspects of military life, some of it less than fair or accurate. No organization in democratic public life stands immune to such critique, a fate that soldiers share with other professions in political culture and statecraft.

"Tradition" among armies in central Europe signifies the dissemination to soldiers (and civilians) the values, norms, and symbols that "join generations together with a bridge between the past and the present." This statement stands in the regulation on tradition, published nearly 30 years ago by the Federal German Ministry of Defense. *Innere Führung* forms the core of the so-called Bundeswehr eigene Tradition, one of the three pillars of tradition in the Bundeswehr (the others being the Prussian reforms of the era 1807–1819 and the 20 July 1944 assassination attempt). Today this *Bundeswehr eigene Tradition* strikes me as being the most important of the three pillars, which was surely not the case when I first began to learn about German military tradition as a doctoral student at the end of the 1970s. At the heart of *Innere Führung*, in turn, is the German Basic Law, and especially its clauses as to human dignity, as well as such political rights and virtues as citizenship and service within the limits of soldierly obedience in the modern world.

In practice, where the integration of the soldier operates in state, society, and the international system, be it in parliament as in the foundation of the Bundeswehr in the 1950s, or in Berlin of the last decade of the Bundeswehr im Einsatz, or in the internet today, the choice of valid norms, values, and symbols—and the construction of the bridge between their past and present meanings—is also a tradition of life here based on the political culture of this country, even with the contradictions and potential for disintegration in politics, society, and culture. Most central is the point that the selection of what is valid and what is invalid in the soldier's code of tradition must unfold according to the principles of the German Basic Law, actively reflected on and lived, rather than some codex of so-called timeless soldierly virtues, utterly unconnected to the society that this military serves. (Any lesser measures do militarize civilians and deprive them of their constitutional rights, while simultaneously relegating soldiers to a self-made ghetto.) Such a valid heritage hardly can be identical for all German soldiers and civilians, even if the German Ministry of Defense and many intelligent and thoughtful people at arms and in state and society have devoted decades of work to fashion a unitary definition. But that is the point of an integrating ethos and the tradition that arises from it.

The ideal of this tradition of integration is one I learned from the late General Ulrich de Maizière, who helped me professionally at the beginning of my career. He suggested to me then and thereafter that the Bundeswehr has been a force of integration in at least two ways, both quite central to its success as an institution in the democratic political culture of a united Germany and united Europe. This dual integration has had a domestic and an international aspect. In the first instance, the citizen of the Federal Republic has served in an army integrated in a democratic state, in which parliament integrated constitutional rights into military professionalism, while military professionals integrated themselves into a pluralistic society, with all its ups and downs. The citizen in uniform has served not in a democratic army (as it is wrongly called) nor, of course, in an army as a state within a state, nor in an army at the service of a totalitarian ideology stripped of civil rights. While the military has not been the sole school of democratic citizenship, as some called for at the end of the 1960s, the integrative force of the citizen in uniform as an army of the German parliament in a pluralistic state has resulted in a success of political culture and institution building that surely eluded the efforts of German liberals and socialists in the 19th and 20th centuries. A measure of this success came two decades ago with the Bundeswehr in German unity and the integration of the new citizens of the Federal Republic in the existing state.

The second aspect of this tradition of integration arises from what can only be called the cosmopolitan outlook of the German soldier as a result of decades of service abroad in integrated military structures and international organizations. One has only to go to Holloman Air Force Base in New Mexico (with its collocation of U.S. Air Force and Luftwaffe units) to see the reality of this generalization. Or come to my seminar in Monterey, California, where Bundeswehr officers routinely get high academic honors when they graduate, despite acquiring comparable accolades in local society and across the recreational tangent from Cannery Row, to Las Vegas, and the Grand Canyon. Without this international integration of German soldiers in the wider world of Euro-Atlantic nations and their values, I would not stand before you today. This tradition of a cosmopolitan soldier accounts for my deep personal affection and kinship with soldiers of the Bundeswehr, who have been my mentors, colleagues, and friends for more than three decades. It also connects today's German soldier to the most enduring and enlightened elements of the 18th-century spirit of Potsdam. But the word cosmopolitan is linked to integration in the wider and presently conflicted sense of society and values, to which I want to turn.

The Tradition of Integration

Let me add a biographical example to my reflection on a soldierly tradition of integration. First, though, I must preface this point with something told to me by one of the great figures associated with this place, Professor Dr. Klaus-Jürgen Müller, whose book on the army and Hitler played a great role in my intellectual development. When I finally met him here in 2007 to celebrate the 50th anniversary of the MGFA, he admonished me always to include the Habsburg Empire in my teaching of German military history. As a sign of my respect for him, and also because I also spend a lot of time in Vienna at the Austrian Defense Academy, and because I married a Slovak from Bratislava, Pressburg, Pozsony, I would like to reach across the Danube for a moment as we think about integration and tradition and the threat to both by enemies on the far right wing of modern politics in central Europe.

Josef Roth surely does not belong to the canon of tradition in our Bundeswehr, for he was neither a member of the Prussian nobility and bourgeoisie who modernized the Prussian state after 1806, nor was he a man of the Twentieth of July in the strictest sense; his death in 1939 meant that he could not participate in the reconstruction of Europe in the wake of the Second World War, though his prose and worldview have become a timeless part German culture. His politics do not fit those of the present-day Federal Republic, as he swerved from left to right in a manner that mirrored his professional life and his own personal misfortunes in the era of the 1920s and 1930s.

But Roth was a man of remarkable accomplishments as an author and a keen observer of the political and social worlds of his time, which included the cosmos of soldiers and the force of dynastic and soldierly tradition in state and society. According to his recent biography, he served not without pride as a soldier, despite suffering, privation, and the bitterness of the lost war. And both his writing and his life's experiences distinguish him as a case study in the promise of integration, the perils of its lack, and the transformative capacity of tradition amid its contradictions when placed against the record of the past.

Roth's writings about the nature of tradition, state, society, culture, and citizenship, the lives of real soldiers, and the role of the outsider have as much to say to our time as it did in his own. The novel *Radetzky March*, published in 1932, tells the story of the Habsburg Monarchy from the 1850s until its end in 1918 in the three generations of a Habsburg-Slovenian-Moravian minor noble family. It also embodies an examination of such traditional military values as bravery, honor, duty, and comradeship, as well as the fate of these traditions in the lives of several cohorts of Habsburg soldiers and bureaucrats as they were bound to Emperor Franz Josef, his army, and his state administration. The story includes the misuse of historical events at the battle of Solferino in 1859 to fashion a dynastic and military tradition.

Roth shows the impact of these events in lives of soldiers, as well as the resonance of those who distinguish themselves in battle and their heirs. At first glance, the novel contains a highly skeptical view of this use of the past and its role in the formation of tradition as a political force. Yet the novelist embraces as an overriding good this same tradition of the dual monarchy for its integration of nationalities and ethnic groups in a greater whole. A Jew from a middling market town in eastern Galicia, Roth knew a thing or two about the promise of civic and social integration.

Radetzky March was published at the end of the Weimar Republic, where Roth made his reputation as a journalist, short-story author, and novelist before emigrating to France the day that Hitler assumed the chancellorship in Germany. The novel can be said on one level to be an expression of a naïve, sentimental cult of tradition and an unseemly penchant for faded glories of vanished dynasties that in both the first Republic in Austria and the Weimar Republic that ended poorly for all concerned, especially Roth. The spirit of Potsdam on 21 March 1933 comes to mind, of course—and provides a signal clue that Roth's story is anything but an old monarchist's stab-in-the-back fantasy.

Indeed, to lump the tradition in central Europe of the dual monarchy as interpreted by Roth with the Frederick cult that operated here at the same time and provided the Nazis with useful tools with which to warp the past would be facile. For one thing, Roth's pining for the recently departed Habsburg emperor had much to do with the promise that membership in the imperial polity and its cultural sphere had extended to him, both as an individual with talent and as a representative of a sub-population and a supra-national or even non-national idea. While the Jews, particularly of Galicia, often were subject to administrative discrimination and physical violence through the centuries, a dedication to the integrative goals of the Enlightenment—European and Jewish—had, step by step, finally culminated in full citizenship for Austria's Jews. Loyalty to the emperor and the empire's values meant, at least in theory, that all social benefits (and responsibilities) were open to the Jews. Franz Josef may have harbored the same "fashionably" anti-Semitic opinions that characterized so much of central Europe at the turn of the last century, but he meant to continue the modernization of state and society that Josef II had begun. When the new broom, Jew-baiter populist Karl Lueger, won the mayoral election in Vienna in 1895, Franz Josef tried to stop the result for more than two years in no small part to ward off the divisiveness that this political tactic engendered. Roth, like many Habsburg Jews, was grateful for the chance to join the ranks of distinguished (often self-distinguished) men in the dual monarchy.

By this same dynamic, Roth symbolized much that the Nazis and others enemies of Jews and their integration into society hated very deeply about the "outsiders" who had traversed the cultural gradient from "the steppes of Asia" to the swank districts of Charlottenburg, Berlin West, and the Parkring in Vienna's First District: the so-called *Ostjude* who managed to swap his beard and caftan for middle-class dress and urbane manners—and acclaim. His success in the cosmopolitan world of literary Vienna and Berlin further incites National Socialist skepticism about integration, identity, and the Enlightenment in general, all with their voluntary and merit-oriented under-pinnings. Right-wing extremists then and now dispute the claim that Roth or anyone like him might make on social membership—conflating, as they do, citizenship and nationality/ethnicity, which they view as necessarily exclusive. Roth had little use for the national-ist politics of his time; Zionism left him bewildered just as the point-ed populism of the years on either side of the Great War struck him as un-Habsburg (and unworthy). His loyalty was to the imperial state that allowed and encouraged him to partake of its opportunities.

A word is in order about Roth's service to this state, the key indicator of citizenship in practice. Roth came to Vienna to study *Germanistik* in 1914, just as World War I began. He did not become a soldier immediately, though he seems to have subscribed to the gen-erally pro-war sentiments of the day. He became a press officer in 1916 among many literate and literary persons like him in uniform that the army of the dual monarchy wisely used in the role of what today is called strategic communication. This assignment often is dismissed as service at something less than the front line (an inaccu-rate implication in Roth's case), but it fitted into the necessity of ar-mies in an age of mass politics and mass communications. Now, after the war, he tended to embellish his military biography with some ficti-tious events, a fact that should not concern us overmuch, since there are others—soldiers and civilians—who have long done likewise in this country and mine, while pretending that they admire the tradition of the soldier. One might even read into Roth's inflations more of the same longing for a bygone empire and social system, and a tacit wish that more might have been done to preserve it. Either way, Roth real-ly was a soldier and saw war on the eastern front. He chronicled the fighting and the experiences of his comrades in news reports and poems from the front. These writings give voice to the times.

Most significant for our purposes is the fact of Roth's military service at all and its implications for reflection on the soldier and what I have called here a tradition of integration which is part of the valid heritage of the Bundeswehr in the year 2011. Now just as I have included Roth in an exercise that normally draws a line from the

Prussian reformers to the men and women of the 20th of July, while making a difficult arch around the years from, say, 1914 until 1945, I include Roth and his military service and its literary monument as a provocation to a group that really has little to offer us in our reflection today. Let me plain: I do not propose that the Habsburg dynastic tradition as interpreted by one of its most able observers in the first years of the 20th century be added to the canon of the Bundeswehr as some fourth pillar of its valid heritage. My Austrian colleagues claim the Habsburg legacy as their own, of course, but it is a tradition that concerns more than merely citizens of today's Republic of Austria, to be sure.

I include Roth and *Radetzky March* to highlight several points. First, the tradition of integration of Europe's peoples stands as major task of policy, leadership, and defense organizations in the present and future. In this task, the past has something to say to us, and says so in beautiful German prose. The Bundeswehr has already set an admirable standard with this European and North Atlantic tradition of integration, when the issue concerns ethnic groups—citizens seen as being from beyond the margins of what integral nationalists and radical right-wingers deem to be "cultured and civilized society."

Second, while I am not sure whether Goebbels had Roth's books burned on Bebelplatz in 1933, Roth's depiction of the hopes and disappointments of soldierly tradition contrast with the Nazis' deformation of tradition and soldiering in the era 1933–1945. His depiction of soldierly tradition especially diverges from how some neo-Nazi, brown esoteric fanatic, or radical right-winger might seize upon what he or she deems as the legacy of the Wehrmacht in the here and now. From this point, let me turn to more conventional definitions of soldierly tradition in the Bundeswehr and conclude with a warning as regards things to come and our role in the tasks of today and tomorrow.

Misunderstandings Amid the Search for Tradition

The search for a valid soldierly tradition belongs to the history of ideas of modern German military institutions from the 18th century to the present—another noteworthy heritage of the German soldier that we should celebrate as well. But the civil-military use of the term "tradition" in connection with soldiers and defense institutions as we know them is of far more recent vintage. One will look in vain in the annals of the late 18th or early 19th century for a single, compact codex on the tradition of the soldier in the idiom of the era that in any way resembles the ministerial guidelines of 1982. The use of the term "tradition" among soldiers and civilians on a wide basis in this country originated more in the late 19th and early 20th centuries; previously, the values and symbols we associate with the soldierly tradition were inscribed in dynastic and estate codes of duty, education, and training in the realms of courts, estates, and the subjects who served them. Moreover, the criteria for a valid military heritage have scarcely remained static in modern German history, or in European history overall because of rapid change in politics, society, and the face of combat and war.

This point requires further illumination amid a critique of some noteworthy misunderstandings connected with soldierly tradition. For many with little insight into the history of military tradition as a feature of democratic civil-military integration in the FRG, the soldierly heritage has been defined in negative terms in the dimension of things (that is, a helmet or a cap badge) rather than values. In this school of thought, the Bundeswehr represents a "break with tradition" because it is not "Prussian" enough in its armory of regalia and customs, as signifiers of underlying soldierly values: The Wachbataillon does not mount the guard on the Linden as done in 1914, or 1943, or even 1988; the Class-A uniform is a cloudy grey as opposed to field grey; soldiers do not address their superiors in the third person; soldiers do not wear walking-out uniforms with a gleaming bayonet on a lacquered belt outside the barracks in town and beyond; there is no parade march—and when one goes to a Bundeswehr ceremony, there is far too much chamber music instead of Johann Gottfried Piefke's marches or, worse, the marches are from John Phillip Sousa. In this limited, blinkered, but widespread view, the tradition of the soldier is circumscribed solely by customs, ceremonies, insignia, regalia, and other external aspects of soldierly and garrison life in the realm of symbols forged from Damascus steel or plated copper.

Please do not misunderstand me here: German soldiers naturally deserve such symbols and ceremonies, just as they exist in the armed forces of your democratic neighbors. But one does ill to mistake these things as magically possessed of some greater value than the core principles and traditions of this army in a democracy imbedded in the political culture of the Federal Republic and a united Europe. These external aspects of garrison life assume the meaning, at least for certain skeptics of *Innere Führung*, as the measures of "timeless soldierly virtues" or what in the United States often is described as the "code of the warrior," pointedly at odds with a soft, pluralist society. At its core, this notion represents the unfortunate (and typically undemocratic) coincidence of cultural pessimism and military romanticism.

In this same vein, for those ignorant of the reality of German history and the history and tradition of this army as a force of integration as I have described it, the Bundeswehr has bogus traditions because it does not honor the institution and personalities of the Wehrmacht. This version of the Wehrmacht, by the way, signifies an Anglo-Saxon institution of curious character (see the biography of Rommel or even certain Waffen-SS soldiers in the English-speaking world), which its fans know from newsreels and from antiseptic accounts of the past in which the tactical level of war is foremost and the armed forces exist in a separate realm from society and political culture. For those who would trash the German Basic Law to fulfill their political fantasies, this sanitized, naive version of the Wehrmacht is made to be full measure of military professionalism in some pure, ideal form in which *Innere Führung* is then deficient, if not deleterious. In their semi-Huntingtonian vision of the perfect soldier above and beyond the realm of political culture—and a pluralist society—this form of field-grey professionalism adhered in the actual record of the past to standards that cannot in the remotest sense be described as ideal.

In the event, the veterans of the Wehrmacht became citizens of the Federal Republic of Germany in a process that is no less historically significant for what has been until now—though perhaps not tomorrow—the peace and prosperity we enjoy in Europe. To be sure, in the era in which the Bundeswehr first took shape, there existed also the (then) partially integrated veterans of the Wehrmacht, Waffen-SS, and Hitler Youth in the young, untried democratic West German society. At that time, the original fear lurked that the Bundeswehr could serve either as a revival of the apolitical and anti-democratic Reichswehr or, at worst, a Werwolf organization nipping at the heels of a young democracy. My doctor-father, Gordon Craig, expressed this worry to his diary in the middle-1950s, as other members of the Princeton faculty did in public, looking to the past, especially the interwar period, as a prologue of what would befall the second German Republic in its first years.

This fear proved unfounded, of course, but the process of defense-institution building in its civil-military values and symbols took years beyond 12 November 1955 and has generally been too simply characterized as the struggle between reformers and traditionalists. The search for tradition in the 1950s and 1960s comprised an attempt to offer a set of professional values to very skeptical company-grade officers of the former Wehrmacht now in Bundeswehr uniform, as well as the young troops they trained. On an official level, this effort sought to square *Innere Führung* with the adherents of certain features of the old cult of soldierly ethos. More broadly, it reflected the embrace of the new political and social order amid the wounded pride and confusion that marked some of the less-well democratically integrated citizens of this country, who for a long time regarded Stauffenberg as no hero at all, though they otherwise upheld the political order of the young Bonn republic. I knew the people who formulated this policy and wrote a book about it. As a young person, I shared their political world as a high-school and college student here, so I respect their accomplishment.

In the three-plus decades since I first met these men (all veterans of the Wehrmacht in the Bundeswehr, by the way), I have seen not wholly dissimilar civil-military events elsewhere in Europe and have struggled professionally to deal with them. While one cannot easily compare especially the role of state and party institutions and even soldiers in the mass murder of European Jewry and other victims of the Nazi order in Europe to the repressive party-state apparatus of the old East bloc, there are kindred challenges in transforming the hearts and minds of soldiers in an emerging democracy. The measure of a valid heritage in this country from the 1950s through the late 1970s embodied the political culture of integration in its internal dimension of rendering the Wehrmacht veteran and young person born in the Third Reich into a citizen in uniform of the FRG. Such a policy embraced the ideal that the men and women of the Twentieth of July as well as the simple, honest soldier at the front were equally worthy figures of a new tradition. Such policy also reflected the political culture and the consolidating defense and military institutions of the era, something that should not be gainsaid even today, though as time passed, this policy came under fire.

The changing image of the Wehrmacht and its legacy in the political culture of the FRG symbolizes but one aspect of the general transformation to a more critical view of the past and of professional choice in the face of the Nazi dictatorship as seen from decades of peace and a consolidating democratic political culture. The cold-war compromise that governed the soldier's official heritage then became a subject of controversy in the midst of domestic civil-military conflicts that have unfolded in episodes since the 1970s. (The most recent has been in 2005 with the *causa* Mölders, which I cannot examine in this talk today.)

The changing civil-military view of the valid soldierly heritage—as well as the misunderstandings that are a constant of this process—embody a debate in a pluralist state and society about the meaning of the past in the dimensions of constitutional fundamentals, citizenship, and military professionalism. This generalized issue today is hardly confined to Germany; it operates in my professional experience in such nations as Austria, Poland, the Czech Republic, and Slovakia. The meaning of the legacy of the Wehrmacht in contemporary history has generally formed the point of controversy in this question, which, nonetheless to my mind at least, has reflected the success of defense-institution building and political culture in this nation.

The assertion that the Bundeswehr "is not military enough" because it fails to honor the Wehrmacht embodies an extraordinary ignorance, as well as a red herring. Such statements no longer arise from the Stammtische of veterans' organizations in the political turmoil of the 1960s, but from neo-conservatives and NATO burden-sharing fanatics with little interest and concern for real content of military professionalism, a question that leads to security and defense policy generally and my concluding words.

Conclusion

The fight over tradition has often been not so much about the historical legacy of the soldier and the fundamentals of his or her professional codex, but frequently about the attitude of political and social groups toward security policy and the use of armed forces as an aspect of foreign policy. This phenomenon reflects but another aspect of the tradition of integration of which I spoke earlier. Tradition, military symbols, and soldiers' identity all become a means for various political groups to argue about issues of policy that often have little to do, really, with the political and professional identity of soldiers. (More often, the contours of the debate owe more to what the opposition dislikes in the white paper of the moment.)

There is nothing especially wrong with the fact that the political discourse becomes locked in a dispute about symbols, but this phenomenon often accentuates the sentiment among soldiers in this state and society that the civilian world and the world of the party politician do not accord them the same respect and even affection as operate, say, in France, Poland, the UK, or the United States. Such a civil-military phenomenon of the disaffected soldier of the lost column or of the abandoned outpost, or, at worse, stabbed in the back after a lost war, bulks especially important today in the face of the Afghan campaign and the proliferation of roles and missions for NATO soldiers, especially with internal security in a globalized world bereft of peace. The problems of policy and supreme command and control of the last several years of the Bundeswehr im Einsatz and the sacrifice demanded of the German soldier in NATO and the European Union in combat in Afghanistan represent a fresh challenge in the evolution of this army in a democracy and its professional ethos.

One may adhere to one's own view as concerns the political value of the NATO Afghan operation, but what remains unacceptable, to me at least, is to degrade, to neglect, or otherwise to belittle the need of soldiers for their sense of professional identity within the democratic political culture of this nation in the face of combat amid security-building operations. This imperative means that civilians should be at pains to help maintain a valid soldierly heritage, not by fawning over soldiers and their myths and legends in the at times false manner as it unfolds in my country, but more or less in accord with the tradition of integration in the self-image of the Bundeswehr as a feature of the political culture of this country. The suspension of conscription, that is, the rise of an all-professional force, as has begun here makes this requirement more acute, yet still.

If we do not accept our responsibility of citizenship within this imperative of the civil pillar of the soldierly heritage, then someone else will fill the gap in the realm of historical ideas and symbols of the soldier in state and society. Such has already happened in my country by those who abuse the history of the soldier for domestic political ends.

So we return to the Nazi spirit of Potsdam in the spring of 1933 and forces that would nullify the tradition of integration with the revival of old hatreds and patterns of thought in the shadow of the swastika and who would once more burn Josef Roth's books in their fantasies of a new Reich. To be sure, such political figures, movements, groups, sects, and cells, who—quite by accident, in my own experience of the matter—see SS Obergruppenführer Thedor Eicke as an embodiment of professional military ideals worthy of tradition, lay claim to the heritage of the German soldier outside the fabric of this state and this army, but they do operate within the structure of German society, European society, and U.S. society. These persons under the black, red, and white banner, in grey flannel, or with crew cuts and paratrooper boots would negate all that I have suggested here as regards the role of the soldier in integration in its wider sense. They would fashion anew the cult of tradition in service of a totalitarian and racist ideology and the maintenance of a soldierly tradition as lives on in the nooks and crannies of YouTube but which the Federal Republic of Germany and its soldiers have banished. The Bundeswehr has formed its own tradition, based on the German Basic Law and the history of the armed forces.

Today our meeting here to honor the liberation of Auschwitz and a victory over the perversion of soldierly ethos symbolizes the strength and durability of the tradition of integration in this record as lived by German soldiers in their number, whom I have the great honor to call teachers, mentors, colleagues and, most of all, comrades. The present crisis of political violence and political and economic dislocation would be entirely familiar to Josef Roth, whose aspirations for membership in a multi-national, or even non-national state should challenge us to reflect on the duties and challenges of forging a European or even Euro-Atlantic soldierly tradition, especially in the shadow of disintegration that plagues our world.

II.   Transatlantic Connections

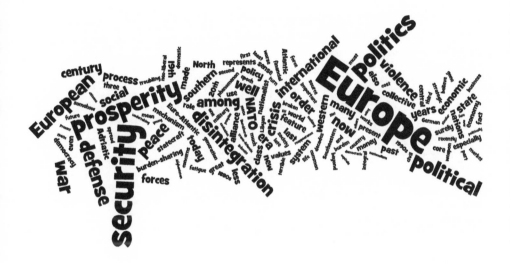

6. The United States and European Military Power[*]

"The Big Picture," a 1950s television documentary produced by the U.S. Army as a flourish of Cold-War mass persuasion of the American public, treated the soldier in Europe as a constant theme of military roles in the atomic age. In one of many episodes on U.S. Army, Europe, scenes of U.S. soldiers in West Germany portrayed young American draftees housed in ivy-covered former Wehrmacht barracks in the German southwest, enjoying tourism on the Rhine, and playing concert music along with West Germans.

Nowhere in this stylized black-and-white reportage loomed the stockpiles of U.S. nuclear bombs or artillery shells in the Palatinate or Bavaria, nor was there any evidence of the brutal struggle of a decade earlier in which Germans and Americans had slaughtered each other in the final months of World War II. Rather, the pictures resembled newsreel footage from before 1939, in fact, in which American tourists, so long as they tended not to be Jews, flocked to Hitler's Germany. So shortly after the war, U.S. forces remained in West Germany, but not as belligerents. The former enemy had, in "The Big Picture," become a ward and an ally, the appeal of whose culture had a transformative effect on American draftees, who seemed to have, themselves, become German through music and architecture.

In the intervening decades, however, the easy bonhomie among U.S. and German citizens and soldiers—and the mutual understanding, appreciation, and respect that also came with such prolonged interaction—has faded like the original film that captured these scenes. The children or grandchildren of the GIs who got to know West Germany of the 1950s no longer have served in a conscript army (if many of them serve at all); they have little or no such opportunity to experience European culture while in government

---

[*] Originally published as Donald Abenheim, "Die militärischen Beziehungen zwischen den USA und Europa," in Jörg Echternkamp and Hans Hubertus Mack, eds., *Geschichte ohne Grenzen? Europäische Dimensionen der Militärgeschichte vom 19. Jahrhundert bis Heute* (Berlin/Boston: De Gruyter/Oldenbourg, 2017) pp. 271–306.

service. Since the 1990s, the Cold-War European garrisons, which as late as the middle 1980s boasted in excess of 325,000 troops, as well as civilians and family members, have almost all vanished into oblivion. In the unsettled geopolitics of the early 21st century—after a decade of jihadist counterinsurgency, post-conflict reconstruction campaigns, domestic economic stagnation, and a much-promoted U.S. "pivot" to Asia as a focus of defense posture—this overwhelmingly positive experience of the world, especially Germany, has given way in the United States to the war-weariness and partisan vitriol of the right-wing U.S. Tea Party that demonizes all things connected with Europe.

By the same token, young German soldiers in 2014 in a small number may only have served along U.S. troops in Afghanistan, but, suffused in a daily experience in which the United States is increasingly a distant, if more affordable, vacation destination, have little knowledge of the mutual relationship between the U.S. military and Europe in the realms of the record of war, the military mind, geopolitics, and even culture. This crucial relationship forms the topic of this chapter and an indispensable part of the story of war, state, and society in modern Europe.

Forces of Military Convergence

The role of Europe as a leading idea of military professionalism and the strategic center of gravity in the evolution and character of the U.S. military spans from the beginnings of the U.S. armed forces in the 18th century until the present—be it as a professional example to be emulated or abhorred, as a mortal enemy to be conquered, or as an extravagant waste of American tax payer's treasure as free-riding allies to be rejected or as a region suddenly to be rediscovered as a vital national interest. As the intellectual ancestor, rival, or ally as well as the scene of decisive battles and enduring strategic encounters, Europe—in terms of state, society, and armies—bulk large in the self-image and institutional character of the American military.

The story of the U.S. soldier and Europe starts out with an American rejection of European political norms and social customs amid emulation in military training, soldierly habits, and professional ideals. From the mid-20th century on, the experience of alliance between North America and Western Europe has predominated. This process in its various phases has fostered what may be called a soldierly convergence between the continents, all talk of American exceptionalism and a European civil-political culture in the 21st century notwithstanding. This coming together of men-at-arms (later of men- and women-at-arms) on the two continents, despite all that might seem to militate against such a conclusion, forms the central theme of the work at hand, and tells a story of how political and social isolation gave way through conflict to a common record of war and peace. Within this soldierly convergence has also operated centrifugal forces in their variety that are examined here and that have acted to drive the two continents apart.

The American soldier has formed a theme in much of European politics and society since the beginning of the 20th century, if not earlier. Despite the 21st-century self-image of leading Europeans, heavy with the moral superiority of civil power, a contempt for power politics, and scorn for the use of armed force, a united Europe that has gone from self-destruction in the age of total war to prosperity and peace is unthinkable without American defense policy as well as soldiers and arms. From Moltke's dismissal of the U.S. Civil War as an armed mob, to the affection of German women for U.S. occupation troops in the Rhineland of 1919 or, more properly, after 1945, when African-American U.S. troops became a fixture of West German life, to the German-Jewish émigrés who returned after 1944 in the U.S. military government, the U.S. soldier, along with presidents and figures of popular culture, acquired a distinctive role in the European mind as a symbol of U.S.-European relations.

The story of the United States as a European military power has unfolded on two levels: first, the rise, maintenance, and, lately, the eclipse of U.S. arms on the continent of Europe in the age of total war as told in military biography and campaign narratives of combat;

and second, in the realm of ideas, mentality, and culture. These categories cannot be fully understood as separate and discrete matters; statecraft, military institutions, soldiers, society, and culture form a whole that is as much a part of this account as the formation of strategy, the lives of generals, the waging of decisive battles, and the evolution of tactics and weapons.

The U.S. Military and Europe from the 18th Century until 1917: American Exceptionalism and its European Soldierly Dimension

The first phase of the U.S.-European relationship in the realm of statecraft, society, and arms concerns the role of the European soldier and armies in the institutional consolidation of the U.S. military in the 18th and 19th centuries. While the founders of the American state in the pivotal period from the 1760s until the 1790s scorned dynasties, estates, absolutism, mercantilism, and the civil-military system of Britain and the continental powers, Europe nonetheless provided the first generations of American soldiers and military thinkers with leading ideas about the nature of war, soldierly ethos, and the science and art of strategy. "The American ways of war," Russell Weigley writes of the late 18th and first half of the 19th century, "were offshoots of the European ways of war, and American strategic thought was therefore a branch of European strategic thought."

This experience manifested a simultaneous professional rejection amid emulation in the civil-military realm, itself part of the cosmos of U.S.-European relations of the 18th and 19th centuries. The founders of the new republic distanced themselves in constitutional practice and rhetoric, if not always in fact, from the mother country, while retaining the tradition of the militia and the citizen soldier. Central to this practice loomed the danger that European empires in North America posed to the 13 colonies and thereafter to the young United States. Defense against invasion across the young nation's northern, western, or southern borders from the British, French, or

Spanish empires formed a focus of military energy as well as the traditional *Feindbild* with resonance into the 21st century.

This sense of perpetual threat led, in John Shy's seminal, *The People Numerous and Armed*, to a quest for absolute security in the face of such vulnerability. This aspect of strategy diverged from the continental European experience with its more limited goals of policy in the cosmos of the great powers, but the former nonetheless became a central tenet of American military thought.

On the other hand, as commander in chief of the continental army in war of independence against Britain in 1776–1781, George Washington employed European drillmasters to organize and train his citizen army. He and his subordinates eschewed guerilla war and an irregular armed force against the British, adhering, instead, to European norms of military organization, professional ethos, and conduct in battle. This new army became a smaller version of its British opponents in its inner structure, tactics, and even strategy, reinforced by the coalition with France to achieve victory in 1781. This American adaptation of aspects of dynastic, absolutist armies notwithstanding in the extremis of war, the peacetime military force founded in the early 1790s, returned to the medieval tradition of a "well-regulated militia," enshrined in the U.S. Constitution.

American military institutions in their early years, as Weigley points out, drew heavily on medieval English, Swiss, and dynastic European prototypes in their dualist ideal of the militia versus the military professional. The infancy of American arms in the 18th and especially 19th century oriented itself toward these two European models, either the citizen in uniform or the soldier as technician of tactics, while rejecting the estate-based military system of absolutism, with its large standing army led by nobles hostile to constitutional government.

While the fighting and military organization in the first wars in North America in the 17th and 18th century might have differed in their strategic scale, social basis, and constitutional principles from war in Europe in the age of absolutism, the rise of war of the nations after 1789 eventually led to a convergence between North American and European war and military professionalism in the course of the 19th century. This coming together of the continents in the military mind and textbooks especially showed itself in the dimension of military education as the basis for strategic thought and institutional practice. Although before his departure from office in 1796, Washington had wanted to found a military academy for the education of officers on the European model, this institution only came into existence in the year 1802 under the administration of Thomas Jefferson, who opposed a centralized federal government and armed and naval forces. Located on the Hudson River, 60-odd miles and a day's journey from New York City, the new school focused on nation-building through military engineering and the citizen soldier. This ideal diverged in spirit from the enlightened generalism of Scharnhorst's and Humboldt's educational principles in the Prussian Kriegsakademie founded in 1810.

Presently, the value of the citizen soldier became confused in practice in the small U.S. Army of the early 19th century, an institution of comparative political and numerical insignificance to the armies of continental Europe, at least before the U.S. Civil War (1861–1865). The citizen soldier became overshadowed by the military technical specialist, with a strong French heritage peculiar to the early 19th century. Such founders of the U.S. Military Academy (USMA) as Sylvanus Thayer and Dennis Hart Mahan oriented the instruction in the 1820s and 1830s to the legacy of the defense à la Vauban and the offense à la Napoleon, with a curriculum imported from the French army engineering and artillery school at Metz. The most successful graduates of the USMA served as military engineers, built fortresses along the nation's seacoasts against a European invasion from a North America base (these structures being the word in stone of the Monroe Doctrine of 1823 to isolate the new world from European imperialist predations), and otherwise nurtured a belief in military science as the basis of the soldier's ethos according to Jomini's immutable principles of war.

In the second instance, the French theory and application of tactics transplanted to the Hudson Valley glorified the quest for decisive battle on the model Austerlitz in 1805, as well as the value of field fortifications in combat. The army's defensive orientation in the coastal fortresses of the so-called Third System (from the wake of the 1812 war until the Civil War) gave way to the expansion according to Manifest Destiny in the Mexican War of 1846–1848.

The Crimean War soon thereafter in the early 1850s offered a chance to renew the bond between the education of U.S. officers and the wars and armies of Europe. The dispatch in 1853–1854 of an elite group of West Point officers to study the effects of the fighting on the Black Sea, in which fortifications figured prominently at least at the tactical level. This mission followed in the tradition of the senior Mahan's French service three decades earlier. The Crimean conflict heralded a new epoch of war in the mid-19th century, in which the scale of fighting expanded and the implications of this process, along with the effects of the industrial revolution on state and arms, became a focus of military thought and professional expertise.

The contradictions between a defensive orientation of military learning and the imperative to formulate an offensive strategy in the course of the U.S. Civil War illustrates the ambiguous character of American and continental European military ideas and institutions in the mid-19th century. Continental Europeans may have rooted for the victory of the Confederacy in the Civil War, and otherwise abhorred the policy and society of the Union states; general staff officers in Prussia/Germany could dismiss from afar the ineffectiveness of U.S. arms in the early years of conflict (i.e., no decisive battle on the Prussian model) based on a militia organization without the comparable political will and institutional brains as in continental Europe—all as a manifestation of wrong-headed democracy on the military profession. Such critics of American society and technicians of the new operational level of war failed to understand fully the baleful, knotted effects of mass political ideology and the industrial age on the intensification of warfare, for which a military-scientific or strategic idealism of tactical and operational expertise offered little mastery. Sherman's march through Georgia in 1864 and the transition in the Franco-Prussian war from regular war to irregular combat, echoed in the anger and hatred of the commune in Paris once the regular French army had disintegrated in 1871, portended this expansion of war that facilitated the convergence of U.S. and European strategic thought and practice.

At the close of the U.S. Indian Wars in the 1880s, a new school of U.S. military thinkers emerged to formulate strategic theory. The horizons of such an effort reached far beyond the North American boundaries. This project took place amid the revival of national interest in strategy as well as military and naval affairs within the age of imperialism. The leading lights of strategic theory in the post-Civil War era included the former general and peacetime colonel Emory Upton and U.S. Navy Captain Alfred Thayer Mahan, whose writings drew on Prussian-German and British examples rather than those of France. Their work formed the basis, in part, for the eventual advent of the U.S. as a military power in Europe in the 20th century. Disgusted with U.S. constitutional principles and the citizen soldier as having made the U.S. Civil War more violent and wasteful, Upton reified Moltke the Elder's institution and doctrine to an American ideal of professional ethos and organization very much at odds with domestic politics of economy, isolation, and pacifism. Son of the French-inspired reformer of the USMA curriculum, Mahan formulated a military-scientific interpretation of British naval mastery as "sea power," a doctrine in the era of imperial expansion at the end of the 19th century that presently made the claim of the United States as a great power and the mark of American strategic thought on Europe decades before U.S. troops first appeared on the old continent.

The war against Spain over Cuba and the Philippines in 1898 manifested the strategic goals of Mahan's navalism and imperialism, as well as new challenges of strategy across the Caribbean and the Pacific Oceans. The operational problems of U.S. Army and Navy command and control, combat, and logistics in the Cuban and Philippine campaigns gave life to Upton's Prusso-centric critique of military organization two decades earlier and furnished the basis for army reforms in the decades prior to 1917 and the U.S. entry into the Great War.

The American Soldier and Europe in Total War, 1917–1945: Expeditionary Force, Retreat, Renewed Conquest, and Postwar Roles

The era of total war in the 20th century witnessed the advent of the United States as a political and military force in Europe. This pivotal phase saw the convergence of U.S. and European military thought and transformed U.S. statecraft and military posture in a doctrine of total war, to say nothing of the impact on European politics, society, economy, and culture. The era 1917–1945 ushered in the role of the U.S. soldier as a global force, with the fate and security of Europe as center of gravity in the further maturation of U.S. military institutions. Heretofore unseen challenges of strategy, operations, technology in war, as well as alliance cohesion appeared in the experience of the American military, to say nothing of the battlefield experience of the soldier and the non-combatant with whom he came into contact.

But at first, in the years 1914–1923, this process operated in a dizzying pattern of long hesitation followed by a brief, loud, all-out campaign with the highest ideals, that collapsed, in turn, under the burdens of domestic and power politics, and finally culminated in a disorganized withdrawal of military force in favor of commercial power—none of which provided a sound basis for lasting security. As Weigley notes about this second stage in the U.S.-European mutual influence in war and peace, until this moment, the United States and its armed forces had been peripheral to European system of states and its armed power.

The eventual entry of the United States into World War I unfolded after a decades-long naval buildup, a congressional reform of the Army and the Navy in 1916, and the U.S. military intervention in the Mexican Civil War in the years 1913 and 1916–1917. Not unlike imperial squabbles over Samoa and the Philippines at the end of the

19th century, the fate of Mexico in civil war, at the same time of the construction of the Panama Canal, led to friction with Germany far from the European continent in the tradition of the Monroe Doctrine. The end of neutrality and the American decision for war against Germany and the Central Powers in April 1917, championed by Woodrow Wilson, hinged on freedom of the seas, which had been put at risk by the German Third Supreme Army Command's decision for unlimited submarine warfare.

Amid an outpouring of martial fervor (and a not small portion of nationalist hysteria), Wilson promoted wide-ranging war aims, with promises of a democratic peace and national self-determination for the peoples of Europe. General Tasker Bliss, who represented the United States in the Entente Supreme War Council, General John J. Pershing, who commanded the American Expeditionary Force in association with the French Army, and Admiral William S. Sims, who led the U.S. naval forces attached to the British Grand Fleet, heralded a revolution in the military and naval affairs of the United States— which was effected by the million or so U.S. troops who presently did duty in western Europe and elsewhere. Bliss, Pershing, Sims, and similar figures embodied a discontinuity in the previous experience of the senior-most officers in the aspects of strategy, alliance cohesion, and the command of forces outside of the continental United States.

Despite the series of organizational and operational reforms that had unfolded since the turn of the century, the U.S. Army and the U.S. Navy as well as American industry and society could scarcely forge all the weapons and equipment this new effort demanded within a year's time; the American armed forces were just as hard-pressed to mount the command, training, and fighting power to match the degree of the European nations at war. These handicaps notwithstanding, Pershing's American Expeditionary Force within the strategic and operational framework of an "Associated Power" of the Entente integrated new American ground and air units in 1918 for training within the French Army, where there operated a legacy of republican kinship ("Lafeyette, we are here!") and a shared tradition that recalled the 18th century. This tradition of shared values and comradeship in arms was rendered a thing of myth and legend by the avant-garde of American volunteers before 1917 in the French Foreign Legion and the French flying forces.

This operational and tactical integration of the U.S. ground troops in the Anglo-French battle line did not become a total subordination or dissolution of U.S. forces, as much as the French high command had wanted to spread U.S. soldiers in the French order of battle. Despite many challenges of alliance cohesion and operational mishaps, by the fall of 1918, a U.S. force of more nearly 900,000 helped defeat German forces in the west. Pershing, on his own—and contrary to diplomacy as well as common sense—wanted to press on, after the model of Ulysses S. Grant in 1865, for a total German surrender rather than the more limited Entente aim of an armistice.

The integration of U.S. naval forces in 1917–1918 into the British Grand Fleet broke with the legacy of Anglo-American conflict in the 18th and 19th century. This policy unfolded as well against British suspicions of 1916 mandated U.S. maritime building plans, "second to none," with an anti-British and -Japanese orientation, made worse in turn, by those U.S. Navy figures who saw the British Empire as an enduring menace. Sims, however, pushed this antagonism aside and threw the weight of U.S. naval units more or less under British command and control into the fight against German submarine warfare, while maintaining cordial relations with the Royal Navy.

The success of arms in battle and alliance cohesion of the years 1917–1918 against the Central Powers endured only briefly into 1919 in the abject absence of coherent statecraft among the victors at Versailles, Saint Germaine, Trianon, and elsewhere while the primacy of isolation reappeared in U.S. domestic politics. This un-blooming was visible in Wilson's lost battle with Congress to enshrine the covenant of the League of Nations and among U.S. senior soldiers, to say nothing of the peoples of Europe, who witnessed in revulsion the Versailles negotiations and the flawed peace. The belief took hold among American soldiers in the mirrored halls of Versailles that the recent war had been a trick, foisted by a cunning Europe on an innocent America. This generalization especially obtained in the trans-

Atlantic diplomacy of U.S. financial aid of the Entente and the reparations from the conquered during the 1920s, all of which poisoned domestic politics and the international political economy.

Nowhere was this disillusionment as tangible as in the Franco-American fight over the roles and missions of the 15,000-man U.S. occupation army in Koblenz, which resisted French Army-promoted Rhenish separatism, while the small American command vainly embraced a pro-Weimar agenda. The disintegrating peace of the years 1919–1922 culminated, in the wake of the U.S. Senate defeat of the U.S. membership in the League, in the little-remarked withdrawal of the garrison on the Rhine as a prelude to the French-Belgian occupation in 1923. While U.S. troops departed, their service in Britain, France, and Germany from 1917 until 1923 in such numbers, they had left a deep impression on European society and culture as to the character of American state and society visible in a citizen-soldier army.

Once the last doughboy vanished into the Atlantic mist, he was followed onto the continent in the mid-1920s by Charles Lindbergh, a high-minded U.S. diplomacy of arms limitations and treaties that banned war, and number-crunching monetary and commercial onslaught on the European estate, class, and consumption. The welter of film, music, five-and-dime stores, auto exhaust and Taylorite management doctrine unleashed by the Americans in Europe seemed to obscure the wreckage of the battlefields of the Great War, themselves the object of American tourist pilgrimages. Accompanied by diplomatic hectoring about reparations and empty treaties to impose world peace rather than a sensible, realistic statecraft to uphold the covenant of the League, American postwar security building resulted in a false prosperity that did precious little to eradicate the sources of conflict in the European system and then, itself, collapsed in the fall of 1929.

The depression in the United States hardened anti-interventionist and anti-European sentiment in domestic politics in the first half of the 1930s. The neutrality laws enacted by isolationists in Congress sought to preclude war by tying the hands of the presidency in foreign policy. The government parsimony and chimeras of perpetual peace kept the armed forces at negligible strength, and caused the services to fight each other bitterly for funding, especially as concerned aviation roles and missions. Atop the sand table, some thought was given by certain figures in the senior military leadership from 1934 onward to a future Europe upturned by Hitler's Germany and its revisionist allies, but no political will existed then to rearm fully while anti-interventionism, pacifism, and isolationism dominated the public until 7 December 1941.

President Franklin Roosevelt only truly awakened to the menace of the European dictators amid the Czech crisis of 1938. The outbreak of war in Europe in 1939 caused Roosevelt to adopt a policy of indirect support for the UK, by no means endorsed by public opinion, a significant part of which was anti-British, while the government formally adhered to neutrality. With the fall of France in June 1940—the shock of which cannot be gainsaid in the spirit of the U.S. military and its image of Europe—this pro-British policy gained velocity, especially with the start of military-to-military contacts between the United States and the U.K. Joint staff cooperation deepened, accompanied by such measures from FDR to strengthen the British as the destroyers-for-bases deal (September 1940); the Lend-Lease program of arms transfers (March 1941), and the convoying of merchant ships in the Atlantic (summer/fall 1941). The latter step had brought the United States and Germany to the brink of undeclared war in the Atlantic when the Japanese attacked Pearl Harbor and the Philippines in December 1941.

The basic outline of U.S. grand strategy as well certain features of its operational character in the Second World War had already taken shape in early 1941; these processes matured, according to Maurice Matloff, in three stages through 1945 amid significant conflicts among the allies about ends and means. In the first stage through 1942, a defensive strategy marked by the scarcity of forces and materiel in expectation of an industrial and manpower build-up, the British and the U.S. regarded the defeat of Germany as the first priority, with Japan and the Pacific Theater taking second place. Once the USSR was attacked in June 1941, the problem of three and more great powers in alliance eventuated, with an "arm's-length" cooperation with the Soviets.

While general agreement might operate among the three allies about a victory over Germany, the formation of consensus about strategy caused endless conflict, which bulked great implications as concerned the fate of the European state system and the U.S. role in it. The United States began the war in December 1941 once again as a junior partner, this time to the British, while FDR regarded the French as a strategic nuisance. Anglo-American emphasis on maritime and air power strategies and the indirect approach collided with the annihilationist and continental school of strategy in the U.S. Army and the newly formed Joint Chiefs of Staff. The latter desired a rapid invasion of the European continent (Operation Bolero) and a knockout defeat of Germany in total war, whereby the virtues of the Soviet alliance loomed uppermost as the opposite flank of such strategy. The overwhelming blow would enable the United States, in turn, to withdraw from Europe quickly, its work at an end, as in the era after 1919. The first U.S. troops to reach Europe were those of V Corps, which debarked in Northern Ireland in January 1942. General Dwight D. Eisenhower was named Supreme Allied Commander, Headquarters European Theater of Operations in May 1942. This title notwithstanding, Roosevelt, leaned to the British strategy, with the initial campaign in the Mediterranean (Operation Torch, November 1942) a show of maritime power and cross-channel invasion only as the climax in the campaign against the Reich. This strategy found disfavor with the U.S. Army leadership, to say nothing of the suspicions it raised with the Soviets about the absence of a second front.

This juncture in 1943 heralded the second stage of the formation of allied strategy, in which the build-up of forces and arms enabled an offensive approach in three dimensions, with the main line in the maritime sphere. This process further exacerbated the tripartite squabble about Mediterranean-centered operations versus a sledgehammer blow to West and Central Europe. The North African campaign held the route of Anglo-American advance to the south, with further milestones of the Sicilian campaign (Husky) in 1943 and then onto southern Italy (Avalanche) itself in September 1943. This line followed the route set out by Churchill in the face of great dissent in the U.S. high command, which added to American civil-military tensions and ill feelings among the three allies.

By the spring of 1944, however, the center of gravity in the making of strategy shifted to U.S.-Soviet condominium, with British goals increasingly locked in the periphery of the Balkans, once the Big Three decision was taken for the cross channel operation (Overlord) as well as a Soviet offensive in the East. The western assault was to be led by General Dwight Eisenhower and constituted the third, final and decisive stage in the making of anti-Hitler strategy.

Eisenhower as Supreme Allied Commander represented the maturation of senior U.S. officers to the dictates of alliance cohesion versus the supremacy of narrow national interest in the force of arms as well as customary or even mythological strategic ideas handed down from the 18th century into the early 20th. He signified a new kind of U.S. officer entrusted with the fortunes of war and peace in Europe, enjoined to juggle various national interests as supreme to operational and tactical concerns of modern war. His biography might also be said to embody the convergence of strategic ideas and practice in the United States and Europe, mentioned above, in the most profound way.

With these events in 1944 until 1945, American military supremacy dawned in the fate of Europe, though this development is more obvious in the retrospective than to contemporaries. The making of strategy in Europe had entered into a new, decisive phase in which the United States would play a significant or leading role, which contrasted with the preceding episodes of U.S. isolation, a peripheral power or a junior ally.

Most significant here was President Roosevelt's grand vision for a postwar world order. This idea resembled something of the lost hopes of Wilson's adherents in 1919, rather than the reality of what indeed transpired in Europe by 1947. FDR imagined the pacification and disarmament of continental Europe as part of a world order held in balance by four great powers—the United States, the UK the USSR, and China. This system would allow the United States to withdraw from a neutralized, harmless Europe held in check by the powers on its flanks. These fantastic goals notwithstanding, such policy in practice in 1944–1945 encountered growing friction in reality with British weakness, French obstinacy, Polish recalcitrance, and Soviet resistance, to say nothing of Roosevelt's own failing health and death.

U.S. forces fought their way from Normandy to Aachen in the summer and fall of 1944, amid battles in such places as Arnhem, the Huertgen Forest, and the Ardennes, where a German counter-offensive in December 1944 led to 76,000 U.S. casualties. The U.S. offensive resumed in 1945 with an annihilationist strategy worthy of U.S. Grant in the final phase of the U.S. Civil War that unfolded from the Ruhr and Rhineland to Pforzheim, Nuremberg, Munich, and Berchtesgaden, at the same time that the air campaign reduced Berlin and the towns of the Ruhr and Rhine to ruins. The violence of the climactic phase of the war, which shouted out the false promise of final victory with little thought given to the aftermath, only made the dilemmas of war termination and the building of the peace more intense as this fighting reached its peak and faded. This problem grew more acute as the international system shifted atop the rubble of war in Central Europe, with the waning of British power and the Americans and Soviets face to face on the Elbe. There followed the rapid withdrawal of U.S. forces from Europe, first for the Pacific campaign and then general demobilization—some 2 million on V-E Day, of which by June 1946, only 290,000 troops remained in Europe, organized in three infantry divisions, subsidiary units, as well as the three mobile brigades of the constabulary.

Planning in the U.S. government for the four-power occupation of Germany embarked in fits and starts from 1942 until 1944, also with the *idée fixe* that the United States would soon withdraw entirely after war's end. The U.S. Army leadership vociferously resisted postwar security building, both because FDR wanted a strong civilian hand in the undertaking and because senior soldiers more or less had forgotten the record of such a constabulary force in 1919–1923. Nonetheless, soldiers and civilians gained practical experience in the administration of conquered territories in North Africa, Italy and France before reaching German soil in 1944.

In all of these cases the problems of the transition from combat to post-conflict reconstruction emerged quickly and stood at odds with the lesser aspects of war and garrison life, save for the few trained in the rigors of military government. Many of these civil-affairs personnel were naturalized German Jews; all tended to be citizen soldiers with a firm grounding in civil society and the professions. In conquered Western Germany, more so than in the previous cases, these problems manifested themselves in such details as the geography of the occupation zone versus that of the other victors; the character and legacy of the Nazi party state and German society generally as seen through the lens of the American soldiers and civilians; the ill effects of the beginnings of the Soviet-U.S. antagonism as well as friction with the French; to say nothing of the impact of peace on GIs weary of Army life. The latter was upended by the temptations of being the victor and bored by the ambiguities of constabulary service.

While the goal of the occupation to eradicate the sources of war and aggression in Germany might have been laudable, the means to do so through such policy as Joint Chiefs of Staff (JCS) Directive 1067, with its notorious non-fraternization dictum and scorched-earth airs, constituted a political and social experiment on a breathtaking scale even for Americans and their culture of optimism and renewal. Denazification, demilitarization, and democratization collided with reality and seemed doomed to failure in the years 1945 through 1947–1948; yet these undertakings succeeded—because of forces outside the comprehension and control of bureaucrats and soldiers-turned-governors in an inter-agency–choked provisional state atop the ruins of the Reich. The U.S. zone of occupation as it emerges in these years comprised the areas of present-day Bavaria, Hessen, and parts of Baden-Württemberg.

Somehow a policy of practicality, generosity, and leniency and a more and more hands-off approach lessened the draconian declaratory objectives of the beginning of occupation. To be sure, the term "reeducation," that is, the general attempt to expel the Nazi mental rubbish from young minds through schooling in civics and a liberal reading of contemporary history—as well as the pluralism of baseball games—might have offended the now déclassé educated middle-class scion who had been a financial contributor to the Reichsführer SS. Nonetheless, the appeal of prosperity, popular music, and technological progress in the American way of life for younger West Germans undermined enduring anti-American stereotypes among the young as well as the old elites. Most defeated Germans, the shadow of the swastika notwithstanding, endorsed the goals of the U.S. occupiers in the long run because little practical alternative existed, save perhaps the Stalinist one across the barbed wire to the east; the character of German state and society in 1946 was anything other than that of 1919. No unbroken elites stood ready to defend their privileges with a horde of military desperadoes, because the curse of genocide, total defeat, and the landscape of rubble precluded resistance as much as a U.S. constabulary force could. All the same, the occupiers feared a Nazi revival well into the foundation of the young Federal Republic.

With the Nuremberg trials, the currency reform, and the onset of the Cold War of the Soviet-U.S. enmity and national division on the one hand in the period 1946–1948, civil-society reasserted itself, on the other hand, in a bottom-up manner in western Germany under the banner of democratization. It did so, joined with the self-correctives in common sense in the face of innate stupidity of a policy that prohibited American soldiers from showing kindness to children, to say nothing of young women (that is, somehow to eradicate the sex drive—an especially American project). The same misbegotten policies ultimately authored failures of occupation procedures that, in some cases, either inadvertently recycled too many Weimar-era political figures; or left too many former Nazis untouched or even rewarded, as in the view of Hans Hellmut Kirst's *08/15*; or punished and disenfranchised the innocent in the view of von Ernst von Salomon's *Der Fragebogen*. All the same, the image of the American soldier changed, for the most part, from the ruthless murderer in uniform controlled by Jewish bankers, as in the Nazi propaganda reinterpretation of *Gone With the Wind*; or, as the faceless automaton with an oversupply of mediocre weapons and fighting machines without real combat élan as seen by German general staff officers.

Rather, as the first months of the occupation passed into a routine of years, the olive drab cohorts of sad sacks, pistol-toting West Pointers, émigré Jews in uniform, mid-westerners, southerners, and African-Americans with good teeth, and wearing bathrobes for military use, and disposing of an unending supply of jeeps, food, chocolate, cigarettes, and jazz, more for the benefit of fatherless children and destitute women in need, formed an occupying army that defied stereotypes of earlier European conflict reaching back to Wallenstein, Tily, and Gustavus Adolfus.

Unlike in the epoch 1919–1923, the imperatives of American policy as a world power in the atomic age, the role of the U.S. soldier in this policy, and the fate of western and central Europe between what presently became ideological blocs astride the northern hemisphere allowed for no departure of U.S. forces homeward within two years of war's end, as Roosevelt had proclaimed in February 1945. Rather, by the end of 1947, once George Kennan's "Long Telegram" on the sources of Soviet conduct made the rounds in Washington to emerge as the Truman administration's policy of containment of the USSR, the Greek Civil War caused a trans-Atlantic diplomacy of U.S. engagement that echoed in the capitals of Western Europe. The upshot was the Truman doctrine of U.S. aid to those resisting communism (March 1947) and the European Recovery Program (June 1947) to help the war-ravaged nations of western and central Europe back to prosperity. At the time these initiatives began, the U.S. European command had slightly more than 100,000 troops at hand. This number continued to shrink as the postwar reduction of U.S. forces took further hold in an attempt to reduce the national deficit from wartime.

These policies amid the absence of peace and the imperatives of security meant that the duties of the occupation were fast evolving into something new. Neither a policy of hemispheric isolation festooned with treaties banning war; nor the failed collective security of 1919; nor the pentarchy of the old powers, which had expired with the suicide of Hitler's Europe, could be resurrected. Rather, the United States committed itself to the construction of democracy, prosperity, and security for western and central Europe and the containment of the Soviet Union in the atomic age. This diplomatic revolution meant that the U.S. soldier had to remain in Europe in a phase of neither war nor peace that portended challenges of policy and strategy that derived in part from the former epoch, but on a new scale and fateful potential that was quite without precedent.

Europe in the Cold War, 1945–1973: U.S. Military amid the Perils of Deterrence and Alliance Cohesion

The imperatives of strategy and the advent of the military posture of forward defense in the years 1947–1955 led away from the post-conflict, constabulary role for the U.S. military to a mission of a deterrent land, air, and naval forces stationed on a large scale in West and Central Europe. This decades-long process of standing guard on the Cold-War front contrasts in the record of soldiers and arms with the epochs that preceded it—and with those that have followed it. Contrary to dark prophecies of 1945–1947 about the reappearance of the interwar pathology, peace and good fortune evolved in western and central Europe not only because citizens had become pacifists, who embraced the ideal of a united Europe on a pluralist basis, but in large part because of the four decades in which U.S. troops in NATO were present. The division of Europe, whatever its many sins wrought, lessened the potential of war on the continent in a manner that had been impossible in previous eras. This policy allowed for the consolidation of the Atlantic order of democracy, the breakthrough of the social market economy on the continent amid extended nuclear deterrence, and alliance cohesion.

The evolution from occupation to alliance for U.S. forces in Europe unfolded in the years 1947 through 1950 in response to a series of crises. These shocks included the Czech coup (February 1948), the western German currency reform, (May 1948); the Berlin blockade (Summer 1948 onward), the Soviet atom bomb (August 1949), the fall of Chiang Kai-Shek's China (December 1949); and the outbreak of war in Korea (June 1950). These events hardened the will of the Truman Administration to hold Western Europe from the Soviets; to allow West Germany to consolidate in the west; as well as to foster the unity of Western Europe generally as a bulwark against war. The Washington Treaty (April 1949) had been preceded by a statecraft of mutual aid among the Western Europeans, which prompted the U.S. Senate to disregard its tradition of shunning "entangling alliances," and, in fact, to embrace in 1948 the prospect of a collective defense treaty with Europe (Vandenberg Resolution). Once the Washington Treaty was signed a year later, the allies embarked on the twisted path to an integrated security and defense alliance.

While the clauses of the Washington Treaty reinforced the values that underlay this alliance, (Article II); the means of consensus, consultation, and equitable shouldering of duties (Articles III and IV); and the primacy of collective defense (Article V), the politics of burden sharing and the impact of nuclear weapons immediately came to the fore in the creation of this integrated structure. These problems predominated because the Truman administration had greatly limited the size and budget of U.S. arms until the eve of the Korean War (June 1950), thereby forcing the question of where and how to find further forces for Europe—or whether to do so at all, in favor of an off shore strategy of limited commitment. (At the same time, the exigencies of economy and security dictated that Western Europe recover without too great a burden of arms and soldiers.)

Until the outbreak of the Korean War, these imperatives indicated an indirect, maritime, and air atomic strategy to defend Europe. U.S. troops in West Germany, for instance, in December 1949 were no more than 84,000 strong. These limitations also raised the issue of how the Western Europeans would arm themselves—and whether or on which terms to include Western Germany. The strategic document, NSC 68, of early 1950 broke through the Truman budget ceiling by means of a buildup of atomic and conventional forces, which sprang into general mobilization in the summer and fall of 1950 with the Korean War.

The North Korean assault blasted aside fears of arming West Germany in the Truman Administration and in western capitals, save Paris. To forestall a Soviet offensive as well as to allay French fears of Anglo-Saxon abandonment in the face of a revived Germany, the Truman administration in August 1950 sent four additional divisions to reinforce the FRG. These troops became the bulwark of what was soon known as "forward defense," a defensive line on the Rhine versus the English Channel. The United States also began security assistance to its NATO allies through the equipment and training of Western European forces on a major scale. Fourth Republic France, already receiving significant U.S. arms for the Vietnam War, allowed the creation of a series of U.S. bases and headquarters on its territory in November 1950. These bases formed a communication zone to reinforce West Germany; at the same moment, the U.S. Seventh Army, which had been deactivated in 1947, was called into action again with its headquarters in southwest Germany.

Secretary of State Dean Acheson hinted that these U.S. reinforcements would later be withdrawn as the Western Europeans shouldered more of the burden once they returned to their prewar strength. This decision, in spite of the war in Korea, caused much dissent in the U.S. Senate among Truman's critics, where Republican Senator Robert Taft, in contrast to his colleague Arthur Vandenberg, questioned the constitutional wisdom and strategic purpose of such a Europe first strategy and posture of forces. From June 1951 until October of that year, the headquarters of V and VII Corps deployed to Europe as part of the Seventh Army. One armor and three infantry divisions followed them by the end of 1952. U.S. European Command HQ unfurled its flag in the IG Farben building in Frankfurt, where it was renamed U.S. Army, Europe. By the end of 1952, the number of U.S. ground troops in Europe climbed to 252,000.

The imperative to share the burden led to the enlargement of the alliance area to enlist West Germany in the defense of the West and hence to abandon German demilitarization. The United States and France jointly pushed for a European Army (European Defense Community) as the squaring of the circle of Atlantic defense in the years 1950–1954. Dwight Eisenhower became the Supreme Allied Commander in 1951 as a major step in the creation of the integrated military structure followed quickly in 1952 by the Lisbon Force Goals, more or less within the concept of NSC 68, as well as the accession of Greece and Turkey to the alliance.

Such momentum endured only briefly into the middle-1950s, as the death of Stalin, the end of the Korean War, the advent of thermonuclear as well as tactical nuclear weapons in western arsenals, and the defeat of the French in Indochina (despite U.S. aid) stalled the first push of integrated defense short of its force goals. The Eisenhower administration (1953–1961) unveiled its New Look strategy of massive thermonuclear retaliation for a more nuclear NATO. This policy cut defense spending and shrank U.S. ground forces from their mobilization levels of the Korean conflict, even as the FRG joined NATO and the new Bundeswehr slowly came into existence amid much controversy at home and abroad. A half-secret plan of 1956 to cut sharply U.S. forces in Europe (the Radford Plan, named for the Chairman of the Joint Chiefs of Staff) soon collided with the 1956 Hungarian uprising against the Soviets and the Suez debacle of the same year, in which a combined French-British-Israeli offensive against Egypt ended in catastrophe of allied discord and nuclear threats.

With NATO in disarray and extended deterrence left a shambles by these events, yet more crisis eventuated the next year with the Soviet Sputnik satellite in late 1957, trans-Atlantic security endured further strain with Nikita Krushchev's attempt of 1958 to end four-power rule in divided Berlin as well as the crisis in Lebanon. These setbacks unfolded just as the first postwar contraction of the U.S. economy made the cost of overseas troops a balance-of-payments problem amid Congressional alarm about defense rendered more acute by a supposed missile gap in the shadow of Sputnik. Nonetheless, the imperative to show alliance cohesion trumped concerns about budget cuts and balance sheets of burdens borne, thus prompting NATO to redouble political consultation as well as embrace the dual use of nuclear weapons with allies championed by SACEUR General Lauris Norstad.

No less important than the former personality was the service, starting in October 1958, of rock star Elvis Presley as a scout with the Headquarters, 32nd Armor Regiment, 3rd Armored Division in Friedberg in Hessen. All Cold-War mass persuasion in allied nations notwithstanding, he signified how shared values had transformed trans-Atlantic relations from the nadir of two decades earlier as West Germans, particularly the younger generation, become enthralled by the U.S. middle-class consumerism and the willingness to discard traditions and customs of social rank and status.

At the same time, however, in 1950s society, hissing German voices deplored the impact of racial mixing on German womanhood because of U.S. African-American troops. Racist cant only slightly removed from National Socialist histrionics about jazz posited that only German women of loose morals and low estate, versus those of proper breeding and a respectable home life, would seek out a GI as a husband—thence to endure the heart break that comes with loss of blood and soil when such Fräuleins encountered the inequalities of U.S. society beyond the dazzle of chromed automobiles and the horn-of-plenty in the post exchange(PX). Indeed, a film of this era, "Town without Pity," memorialized the issue of sexual violence by U.S. soldiers and promiscuous—or perhaps merely modern—German women.

There were also those ex-Wehrmacht soldiers as neighbors to American garrisons, who, with the *Landser Heft* in hand and Moltke's screed of the last century on their lips, regarded U.S. soldiers as ill-disciplined pansies compared to the field-grey, battle-hardened Ivan-slayer of the eastern front. This disregard by Hitler's former troops for the new Bundeswehr was similarly outspoken, but such verdicts had a nationalist, if not irredentist, character.

Nonetheless, U.S. troops, their music, and their kinship with their neighbors "on the economy" as well as the official willingness on the U.S. and West German sides to ameliorate openly the collateral damage of the stationing of forces (or wild-boar rooting or rutting anywhere in the vicinity of U.S. bases) had a major strategic effect—much in contrast to the Soviet soldier stationed in East Germany and elsewhere in Central and Eastern Europe, whose installations and civil-military interactions, marred by secrecy and a cult of silence toward subject populations bristled with remnant mistrust and mutual suspicion, all protestations of the "fraternity" of socialist nations aside.

The deployment of dual-use nuclear weapons among NATO forces in the late 1950s, as well as the nuclear crises that unfolded into the early 1960s gave rise in western European civil society to an anti-nuclear, pacifist movement, which became a leading force in statecraft and the domestic politics of security and defense. The Committee for Nuclear Disarmament in the United Kingdom and the Kampf dem Atomtod movement in West Germany were but two of these groups that became mainstays of society and culture, spawning further political movements and stylizing popular expectations of the trans-Atlantic relationship as a fixture of European life.

The new decade of the 1960s brought ongoing strains in policy, strategy, budgets, and force posture that by now had hardened into enduring aspects of the alliance. As the Berlin crisis worsened into 1961 amid discord among the allies over the future of nuclear deterrence in the hands of the Kennedy administration, U.S. garrisons in Europe were greatly reinforced, just as De Gaulle's France began to withdraw its first units from the integrated military structure amid the Algerian war. In a shift from what was deemed by critics as the dead end of megaton threats of massive retaliation, useless in the face of limited nuclear conflict and guerilla war, the new administration augmented U.S. and allied conventional forces and thus endeavored to raise the nuclear threshold in the face of growing Soviet nuclear strength as part of flexible response. Critics of the new policy in Paris and Bonn saw this innovation as greatly weakening the U.S. commitment to European security, while limiting nuclear war to Europe.

This conflict became more tangible with the construction of the Berlin Wall in August 1961. The Berlin crisis saw 40,000 further troops dispatched to western and central Europe amid the Kennedy administration's emphasis on a conventional buildup. Troops of the U.S. Berlin brigade in October 1961 confronted Soviet armor at Checkpoint Charlie across the recently constructed Wall in what seemed a prelude to world war. The number of ground troops in Western and Central Europe reached a high of 277,000 in June 1962, partially as a result of the domestically unpopular mobilization of the reserves. The policy of flexible response gained further impetus from the Cuban missile crisis of late 1962, whereupon a superpower reduction of tensions and a shift of U.S. strategic emphasis to Asia took hold with the escalation of the Vietnam conflict. Perhaps the time had arrived for the United States to recalculate its investment of money and attention in Western Europe, particularly as European recovery seemed all but complete?

In the event, the growing costs of U.S. garrisons in the face of a worsening dollar led to major cuts of U.S. forces (initially, a third of a division) through the dual-basing of American forces in the continental United States and Western Europe. At the same time, the West Germans began offset payments, more or less through the purchase of U.S. weapons for the Bundeswehr, in order to lessen the costs of stationed forces, a diplomacy of burden sharing that brought anything other than calm in bilateral relations. The Big Lift exercise of 1963 (which sought to demonstrate how forces now based in the United States could be re-deployed to Europe with great speed and effect), on the eve of the escalation of the U.S. role in South Vietnam, heralded further policy pressure to lessen fundamentally the cost and scope of the U.S. commitment to Europe from the middle-1960s on. This trend accelerated with the 1966 decision by Charles De Gaulle to withdraw the remaining French forces from NATO's integrated military structure and to eject foreign bases from French soil.

At the same time, the imperative to raise new units for Asian service hollowed out U.S. forces in Western Europe and led, for instance, to the reduction of command echelons for ground forces with the merger of the U.S. Army, Europe Headquarters, with that of the Seventh Army. The ill effects of the Vietnam War hastened a collapse of morale and fighting power in the waning years of the decade. (This phenomenon in military ranks more or less mirrored the turmoil in U.S. and western society in the late 1960s.) With a page from Senator Taft's script of the Great Debate, Senator Mike Mansfield in 1966 introduced a resolution to withdraw a significant fraction of U.S. forces in order to shock the western European allies into higher defense spending. This struggle went on in the U.S. Senate for several years and culminated when President Lyndon Johnson placed excessive pressure on the West German government of Chancellor Ludwig Erhard to share yet more of the burden—while Johnson scrapped the NATO nuclear Multilateral Nuclear Force proposal at the expense of West German interests.

NATO finally embraced flexible response as its strategic doctrine in late 1967, while the Harmel Report on the future tasks of the alliance adapted the politics of collective defense to Détente at the close of the decade with a principle of the dual track: Détente and collective defense. This program was a tough sell in its day on both sides of the Atlantic, where adherents of Détente believed that NATO was obsolete, and budgetary critics of the U.S. defense posture sought to cut forces. Despite the Warsaw Pact invasion of Czechoslovakia in August 1968, the new Nixon administration focused on lowering tensions with the USSR and ending the Vietnam War. These policies also unfolded amid a steady deterioration of trans-Atlantic security relations, principally because the United States concentrated its energy and attention outside of Western Europe. The U.S. side looked with skepticism on West German *Ostpolitik* as an augury of neutralism that either reflected the reddish glow of nascent Euro-Socialism or, more ominously, a recidivist effort toward a stability-busting *Schaukelpolitik*.

Concomitantly, the U.S. military posture in Western Europe seemed to slump further as the 1960s drew to a close and as the Warsaw Pact armed at break-neck speed. To counteract the perception of a weakening U.S. resolve toward forward defense, in January 1969, the so-called Return of Forces to Germany (REFORGER) exercise began as high point of each military year. This maneuver, however, could not mask problems of morale and discipline in the ranks of the U.S. forces in Europe. This malaise originated in the decline of the dollar as well as the spread of crime, drugs, and racial tension in U.S. *Kasernen* roiled by the combined effects of Ho Chi Minh, Abbey Hoffman, and Huey P. Newton.

The Nixon administration's answer to the weakness of the inner structure of the Vietnam military came with the ballyhooed abolition of conscription, and the introduction of the all-volunteer force in 1972–1973. This reform caused even greater skepticism in a Western European public that the U.S. armed forces had simply discarded their professional standards and marked the descent from the stature of a conquering force and bulwark of forward defense of 20 years earlier. In 1972, the first of German terrorist attacks began against U.S. bases in Frankfurt, and episodes of such bombings and murder against U.S. troops continued through the 1970s and 1980s. These incidents worsened through the rest of the 1970s and 1980s, because of the campaigns German and Italian left-wing terrorist cells, as well as those of Palestinians and Libyans, in some cases supported by Soviet proxies.

The baleful trends in U.S.-European defense affairs climaxed in the year 1973 in what, with hope amid the pullback from Vietnam, U.S. makers of policy had trumpeted as the "Year of Europe." This attempt to mend frayed ties ended in the "out of area" debacle of the Yom Kippur War of October 1973, led by Egypt and Syria among others against Israel—and its disastrous aftermath. The United States shifted its attention and considerable aid monies to Israel in the face of its near defeat at the hands of the Arabs; meanwhile, western European NATO allies denied over-flight rights for U.S. arms and materiel for the Israelis, inaugurating in deed a long-standing habit of thought in Europe that connects anti-Americanism with anti-Semitism.

Against the backdrop of the economic turbulence of the oil embargo—which visited on the Americans the first iteration of the fear of dependency on "foreign oil" as gasoline prices rose from less than 40 cents a gallon to more than a half-dollar, while bringing to West Germany the now-nostalgic car-free Sundays—a systemic crisis in the western economy and society was the most profound effect of war. The course of the fighting also seemed to demonstrate the tactical and operational effectiveness of Soviet weapons and tactics against western forces, a prospect that was somehow even more alarming than operations research conjured missile gaps. All of this unfolded just as the U.S. combat role in Vietnam was ending and U.S. forces labored with post-conflict retrenchment with the all-volunteer force. The young second lieutenant or E-3 enlisted soldier stood in their dilapidated barracks, estranged from West Germans and their fellow Americans at home and compelled to remain on post by the eroding value of the dollar and by the tarnished prestige of the American soldier in Europe in the era of stagflation and Détente.

Détente, Renewed Confrontation, Peace, 1973–1990: Shift from Europe to the Middle East

In 1973, the Nixon administration opened the Mutual Balanced Force Reduction (MBFR) talks with the Soviets in Vienna. The aim was in part to block the Mansfield amendment, but also to animate the diplomacy of arms control as specifically applied to the east/west order of battle on the German and Czechoslovak border. In the event, the Cold War and the relatively stabile, if militarized, order of trans-Atlantic relations was beginning to end—though the contemporary observer could be excused for missing the first faint glimmers of this twilight.

The MBFR effort existed in the shadow of arms control associated with intercontinental nuclear weapons and anti-missile batteries within SALT I in the years 1968–1972. Soviet goals in Détente also found their crowing in the Helsinki final act of 1975, which led to the creation of the Conference on Security and Cooperation in Europe (CSCE) as a pan-European security structure beyond the two blocs. U.S. neo-conservative critics of Nixon and Kissinger's attempt to reorder the state system in the 1970s decried this institution as a legitimation of Soviet hegemony in Central and Eastern Europe, whereas, in reality, the emphasis on human rights in the protocols offered a remarkable boost to civil society in Central Europe. At the time, however, these baby steps of a homegrown civil protest movement in the latter half of the 1970s in Czechoslovakia and Poland were all but overwhelmed by anxieties about the durability of the U.S. defense commitment in the face the modernization and expansion of nuclear arsenals.

At the strategic and operational level of U.S. ground and air forces in Europe, efforts undertaken by Senator Sam Nunn, together with innovative officers in the U.S. Army amid the reform of U.S. ground troops as a total force of reserves and active duty soldiers, led out of the valley of despair. Nunn followed Mansfield as the leading figure in the U.S. Senate to concern himself with the fate of U.S. troops in Europe, but he did so much more as a military technician than as keeper of constitutional prerogatives as in the case of Vandenberg and Taft. Such undertakings comprised a civil-military revival of thought and doctrine on and for the armed forces, as well as a modernization of arsenals, after a decade of neglect because of the Indochina conflict.

This reform evolved from the active defense doctrine of a more or less static posture to U.S. and NATO adaptation of traditional principles of mobile air-land warfare long advocated by the strategic thinkers of the Bundeswehr as the core of German practice. The U.S. side also moved units out of the traditional area in Germany's southwest and into Lower Saxony and the North German Plain as part of an attempt to block a Warsaw Pact steam roller from the Baltic to the English Channel that increasingly seemed the worst case on NATO's central front. This new garrisoning of troops led to local protests in the 1970s that presaged a restlessness in civil society to the civil-military burdens of forward defense, and which manifested a general trend in the face of such undertakings as the expansion of the Frankfurt airport and the construction of new nuclear power stations.

The nuclear issue as a question of civil-military relations of Atlantic defense also loomed ever larger from 1977 onward. The North Atlantic Council's decision to revitalize defense efforts and to boost defense budgets to 3 percent of gross domestic product in the face of the Warsaw Pact arming up led to the modernization of nuclear arsenals ("tactical nuclear weapons") on the European continent–even though these weapons flirted seriously with irrelevancy as new kinds of nuclear warheads (the enhanced radiation nuclear explosive) as well as new kinds of missiles (the Soviet SS-20, and the U.S. Pershing II and ground-launched Cruise missile) emerged from the aerospace production lines of the superpowers. In 1976–1978, the U.S. effort to revamp nuclear artillery and tactical missiles deployed on the NATO central front erupted into a crisis of alliance cohesion over the deployment of the neutron bomb. This episode formed but the prelude to the fight in NATO capitals of 1979–1987 and beyond in the shadow of the SS-20, a weapon that West German Chancellor Helmut Schmidt and others feared would overawe western Europeans and decouple Western Europe from the U.S. Single Integrated Operational Plan, the blue print of combat in nuclear war.

The Soviets for their part anguished that NATO could suddenly decapitate the highest echelons of the Warsaw Command with the blade of the Pershing II. Elite postulates of deterrence theory and collective defense in the late 1970s became engulfed in the groundswell of popular anger against all things nuclear, be it a power plant or a missile, as a new peace and ecological movement of great breadth emerged in Western and Central Europe. On 12 December 1979, the North Atlantic Council endorsed the dual-track decision on Intermediate Nuclear Forces, that is, to arm with new theater nuclear weapons based in the U.K., the Benelux, the FRG and Italy and to negotiate their reduction at the same time in the spirit of the Harmel doctrine.

Détente expired in the crises of late 1979, when Islamist fanatics besieged the U.S. embassy in Teheran, Iran, and the Soviets launched a grand military operation in Afghanistan of the type that had long been the object of dread in Central Europe. While in hindsight the Iranian episode perhaps formed a portent of things to come in a new century, in fact, Western strategists peering at the time through the lens of the past saw the Afghan campaign as the climax of a decade-long erosion of trans-Atlantic strength in the wake of the U.S. "quagmire" in Vietnam. In this view, the Soviet drive to the Hindu-Kush manifested a new version of the Great Game in a bid to change the world order through the seizure of the Persian Gulf.

The Iranian hostage nightmare, the Soviet Afghan campaign, and the enduring petro-malaise precipitated the first telling stages in the U.S. grand-strategic reorientation and the shift of military power away from Europe and toward the Middle East. A new joint command emerged with units readied for rapid intervention in the Persian Gulf, whereby reinforcements in the continental United States held in reserve to bolster the central front also took on missions for conflict in the Middle East. Under the banner of "out of area," the continent's southern flanks and the regions beyond in the Near East assumed a greater role in alliance thinking that became enduringly contentious on this issue.

The fate of the British imperial legacy in the South Atlantic, however, dominated the first part of the 1982. The Argentine-UK war over the south Atlantic Falkland Islands diverted world attention from the INF nuclear arsenal, and drove the Reagan administration to support the British in combat in the South Atlantic with generous security assistance.

Meanwhile, the uprising of the anti-communist workers movement in the Baltic plunged Poland into crisis. The specter of another Warsaw Pact operation as in August 1968, but this time on the Baltic and Vistula, threatened the peace of Europe as the INF missile crisis deepened in its turn. The year 1983 formed the darkest moments of the INF crisis in a spiral of violence, the end of which might well be all-out war. In what appeared to those gripped by these events as an updated version of the crises of 1961–1962, generalized fear of global war loomed from spring into the fall of that year. These moments included the near catastrophe in February–March of the NATO "Able Archer" nuclear release exercise, which the Russians thought might be a first strike; at virtually the same time, the programmatic advent of the Strategic Defense Initiative anti-missile arsenal by the Reagan administration amid Hollywood-style mass persuasion to a poor reception among European pacifists; the so-called Hot Autumn of peace protests against the fall 1983 deployments of the first Pershing IIs and GLCMS in the wake of the USSR having shot down a Korean airliner in the Pacific; Iranian-sponsored Islamists bombed a U.S. Marine Corps barracks in Beirut, Lebanon; and the U.S. invaded the Caribbean island of Grenada to prevent a Cuban or Soviet foray there.

The thermonuclear shadow over Europe began to fade in the middle of the decade, with the reform of government in the USSR and the advent of Mikhail Gorbachev as a Soviet premier who departed radically from the doctrines of his predecessors. The first moments of the diplomatic revolution that heralded an end to the Soviet-U.S. confrontation came with the Reagan-Gorbachev meeting in Rekjavik, Iceland, in October 1986, with its pragmatism of radical cuts in nuclear arsenals. This event was followed in December 1987 with the treaty to scrap the INF nuclear forces that had been recently emplaced; the Soviets announced a year later their withdrawal from Afghanistan and unilateral reduction of 500,000 soldiers and 10,000 fighting vehicles on the main front line of Central Europe. Senior Pentagon planners unveiled a study titled "Discriminate Deterrence," which revived the troop pullback plans concocted by strategists in intervals since the Radford plan of the middle 1950s. Yet at the same time other or, in fact, the same strategists speculated about the need to update short range nuclear missiles in NATO—two highly contradictory statements of policy as befitted a period of break-neck change.

The spectacle of arsenals on the way to the junkyard, however, was soon dwarfed by the migration of peoples westward and the siege of central European communist party and secret police headquarters.

The onslaught across the iron curtain either from Hungary into Austria in the spring of 1989 or the breach of the Berlin Wall in the fall of the same year unfolded in a rapture of joy and pleasure devoid of bloodshed save in the single case of Romania. The cacophony of Trabi-thumping and car horns on the night of 9 November 1989 on Berlin's Bornholmerstraße sounded taps for the Cold-War U.S. garrisons in West Berlin and the Fulda Gap. The peaceful upshot of a decade that had seen the threat of war meant anything other than the final chapter in the story of U.S. soldiers in the fate of Europe. The nonviolent end to the Cold War added luster to the memory of those who had forged the defense bond between Europe and North America in the 1940s.

But the passing of the age of total war on the continent and the advent of unity scarcely heralded the end of the U.S. as a force in war and peace. Franklin Roosevelt's nearly forgotten prophecy of 1944—that U.S. troops would be withdrawn within two years of war's end—echoed in the windy predictions of the first months of the 1990s that NATO would soon vanish as no further reason existed for U.S. military power in the fate of Europe. The convergence of European and U.S. military thought and practice that had become a tradition in the years since the 1940s formed a not insignificant feature of the edifice of trans-Atlantic peace and security. This union had been sealed in combat and in the episodes that followed battle in postwar reconstruction, forward defense and deterrence—the latter, in their specific way, being no less momentous.

The U.S. Military in Europe in the First Post-Cold–War Decade: Engagement Amid Pullback

Despite the many problems and burdens that collective defense and alliance cohesion had entailed from the start, this conjunction of strategic thought and military service in multilateral entities persisted where many Cold-War weapons presently ended up under the scrapper's torch. The chief reason for this continuity of policy was simple: November 1989 scarcely portended perpetual peace for all in Europe and its environs. Rather, the moment tolled a trans-formed conflict in which many of the issues of security and military organization analyzed in the preceding pages reappeared on an expanded geographical scale and in which U.S. security in Europe endured. Yet other, centrifugal forces of unilateralism and a new reliance on the force of arms emerged in U.S. statecraft in the 1990s, which clashed with the rise of a self-styled "civil power" among certain continental European political elites. The upshot of this divergence thereafter pulled the two continents apart.

In March 1990, at the time of parliamentary elections in the GDR that swept out much that was left of the communist government in Berlin and opened the path to national reunification, troops of the 11th Armored Cavalry Regiment embarked on their final patrol of the inner German border between Hesse and Thuringia. This last sortie along a vanishing frontier was followed within 18 months with the dissolution of the USSR itself. In such places as Poland, Czechoslovakia, or Hungary and along the Danube to the Black Sea, a chasm reemerged in the heart of the continent with particular meaning for German policy as well as U.S. policy. This security gap in Central and Eastern Europe assured that the fate of the continent endured as a theme of U.S. security policy and in its military posture, even if the number of troops there shrank rapidly.

This process of push and pull, that is, of renewed engagement versus withdrawal, in the U.S. defense establishment gathered speed from the end of 1990 onward. This phenomenon worked on two levels: a traditional school of trans-Atlantic diplomacy and a politics of values (engagement on a new basis), sometimes in concert with, but often at odds with the military-technical level, that is, the senior defense civilians and uniformed officers of the armed forces, who took a lead in disengagement. The former endeavored to maintain and modernize the trans-Atlantic security bond on an expanded scale beyond the rubble of the iron curtain with fewer, specialized forces, while the military operational level (with some notable exceptions of those stationed in Europe with military-to-military contact to Central Europe) sought to reduce drastically the U.S. military role and downgrade the trans-Atlantic alliance. At the level of foreign and security policy, a general will in key quarters of the U.S. government slowly developed in the first half of the 1990s toward the extension of Euro-Atlantic security and defense organizations to Central and Eastern Europe more or less at the same time that war reappeared in the European system of states in the southeast of the continent.

The foregoing, however, was but a sideshow compared to the sharpening crisis in the Persian Gulf in the wake of the Iraqi invasion of Kuwait in August 1990, as well as the generalized statecraft that sought a modus vivendi with the moribund Soviet Union and then with the Russian Federation. The midsummer Iraqi blow against Kuwait thrust the Middle East and especially the Persian Gulf into the focus of American security policy. This change relegated the peace of Europe further to secondary status as a concern of U.S. strategists, and worsened again issues of alliance cohesion, the fight over the geographical limits of the alliance, and the sharing of military burdens.

The path of U.S. arms to the Persian Gulf as the rationale for a change of strategic focus had been laid well before 1990, and is a story best retold elsewhere. The Pentagon of the late 1980s had already put in hand a major reduction of general-purpose and especially ground forces (the so-called Base Force) that had first emerged under Chairman of the Joint Chiefs, Colin Powell in 1989 and that foresaw a further reorientation to southwest Asia at the expense of Europe. Culminating a development that had begun in the 1970s, the realignment of ground forces toward a mission on the Persian Gulf reached a climax in November 1990 with the redeployment of the VII U.S. Corps, consisting of two armored divisions and an armored cavalry regiment, for service in the Kuwait Desert Storm operation of February 1991. With the U.S.-Arab-European coalition battle line on the Saudi-Kuwaiti border organized under the U.S. Central Command, and not by NATO, this most significant military campaign since the 1960s borrowed heavily from operational doctrine crafted in the 1980s with a strong European antecedents, particularly air-land battle, with an emphasis on the somewhat plodding use of overwhelming force in the air and on the ground against Iraqi arms in Kuwait.

The putative victory in the 1990–1991 Gulf War, with the willful misattribution of battlefield success to the tactical and operational level and its improved weapons, versus alliance cohesion and statecraft, illustrated the willingness of certain figures especially in right-wing think tanks and the Defense Department of the United States to push aside the practices of alliance defense and military organization in its dimensions of statecraft and consultation. This change became associated with a post-Vietnam Pentagon policy first drafted in the darkest moments of the last phase of the Cold War (1983–1984), but which came into its own in first Gulf War: the Weinberger-Powell Doctrine. Its authors, borrowing from the "never again school" in the U.S. Army after Korea that railed against limited war (versus total war), posited an all-or-nothing approach to the formulation of strategy and the use of force.

This school of strategic practice also entailed the ad hoc formation of coalitions of the willing, the model being the Kuwait campaign of 1990–1991, which became in the course of the 1990s a unilateral strategy of "the mission defines the coalition." This neoconservative dogma, a poor substitute for the alliance statecraft and policy that had been championed by Roosevelt, Marshall, Eisenhower, Truman, and Acheson, heightened tensions about alliance cohesion and the sharing of defense burdens, in which European armies and political culture became the butt of criticism with a new degree of agitation and vitriol in the wake of the victory over the Iraqis in the spring of 1991.

Yet forces of cohesion operated as well, not the least because the iconoclastic, unilateral impulse to junk alliance statecraft encountered stark limits in practice. Having confronted more than their share of existential crises since 1949, the advocates of regeneration in the Alliance began the reform of NATO in 1990–1991. They replaced the Harmel doctrine through a series of summit meetings that resulted in a new security strategy toward the eradication of conflict with the USSR/Russia, as well as first steps to further cooperation with the nations of Central and Eastern Europe and recognition of conflict beyond Europe's borders. Most significant here was the creation by the North Atlantic Council of the North Atlantic Cooperation Council in November 1991. This entity furnished Central and Eastern European nations a place adjacent to the North Atlantic Coucil (NAC)—as did the NATO-Russian Council—a step that pushed away the specter of an unmoored *Zwischeneuropa* that haunted the new democratic leadership in Warsaw, Prague, and Budapest. The mostly irrelevant doctrines of nuclear deterrence from the 1970s were transformed by the NAC to the security horizon after first Gulf war with the adaptation of a new strategic concept in November 1991. It was a more deliberately political statement of policy and strategy that recognized the security and defense implications of the early post war epoch with the changing map of Europe and the proliferation of crises beyond it. These first opening measures by NATO, however, only increased the desire of Central and Eastern Europeans for yet closer alignment with the west.

More significant, however, post-Tito Yugoslavia descended into civil war in the course of 1990–1991, an increasingly gruesome conflict that elicited little official interest among senior strategists in the United States until a very late moment. (By contrast, in the wake of German unification, the nations of Western and Central Europe intensified their desire for further continental integration with the Maastricht Treaty in 1992.) Whereas the departure of Slovenia from Yugoslavia transpired basically without violence, the independence of Croatia and presently Bosnia began a blood bath among Serbs, Croats, and Bosnians. In the years 1992–1994, the siege of Sarajevo became the pit of savagery into which the United Nations had sent a peacekeeping force, UNPROFOR, many members of which were European Community and NATO allies, but who, at first, were nonetheless without the political will or military means to stop the fighting. Desultory efforts of a naval arms embargo in the Adriatic, an air exclusion zone in the skies over the conflict, as well as air resupply of Sarajevo had no significant effect, other than to suggest the futility of half measures.

In the United States of the first half of the 1990s, domestic policy and the fate of Asia and the Middle East held sway among the nation's leadership and an easy excuse for a hands-off policy that became further amplified in the slavish recitation of the Weinberger-Powell doctrine. The recession that followed the Kuwaiti invasion had increased the demand for a "peace dividend" and accelerated the reduction of forces in Western and Central Europe. From the end of 1991 until the end of 1994, the U.S. Army, Europe, for instance, went from 143,000 to about 60,000 troops. The venerable array of bases and facilities with lineage and honors reaching back to 1945 shrank greatly, especially in Bavaria, Hesse, and Rhineland-Palatinate, with many German employees of the U.S. forces put out on the street. The German-American biotope of the GI, his neighbors at the *Gasthaus*, the local car dealership, and the German folklore gift shop became a kind of ghost town and an object of nostalgia for those who had grown up with this world.

Once the strongest links in the chain of forward defense, the U.S. VII Corps, itself, was deactivated in April 1992 after its return from the Persian Gulf, where its commander had secured some opprobrium for his lack of dash in the Kuwaiti campaign. The storied Berlin Brigade marched out of Berlin in 1994, as the Russians withdrew from their garrisons in central and eastern Germany. No less momentously, REFORGER shrank from a costly, diesel-drenched annual spectacle to a computerized command-post exercise—a symbolic end of the era of forward defense on the classic pattern.

This dismantling and force reduction may have gladdened the hearts of those in Washington and elsewhere who scoffed at the wish of central Europeans for security guarantees under the NATO compass either because it would consternate the Russians or because Europe played no role in "unipolar moment" geopolitical fantasies that fixated on the Middle East and Asia. Yet in a little-remarked process of nonetheless great portent, which proceeded along with the absorption of the soldiers of the former East German army into an all-German Bundeswehr in late 1990, the U.S. side offered security assistance and technical aid to central and eastern European defense ministries, general staffs, and combat forces bereft of their Soviet senior counselors. This effort had begun in the wake of the CSCE and CFE diplomacy of confidence-building measures of military exchanges, whereby Czechs, Slovaks, Poles and Hungarians received aid from U.S. personnel based in the U.S. European Command in Stuttgart as well as from defense education and military training institutions in the continental United States. This technical assistance to U.S. and NATO standards of defense institution building, however, surely constituted something less than the bonds of collective defense under Article V of the Washington Treaty, a need that was felt to be especially urgent amid the stalemate in western capitals in the face of the Bosnian slaughter and anxiety over the future of the Russian Federation.

The epoch from the middle of the 1990s until the end of the decade threw into reverse those centrifugal forces that had weakened the security bond between the U.S. and Europe. The bloodshed in ex-Yugoslavia and the need to extend Article V eastward prompted the Clinton administration in 1993–1994 to rediscover Acheson's statecraft in concert with Helmut Kohl and Vladimir Putin. The first stage in this process in January 1994 introduced NATO's "Partnership for Peace" (PfP), which represented a step beyond cooperation toward further indirect benefits for Poles, Czechs, Slovaks, and Hungarians of alliance accession (partnership), without the formal extension of collective defense. PfP elevated the central European reform and transformative measures already put in hand by allies on a bilateral basis under Articles II, III, and IV of the Atlantic Treaty; although for critics, the plan smacked of a two-tiered alliance that had been considered by the founders in the late 1940s. PfP soon included not only defense institution building on the western ministerial model, but participation in routine military operations on the basis of NATO interoperability.

The transformation of collective defense, however, became lodged with collective security in the need for peace enforcement in a southeastern Europe suffocating in human misery that signified a reprise of the years 1941–1944. The ineffectiveness of great-power statecraft and the failures of UNPROFOR to protect Bosnians and to lift the siege of Sarajevo led to the abandonment of stand-off measures as well as the first use of force. NATO air actions against the Bosnian Serbs began in the spring of 1994, and the significance of these strikes resided, rather in physical damage done to targets, in the shift by the United States and its European NATO allies to a coercive diplomacy with the escalating force of arms. In the course of mid-1994 into 1995, as multilateral consensus hardened against Bosnia Serb brutality (as well as the horror at Croatian-versus-Bosnian mayhem) the air strikes within NATO declared military exclusion zones took on greater operational effect.

Planners at Brussels and Mons prepared in early 1995 to fetch UNPROFOR out of Bosnia with a newly formed NATO rapid reaction force, which manifested another stage of escalation. In turn, in the summer of 1995 the Serbs answered NATO air with the humiliation of UNPROFOR troops as hostages in the face of the massacre at Srebrenica, whereupon a Croatian offensive against the Serbs that summer—with U.S. support—drove Serb forces from eastern Croatia. Further NATO air strikes of growing destructiveness led the warring parties to a meeting at Dayton, Ohio, where an armistice was inked beneath the glinting fuselages of USAF jets in a message-heavy museum installation. The peace was to be enforced by a multinational implementation force with a significant U.S. contingent. U.S. ground troops thus ceased the march homeward and embarked along the Danube and across the Sava on a peace enforcement and security-building operation to implement the Dayton agreement in the NATO Implementation Force (IFOR), which within a year's time became the NATO Stabilization Force (SFOR). U.S. Army, Europe undertook the largest post-conflict security-building campaign since its predecessors had done so in World War II, the practical experience of which nonetheless had been lost over time.

IFOR/SFOR was quite unlike the recently completed fighting in Kuwait and cut against the grain of combat doctrine as it had emerged in the two decades prior. The operation provided a role for PfP nations, including such ex-communists as Romania as well as such neutrals as Austria, to serve alongside the U.S. military in an ever more integrated, combined, joint military echelons. Not the least, the operation engaged the Russian army peace keeping forces in a bilateral U.S.-Russian Federation command alongside NATO—no small feat considering how the same soldiers a decade earlier stood poised to annihilate each other.

IFOR/SFOR unfolded as an operation of great strategic merit, which the makers of U.S. tactical-operational dogma, with fuzzy memories of muddled postwar policy in the Rhineland in the 1920s and the twisted civil-military prelude to occupation in Western Europe in 1942–1944, chose to ignore. The operation became the butt of scorn of neo-conservatives, military traditionalists of the Weinberger-Powell school, as well as their claques in domestic politics, all of whom sought to downgrade the security of Europe as a concern of U.S. policy.

These American critics notwithstanding, the closer military integration in the Bosnian peace support operation signified the virtues of alliance cohesion and the strategic benefit of enlargement in NATO. This phenomenon found new energy in the years 1995–1997 along the line from the central European capitals to Bonn, Brussels and Washington, D.C. In September 1995 the NAC finally pushed beyond partnership to enlargement with the publication of its Enlargement Study. This policy signaled the revival of Article X accession in the Washington Treaty for central European nations that operated in three stages of accession from the end of the 1990s over the decade to come in the new century. The little-noticed attempt by the French to rejoin the integrated military structure unfolded in the mid-1990s, but it ended in a return to U.S.-French snarling over the fate of a major NATO command under possible French flag at the Naples, Italy, headquarters for allied forces in southern Europe. Further Franco-American discord erupted in 1997 at the Madrid NAC Summit over the question of how many Central and Eastern European nations should accede to NATO. The French insisted on the Romanians and Slovenians in addition to the Poles, Czechs and Hungarians. The U.S. side prevailed, however, with the military technical rationale that the latter three were better armed for the requirements of NATO, an argument that gave insufficient weight to the essentially political character of an enlarged NATO.

While IFOR/SFOR brought respite to the beleaguered peoples of Bosnia-Herzegovina, the curse of integral nationalist, sectarian conflict shifted by 1997–1998 southward to within Serbia itself; that is, to Kosovo, where ethnic Albanians had sought independence from Belgrade in the latest episode of a struggle within origins in the late 19th century. U.S./EU multilateral conflict termination on the Bosnian model to restrain the Slobodan Milosevic regime availed little in the course of 1998, other than renewed massacres and internal deportations that reached a climax in the fall of that year. Beneath the lurid details of President Bill Clinton's impeachment in the U.S. Congress for a sex scandal, the accounts of the carnage in Kosovo finally became an issue in the U.S. by the end of 1998. The United Nations (U.N.) Security Council demanded an end to the fighting, a demarche which prompted the North Atlantic Council to prepare an air campaign just as multilateral negotiations in France between the great powers and the warring sides led the Serbs to reject the military dimension of the agreement.

The NATO air operation "Allied Force" from the end of March until the beginning of June 1999 included a strong contingent of U.S. Air Force and U.S. Navy aircraft in action alongside European allied forces. These aircrews not only flew into the teeth of Serbian defenses that were more resolute than in Bosnia, but also into the challenge of alliance cohesion and burden sharing in wartime that has been a constant theme of this chapter. The latter proved as problematic as any aspect of an already vexed conflict because the reality of war in southeastern Europe diverged from the abstract, albeit comprehensive, preparations for war in order to deter conflict that had been the organization's main calling for decades earlier.

The dichotomy between the ideals of combat doctrine as taught in defense academies and the political, strategic and operational dictates of the Serb-Kosovo conflict in 1999 proved too much for the outspoken critics in the United States of the political-strategic process of graduated response that violent spring. What they deemed as too timid a blow from the air in the face of the entrenched Serbian resistance in the first weeks of the struggle was portrayed by these guardians of Douhet and Mitchell's legacy as treason against the fundamentals of overwhelming force, i.e. the Weinberger-Powell Doctrine as well as the dogma of air power. Atop this cardinal sin these critics heaped a list of tactical-operational deficiencies of European pilots and aircraft in combat wrought by the 1990s peace dividend—that is, the normal demerits from the NATO annual defense planning questionnaire were reworked for a dubious strategic purpose by the adherents of the fata morgana of American unipolar power at the cost of the people of south eastern Europe and the Atlantic alliance.

Once the war in the air devolved into attrition, the theater commander, U.S. Army General and SACEUR Wesley Clark, provoked a civil-military fight that signified a new attempt by the operational level of war to hoist itself to the pinnacle of policy. Clark readied a rocket artillery and combat helicopter-borne offensive into Kosovo to eradicate the Serbian resistance that, for a time at least, seemed invulnerable to allied laser-guided projectiles. More than some of the latter struck the innocent and gave life to anti-war claims that the United States and NATO were monsters as despicable as the Serbian ethnic cleansers. Clark's ideal of full spectrum air-land battle found scant favor with his political masters in the NAC and sparked the displeasure of the U.S. Joint Chiefs of Staff as well as the Clinton White House, which scotched his plans. Though this short war in the air may have been hampered by the defects of alliance crossed purposes, as well as by somewhat less operational striking power in many NATO flying units than the most crack USAF wing, the weaknesses of NATO proved less a strategic liability than those that handicapped Milosevic's war-weary and isolated Serbia. The latter finally yielded to great power control of its southern province so burdened with myths of blood and soil. KFOR, a new combined, NATO joint task force rather than Clark's rockets and helicopters ended the carnage without a shot being fired and presided over what became a division of the province into Serbian and Albanian halves in the years that followed June 1999.

The false starts of coalition war and the burden-sharing problems of the Kosovo campaign notwithstanding, the imperative of alliance cohesion among the adherents of Acheson and Bevin and the new allies from Central Europe led the North Atlantic Council to Washington in April 1999 with a dual purpose: to promote a new NATO strategic concept to replace that of 1991 (the transformed face of security in post-conflict reconstruction) and to endorse the accession of the Poles, Czechs and Hungarians to the Washington Treaty. The enlargement of NATO reached its climax in the midst of NATO's first major fighting campaign that lurched painfully close to defeat as well as to the territory of the new NATO allies. Certain of the latter nurtured affection for Yugoslavia and its statecraft in modern Europe and these governments faced a hostile public opinion in the test of alliance solidarity in 1999.

The conflict nonetheless brought a truce if not a peace to southeastern Europe that had been the locale for the worst fighting since 1944–1945, which for a while had placed an unbearable burden on the fundamentals of trans-Atlantic security, and to which the government of the United States at the beginning of the decade had turned an indifferent eye. The alliance carried out enlargement even in the extreme of battle, and as it finally achieved the relative pacification of southeastern Europe it also anchored *Zwischeneuropa* in the west and thus created the basis for peace in a part of Europe that been the victim of the 20th century.

The record of the 1990s illustrates the engagement and disengagement of the U.S. soldier in Europe in the transformed epoch of war and peace at the end of the 20th century. The decade demonstrated the durability of shared defense institutions and military practice across the Atlantic, even if the shape and size of the U.S. force in Europe shrank greatly and the strategic problems changed from nuclear deterrence to the use of military force within the partially peaceful and partially violent reorganization of the European system.

This defense integration, however, collided with its nemesis of disintegration and disengagement in Europe and North America beset by renationalization, integral nationalism in southeastern Europe, as well as delusions of the "end of history" and unipolar hegemony nurtured on the Potomac, where little insight obtained as to the brooding forces over the horizon or the value of alliances in general. The generation of the 1990s devoted to the trans-Atlantic ideal slowly summoned new energies appropriate for the moment, in common with the peoples of central and eastern Europe, who saw the American soldier as a representative of an open, more or less generous community of values that had beaten totalitarianism and brought security and prosperity to half of Europe.

Conclusion: The Riddle of Mars and Venus in the Empty Barracks

In the year 2011, the Federal German office for real estate and excess government property placed an online tender for the conversion of Campbell barracks in Heidelberg, the former seat of U.S. Army Europe and the 7th Army. The buildings originally constructed in the Third Reich might easily be adapted to civilian use, surely as part of Heidelberg's globalized university—a place of excellence in realms of knowledge, law, and economy where Germany had reemerged in the new century.

As part of the general reduction and re-stationing of forces that started in the early 1990s and reeked of the "exit strategy" in the Weinberger-Powell doctrine, the USAREUR headquarters as a shadow of its former self had finally swapped Heidelberg for Wiesbaden in the new century. The rolling up of American top brass lurched forward with the campaigns of counter-proliferation and counterterror in Afghanistan and Iraq—housed not in central European barracks, but in Saddam Hussein's palaces, as well as in sprawling cantonments and outposts run by multinational civilian military contractors, a throw-away feature of military architecture in the 21st century. The empty barracks and headquarters on the Neckar had somehow joined the town's famous castle and so many other fortifications along the nearby Rhine to become a kind of ruin, that is, 20th-century detritus of total war.

The meaning of this place in the rancor of the years 2002–2008, when seen through the lens of this chapter, threatened either to degrade into Mars-versus-Venus neo-conservative caricature in the post-September 11 falling out between many European governments and the Bush administration in the United States or, more likely, among young people with no real memory of the 20th century, simply to recede into obscurity. Yet the record of how the American soldiers came to Heidelberg and then to leave it finally deserves neither caricature nor oblivion either in the United States or in the European Union. The role of Europeans in the creation and professional consolidation of the American military in the 18th through the 20th century, especially in the realm of theory and education and training, forms a central truth essential to the whole. The role of American soldiers in the age of total war in Europe and its legacy in modern Europe forms the second dimension of this important story.

A community of fate linked American soldiers and Europe in the phenomenon of attraction and rejection in ideas and in geography. While the social and political basis of American in the origins of military institutions diverged especially from continental Europe in the 18th century (republicanism versus absolutism), the soldierly professional ideals of 19th-century continental Europe (the rise of machine war and a managerial elite with its own prerogatives), be it from France or later from Germany of the second Reich, exerted a strong pull on American soldiers. To this dynamic was added the phenomenon of engagement and disengagement as the United States emerged as a world power, and the advent of the U.S. soldier and the American armed forces as significant political institution in the first half of the 20th century. The epoch of total war from 1914 though the short 20th century contained the maturation of American arms to a major force in the international system which culminated in the Atlantic alliance of the years from 1941 onward.

As laudable in hindsight as this alliance might have been from the perspective of the bloodless end of the division of Europe in the years after 1989, its character and evolution in the epoch 1948–1989 were prone to endless crisis that recalled earlier phases of conflicted statecraft and strategy. These crises fell more or less into four general categories that frequently comingled with each other. First, the willingness of the Atlantic allies to form an integrated security alliance presented challenges of statecraft, defense burdens, and the common formation of strategy that had been neither simple nor easy in past force and statecraft.

Second, the necessity to find some coherent strategic response to nuclear and thermonuclear weapons caused unceasing "nuclear crises" about the ends and means of the U.S. nuclear presence in Europe, particularly the impact on those living in the shadow of the nuclear bomb. Such policy made the United States take on the interests of its allies as its own, but this imperative collided with the growing nuclear arsenal of the Soviet Union in the 1950s, thereby testing the limits of extended deterrence. In turn, the alternatives impelled junior allies possibly to acquire nuclear weapons and/or even defect from the alliance into neutrality.

Third, the limits of the eastern and southern lines of North Atlantic defense ("out of area") collided with armed conflict in the Asia (Indochina, Korea, and Vietnam) and the Middle East (Suez, Algeria, the 1973 Arab-Israeli war), which again and again reverberated in the western alliance and led to particular pressures on France as well as divided Germany in the European and international system, which in their own turn caused ongoing crises of alliance policy and cohesion.

In the fourth instance, the traditional rejection of Europe in parts of American state and society, with origins in the 17th and 18th centuries, became quickly evident in Department of Defense and Congressional plans each decade from the 1950s until the 1980s to reduce greatly the U.S. troops, as well as to shift the costs of the collective defense burden more onto western Europeans within the international political economy of the Cold War. The growing focus on the Middle East as the center of gravity of U.S. statecraft from the 1970s onward exacerbated this trend, however, intermittently. Under the heading of "burden sharing," the domestic politics of forward defense, defense budgets, and political economy—embedded, as they are, in conceptions of society and economy in U.S. and western European capitals—made for an unending story with many chapters in which U.S. displeasure with the "insufficient defense effort" of the European allies became a constant theme.

Then, amid the withdrawal of U.S. forces as a continuity within the story of America and military power in Europe, the 2013–2014 Ukrainian crisis and annexation of Crimea by Vladimir Putin's Russia in a shot resurrected many of the issues explored in this chapter as concern an integrated Atlantic alliance, its geographical limits, the posture of U.S. forces in the European system of states, and the enduring role of the trans-Atlantic relationship despite talk of a pivot to Asia by the United States in the wake of the Iraqi and Afghan campaigns. Calls for reinforcements of U.S. forces in Europe in addition to a halt to the ongoing withdrawal of troops and weapons echoed on both sides of the Atlantic amid what seemed to contemporaries as the most significant crisis of war in peace in Europe since the 1980s.

For this reason and more, the story of war and peace in Europe stands incomplete without due consideration of the role that American soldiers have played in the evolution of the European system of states and the 20th century composition of armed forces. A young officer of a united Europe in search of the origins of contemporary issues of soldierly service as well as the posture of command and operations can make little sense of these issues without resort to the account rendered here of how Europe helped to form U.S. military institutions, and how 20th-century America transformed the old continental order and its armies that were wiped out in the era of total war. The upshot of this process has been a military convergence through alliance between North America and Europe, despite propagandistic assertions to the contrary.

U.S. soldiers on counterinsurgency operations have recycled combat doctrine first crafted by French and British officers in the 19th and 20th centuries. European soldiers fight and serve today with the legacy of NATO integration, even if under the EU banner; when on counterterrorism service in Africa or elsewhere the impact of combined, joint operations with an American accent is never far.

While the physical presence of American soldiers in Europe remains an open issue of policy in the wake of the Crimean crisis, the impact of this military convergence in the legacy of arms and contemporary experience remains vital, not because of the U.S. as "some remaining superpower" (a dubious assertion) but because of this shared legacy of ideas and experience in war and peace that has forged a bond that has proven more powerful than its critics dare to acknowledge and that the crises of the past and present have failed to tear apart.

Guide to Further Reading

The themes of U.S. strategic culture, military institutions, and the role of Europe are explored in: Russel Weigley, The American Way of War (New York: Macmillan, 1973); Richard H. Kohn, The Eagle and the Sword: The Federalists and the Creation of the Military Establishment in America, 1783–1802 (New York: Free Press, 1975); Peter Paret, Understanding War, (Princeton, N.J.: Princeton University Press, 1992); Brian Lynn, The Echo of Battle : The Army's Way of War (Cambridge, MA: Harvard University Press, 2007); John Shy and David J. Fitzpatrick, "American Military History" in A Century of American Historiography, edited by James M. Banner, Jr.,(Boston: Bedford/St. Martin's, 2010), pp. 66–77. Studies of trans-Atlantic political, strategic, social, and cultural relations in their variety are: Jonathan Harper, American Visions of Europe (Cambridge:, Cambridge University Press, 1994); Richard Pells, Not Like Us: How Europeans Have Loved, Hated and Transformed American Culture (New York: Basic 1997); Kenneth Weisbrode, The Atlantic Century: Four Generations of Extraordinary Diplomats Who Forged America's Vital Alliance with Europe (New York: Da Capo, 2009); Phillipe Roger, The American Enemy: The History of French Anti-Americanism (Chicago: Chicago University Press, 2002); Frank Trommler et al., eds. America and the Germans: an Assessment of a Three-Hundred Year History (Philadelphia: University of Pennsylvania Press, 1985); Detlef Junker ed., Die USA und Deutschland im Zeitalter des Kalten Krieges: Ein Handbuch (Stuttgart/München: Deutsche Verlagsanstalt, 2001); Frank Trommler et al., eds. Deutsch-Amerikanische Begegnungen: Konflikt und Kooperation im 19. und 20. Jahrhundert (Stuttgart/München, Deutsche Verlagsanstalt, 2001); Donald Cameron Watt, Succeeding John Bull: America in Britain's Place, 1900–1975 (Cambridge: Cambridge University Press, 1984); William Roger Louis et al., eds., The Special Relationship: Anglo-American Relations since 1945 (Oxford/New York: Oxford University Press, 1986).

Prominent among the 19th-century American military thinkers and their connection to the military heritage of Europe are: Emory Upton, Armies of Asia and Europe: Official Reports (New York:

Greenwood 1968); Stephen E. Ambrose, Upton and the Army (Baton Rouge, LA: Louisiana State University Press, 1964); Harold Sprout, The Rise of American Naval Power, 1776–1918 (Princeton, N.J.: Princeton University Press, 1966); John T. Sumida, Inventing Grand Strategy and Teaching Command: The Classic Works of Alfred Thayer Mahan Reconsidered (Baltimore: Johns Hopkins University Press, 1997). Edward M. Coffman treats the modernization of the U.S. Army of the 19th century until the early 20th century in The Regulars: The American Army, 1898–1941 (Cambridge, MA/London: Harvard University Press, 2004). On John J. Pershing, U.S. forces, and alliance cohesion in the First World war, see Russell Weigley, "Strategy and Total War in the United States: Pershing and the American Military Tradition" in Roger Chickering et al., eds., Great War and Total War (Cambridge, MA: Cambridge University Press, 2000), pp. 327–345.

On Anglo-American naval relations and matters of alliance cohesion see: David Trask, Captains and Cabinets: Anglo-American Naval Relations, 1917–1918 (Columbia, MO: University of Missouri, 1972). On the Franco-American case, see Robert B. Bruce, Fraternity of Arms: America and France in the Great War (Lawrence, KS: University Press of Kansas, 2003). On the United States and the interwar system of states, see Jeffrey W Talliafiero et al., eds., The Challenge of Grand Strategy: The Great Powers and the Broken Balance Between the World Wars (Cambridge: Cambridge University Press, 2012). On the U.S. Army in the Rhineland from 1918 until 1922, see Irwin Hunt, American Military Government of Occupied Germany, 1918–1920 (Washington, DC: U.S. Army, 1943).

On strategic thought and alliances of the inter-war U.S. Army, see Mark Stoler, Allies and Adversaries: The Joint Chiefs of Staff, the Grand Alliance and U.S. Strategy in World War II (Chapel Hill/London: University of North Carolina, 2000). For the inter-war U.S. military, Europe and technology, see: Henry Gole, The Road to Rainbow: Army Planning for Global War, 1934–1940 (Annapolis, MD: Naval Institute Press, 2003); David E. Johnson, Fast Tanks and Heavy Bombers: Innovation in the U.S. Army, 1917–1945 (Ithaca,

NY: Cornell University Press, 1998); and the classic work of Maurice Mattloff et al., Strategic Planning for Coalition Warfare, 1941–1942 (Washington, DC: U.S. Government Printing Office, 1953), a volume in the official U.S. Army history of the Second World War. Also see: Maurice Matloff, "Allied Strategy in Europe, 1939–1945" in Peter Paret, et al., eds., Makers of Modern Strategy: From Machiavelli to Nuclear Strategy (Princeton, N.J.: Princeton University Press, 1986) pp. 677–702.

The U.S. occupation of Germany is treated in Harold Stein, American Civil-Military Decisions: A Book of Case Studies (Montgomery, AL: University of Alabama, 1963); Earl F. Ziemke, The U.S. Army in the Occupation of Germany, 1944–1946 (Washington, DC: U.S. Government Printing Office, 1975) and Klaus Dietmar Henke, Die amerkanische Besetzung Deutschlands (München: Oldenbourt, 1995). Also see among a growing literature of the most recent scholarship: Christian Thomas Mueller, US Truppen und Sowjetarmee in Deutschland: Erfahrungen, Beziehungen und Konflikte im Vergleich (Paderborn; Schoeningh, 2012). On social and gender relations between U.S. forces and Germans, see Petra Goede, GIs and Germans: Culture, Gender and Foreign Relations, 1945–1949 (New Haven, CT: Yale University Press, 2003).

On the origins of NATO, security assistance, and burden-sharing, see: Lord Hastings Ismay, NATO : The First Five Years, 1949–1954 (Paris: NATO Press, 1956); Lawrence Kaplan: A Community of Interests: NATO and the Military Assistance Program,1948–1951 (Washington, DC: U.S. Government Printing Office, 1980); Wallace J. Thies, Friendly Rivals: Bargaining and Burden Shifting in NATO (Washington, DC: Sharpe, 2002); Helmut Hammerich, Jeder für sich und Amerika gegen alle?: Die Lastenteilung der NATO am Beispiel des Temporary Council Committee (Muenchen: Oldenbourg, 2003); Gero von Gersdorff, Die Gründung der Nordatlantischen Allianz (München: Oldenbourg, 2009).

A variety of scholarly and policy studies of the middle and late Cold War treat the politics of U.S. forces in Europe from the late 1940s until the 1980s. See: John Newhouse, U.S. Troops in Europe:

Issues, Costs and Choices (Brookings, Washington DC, 1971); Phil Williams, The Senate and U.S. Troops in Europe (New York: Macmillan, 1985); Simon Duke, U.S. Defense Bases in the United Kingdom: A Matter for Joint Decision? (New York: St. Martin's, 1987); Robert E. Harkavy, Bases Abroad: The Global Foreign Military Presence (Oxford: Oxford University Press, 1989); Simon Duke et al., United States Military Forces and Installations in Europe (Oxford: Oxford University Press, 1989); Jane Sharp, ed., Europe After an American Withdrawal: Economic and Military Issues (Oxford: Oxford University Press, 1991). On U.S. Army Europe as well as U.S. Air Force, Europe, and their allies, see: Daniel J. Nelson, A History of U.S. Military Forces in Germany (Boulder/London: Greenwood, 1987); Ingo Trauschwitzer, The Cold War U.S. Army: Building Deterrence for Limited War (Lawrence, KS: Kansas University Press, 2008); Helmut Hammerich et al., eds., Das Heer 1950–1970: Konzeption, Organisation, Aufstellung (München: Oldenbourg, 2006); Bernd Lemke, et al., eds., Die Luftwaffe 1950–1970: Konzeption, Aufbau, Integration (München: Oldenbourg, 2006); Jan Hoffenaar and Dieter Krüger, eds., Blueprints for Battle: Planning for War in Central Europe, 1948–1968, English translation edited by David T. Zabecki (Omaha, University of Nebraska UP, 2012)

On the political and financial aspects of stationed forces, see: Gregory F. Treverton, The "Dollar Drain" and American Forces in Germany: Managing the Political Economics of Alliance (Athens, OH: Ohio University Press, 1978); Daniel Hoffmann, Truppenstationierung in der Bundesrepublik Deutschland: die Vertragsverhandlungen, 1951–1959 (München: Oldenbourg, 1997); Hubert Zimmermann, Money and Security: Troops, Monetary Policy and West Germany's Relations with the U.S. and Britain, 1950–1971 (Cambridge: Cambridge University Press, 2002). Statistics on the strength of U.S. Army Europe in the era 1945 until the present are on the USAREUR website:

http://www.eur.army.mil/organization/timeline.htm

Monographs from the U.S. Army Center of Military History on aspects of U.S. Army Europe in the Cold War and after are: Stephen

Gehring, From the Fulda Gap to Kuwait: U.S. Army, Europe and the Gulf War (Washington, DC: U.S. Government Printing Office, 1998); Robert P. Grathwol, Donita M. Moorhusn, Building for Peace: U.S. Army Engineers in Europe, 1945–1991 (Washington DC: US Government Printing Office, 2002); Also see Robert Gunnarsson, American Military Police in Europe, 1945–1991: Unit Histories (Jefferson, NC: McFarland, 2011).

7. The Present Crisis and the Fate of Security in the Adriatic and Beyond: Some Historical Reflections on Democracy and Security in the Past and Present[*]

The goal of the statecraft and policy of the past two decades among the Euro-Atlantic nations and their international organizations, to say nothing of the desire among the peoples of this region, has been to bring security, peace and prosperity to the nations of Southeastern Europe in the wake of the warfare of the 1990s. Central to this undertaking have been the benefits of both the trans-Atlantic alliance and the construction of a United Europe anchored in the order of nation-states created at great cost from 1949 until 2004. My purpose here, however, goes well beyond the ordinary strategic-communication praise of the security and collective defense benefits of the trans-Atlantic alliance. You have already heard such talks, and anyway, the topic is better depicted on the NATO website and its social media. Instead, I wish to reflect on the unsettled character of security, peace and prosperity, and the growing threats to this fragile new order that are an ever more powerful feature of a crisis-laden present.

The necessary policy of including Southeastern Europe into the zone of democracy, prosperity and security, as say, between Liege and Aachen (that is, the old core of the European common market), has lurched into a crisis of state, economy, and society, wrought of the weakening of the western democracies in the mayhem of the world financial crisis. This process of disintegration is further exacerbated by the failures of memory and the fatigue of the public mind in what seems to be a chain of crises without end. This process obscures what are central insights for the formulation of policy in the peace of Europe: that to slacken and falter in the preservation of values in security and prosperity will not only mean poverty, but chaos and war.

[*] Presentation, Conference on Adriatic Security, Tirana, Albania, October 2011
Thanks to the Albanian ambassador to the North Atlantic Council, the Honorable Leonard Demi.

That a return to the mentality and deeds of the era from the 1880s until 1939 in some new 21st century guise camouflaged in social media and the politics of disorder will have similar or worse results. I do not need to school you in this fact, granted what you have endured in the last 20 years, and which Europe and North America as a whole have learned at huge cost in the last century and more. Yet many who rule today on very shaky thrones and those who blog before they think seem all too willing to forget these insights with a carelessness that is shocking.

Terrible Simplifiers and Friend/Foe

In the late 19th century, the Swiss historian Jacob Burckhardt wrote of the dangers of his epoch of mass politics amid the European era of nationalism and the industrial revolution. Chief among the perils of mass politics that Burckhardt described were its terrible simplifiers, that is, those dubious figures in public life in Paris, Berlin, and Vienna who poisoned political debate in the generation before 28 June 1914 and whose violence of thought and word, in part, made possible an era of the world wars. The principal weapon of the terrible simplifier, integral nationalism, has been the use of an image of the enemy (*Feindbild*) and the role of enemies within the state and society, as the essence of politics. The German jurist and political theorist, Carl Schmitt, reminds us that such a mechanism is central to politics or at least it was in the turmoil of much of the 20th century that we all hoped had ended in 1989–1991.

To be sure, the policies of Europe and the West in the last six decades or so have aimed at ameliorating the most pernicious effects of the terrible simplifiers—mitigating the zero-sum competition among European states and the mass-political proclivity toward tribalism, in Hannah Arendt's sense of the term and for a while, at least, putting the lie to Schmitt's dialectic of friend or foe. But the conditions in which Carl Schmitt flourished (1920s–1940s) with such an idea, that is, the state of emergency and democracy in peril, are returning with frightening speed.

And this image of the enemy more or less on model of such men as the founders in the 1880s and 1890s of the French xeno-phobe Action Française, or the German radical nationalist Alldeutscher Verband, or the Austrian ethnic German, anti Slav Christian Socialists is once more becoming the currency of politics and society, to say nothing of the international economy in the Euro-Atlantic area. This process has unfolded in the last decade amid polit-ical and economic integration of a broad sort in the Euro-Atlantic realm, at the same time that religion and political violence became a dominant feature once more of the international system in the wake of 11 September 2001. No sooner has the scourge of integral—that is, the blood-and-soil variety of—nationalist war on the European con-tinent been (mostly) contained after the suffering of the 1990s, the same tensions now emerge in the specter of racist nationalist violence in places of heretofore noteworthy for prosperity and stability.

This fact is made worse by the reappearance of class conflict of the 19th- and 20th-century stripe. In this sense, the money crisis portends more than trouble for a common currency in use in Paris and Bratislava. The habits of thought and expressions of exclusion that the economic depression has engendered undermine much of the social, political, economic, and even cultural order which, for example, today threaten to undo the progress of the nations of the Adriatic and Southeastern Europe in their consistent efforts to enter Euro-Atlantic political, security, and defense institutions and acquire their rightful place once more in the democratic camp.

Europe in Between and Walls of Gold and Silver: Sources of Disintegration

The march of disintegration, that is, the centrifugal forces at work today contain three interconnected centers of gravity or sources of dissolution that demand our response in policy and statecraft. This process of breakup via exclusion is bringing about a new division of Europe into its prosperous and its debt-laden realms—the sharpening of a conflict between the haves versus the have-nots. The latter play the role of scapegoats or victims of the neo-liberal epoch of the era 1980–2008, which is coming plainly to an end.

The first of these sources of disintegration and decomposition concerns the bedrock of security of the Atlantic Alliance and the shared fate between Europe and North America. The second source of disintegration is the fatigue among the "core Europeans" as concerns the merits of an enlarged, integrated Europe, and the tendency either to erect a new wall of prosperity to isolate the formerly secure peoples of southern Europe through a neo-liberal dogma that is, in turn, enflaming an ever more virulent populism that departs starkly from the political culture of the post-1945 era.

The third source of disintegration is the revival of extreme right-wing politics with resort to violence, a phenomenon that more or less vanished in the maelstrom of the Second World War and its aftermath. Let me explore each of the three in turn.

Burden-Sharing Abroad and Tub-Thumping at Home

Democracy and prosperity require security, which the North Atlantic Alliance has provided at first with nuclear deterrence and more recently with the limited use of military force for limited strategic ends, but with actual fighting and post-conflict security building, in southern Europe, the Middle East, South West Asia and, most recently, in North Africa. However, the combat of the last decade and a half nearby and now in Afghanistan and Libya, for instance, has exacerbated greatly the classical problem that concerns all forms of pluralistic politics, that is, the price tag of policy and the perception of the sharing of this price, i.e. burden-sharing or also burden-shifting. As my graduates from Monterey know, this phenomenon represents an important feature of how NATO works and works very well; but also now, in view of the EU rescue-mechanism for southern European debt, of how the EU works as well in dimension of shared wealth and obligation.

The burden-sharing fight that has been especially vicious among the western European and U.S. sides since 11 September 2001 and has done, I think, great damage by an overemphasis on its negative aspects. Let me be clear: What I will now describe to you represents not my personal and professional view, but the majority posture of those around me and who outnumber me many times over. Here the issue of who shoulders the burden of war and peace is seen by many in a narrow-minded, bookkeeping table, that once more ignores the contributions made by many allies of a qualitative sort, and that sees security, defense, and military affairs as a numerical exercise, as if war and alliance were a mathematical and business undertaking.

This toxic burden-sharing to and fro that began in its present form in the 1990s here in Southeastern Europe, leaped into a hateful phase prior the Iraqi campaign of 2003 and more recently has spread to the Afghan and Libyan campaigns. This process has especially had a poisonous effect on domestic politics in my country. Not for the first time in my experience, does war weariness and anxiety over the ill effects of financial crisis seize on the defense commitment to Europe.

The advent of neo-isolationist political forces, which are at odds with the U.S. alliances and their crucial role within the international system, represents a force of disintegration. A great debate about the costs and burdens of a U.S. defense commitment to the security of Europe has already manifested itself in the electoral season. Opponents of defense spending in U.S. domestic politics always deplore NATO as a Cold-War relic and a waste of money in their general attempt to accentuate social programs over security, defense, and military requirements.

How the "lessons learned" from the Libyan campaign will operate in this connection lies beyond my level of knowledge, though to my mind the Libyan operation shows the enduring strategic importance of NATO to peace and security. However, many young U.S. officers as well as editorial writers and bloggers believe quite the opposite, insisting that NATO is *kaputt*. Thus, the core security and defense alliance that has brought peace and security throughout my lifetime at modest cost and great benefit is damaged by its burden-sharing mechanism gone berserk. The use of this broken tool of burden shifting as a weapon by rabble rousers in domestic politics portends, as one senior U.S. official suggested, a "dismal future" for NATO, which one presumes will end up on some Dunkirk-like beach in the years to come.

Thrift, Xenophobia, and Statecraft:
Fatigue with Greater Europe and the North-Versus-South Syndrome

More alarming than the exhaustion in the North Atlantic capitals with the burdens of collective defense in the 21st century looms the danger to international politics from money gone mad and middle-class values shoved into radicalism. In particular, I mean the agonies of the neo-liberal governance and management that stumbles in circles today under the banner of globalization ripped to shreds by the bank collapses of 2008. The loss of direction of this managerial elite and the riposte of an enraged and duped stock holders and account book owners comprise the second force of disintegration in the international system.

Prosperity linked with democracy has been the basis of security since the economic recovery of Western Europe in the late 1940s and 1950s. This prosperity formed the magnet of the western camp and had lately spread to the regions deprived of such prosperity even before the Cold War. The political and social peace that this prosperity nourished has been nowhere more visible than in so called Rhenish social market economy; that is, the economic miracle in West Germany, the Low Countries, and France that once again formed the core of a common, integrated and united Europe based on a renunciation of revanche and class war.

But such facts play little role in the lives of citizens today, in the second or third generation from these now remote times, whose position in a formerly comfortable middle class has lurched into uncertainty and whose paid vacations along the Adriatic are now at risk. Such nostalgia for the 1950s is nowhere to be found among young people unable to attain this prosperity at all because of what they perceive to be an invasion from open borders of "…cheap, foreign labor from alien lands" marshaled by heartless managerial elites blinded by PowerPoint slides atop their business towers to the harm they wreak on tens of millions.

Enlargement fatigue made virulent by the financial crisis of 2008 portrays the European Union as a distant tyrant when seen from Vienna or Bratislava, along with globalized banks and corporations that answer to no state in the conventional sense and whose profit accrues to the so-called 1-percent plutocratic class.

Meanwhile, with the scenes of civil unrest and strikes in southern European capitals over the debt crisis, the owner of the Mediterranean restaurant becomes a kind of other, somewhat and somehow disenfranchised and burdened with a collective guilt of lacking thrift and middle class virtues, although in this person's case, their energy and prudence are beyond reproach. He or she lurches in the collective subconscious a little farther toward the city gate or the debtor's prison. The former generosity and deeds of inclusion that once operated under the motto of prosperity for all has decayed into a mean-spirited, penny-pinching mentality, in which the friend/foe mechanism of politics can operate more loudly and with less regard for the damage it will surely cause in the future.

Populism, the Right Wing, and Political Violence

The third and most troubling source of disintegration and de-struction is the reappearance of the integral nationalist right wing violence as a feature of European politics. Such politically driven, racist violence has long been a feature of life in my country, to be sure, but it surely was a more or less scarce thing in past decades in Europe. Most important, the Norwegian Breivik, having read Georges Sorel and Gustav Le Bon, among his bibliography of ex-tremism, laid his bombs and mowed down innocent children in a way that was entirely familiar to the epoch from the 1880s until 1945.

Populism easily degenerates into xenophobia, made worse by prolonged warfare as well as the failure of elites to respond to the hopes and fears of the electorate. Most troubling has been the use of religion as a political weapon in a promiscuous way by our opponents, but also by figures in my country, as well. The infection of religious fundamentalism of whatever kind (I mean Christian and Jews as well as Muslims) into the life of the state and the international system wreaks havoc on human rights, tolerance, and peace and, as such, is a phenomenon that few experts predicted a generation ago.

I believe, however, that Breivik was as much attempting to murder the established political order in Western Europe as he was slaughtering Norwegian citizens "with an immigrant background" and brown eyes and dark skin. In this aspect, I also believe that others in their small, but growing number elsewhere in Western Europe and Central Europe who nurture similar ambitions, and that, after ten years of war in Iraq and especially Afghanistan, as well as an economic crisis weakening the west, they sense their moment is arriving. Perhaps they, themselves, do not keep their fingers on the trigger or accumulate the raw materials for bombs, but they encourage and tolerate others, less civil, clad in black jump boots and with skin heads and tattooed "88" mottos, who can be mobilized in a crisis to upend the political and civil order of constitutional human rights.

This fact represents perhaps the least tangible of the three forces of disintegration I have described, but surely the most dangerous and troubling. Political violence on a small scale in the late 19th century portended an era of total war. Our job is to ensure that this pattern does not repeat itself in the present century.

Conclusion

This admonition, overdrawn as it might be, arises from a reflection about the European past informed, in turn, by an active professional involvement in NATO for more than 40 years. My warning also manifests a heartfelt and deep affinity for the people of Central, Eastern, and Southern Europe who have been my students for 20 years (and are my own family for 14 years...), and whose desire for security and prosperity was cheated and betrayed in the 19th and especially in the 20th centuries by epochal forces that may reassert themselves now.

Those who see the post-1945, and even post-1989 order as now being somehow worn out, exhausted, and ready for the upload of some new application as one puts in their smart phone, even when such is untested, should consider the real forces that brought about the era of the world wars and punished this part of the world with particular evil and brutality. The three forces of disintegration that are undoing the order of values of democracy, prosperity, and security in this part of Europe are accelerating. This acceleration is propelled by the blindness of materialism, its pettiness, and shrunken spirit; by an amnesia about the European past; and by an appalling ignorance that these questions of balance sheets and management wizardry, in fact, are not business school case studies, but affairs of statecraft, and thus, of war and peace.

You and I are enjoined to redouble our efforts to show that a broken Atlantic link as in the 1920s and 1930s, will again result in a broken international system, as the justification for the sharing of the defense burden. We must find a more politically sound and sane answer to the spectacle of money gone wild rather than the witless cost-cutting of the year 1930. We must revive the best of Rhenish social market economy somehow so that its blessings will spread more widely, and prevent the marginalization of those nations in southern Europe that were the scene of such suffering in the 19th and 20th centuries.

Most important, we must extinguish through the due process of law and the power of the democratic state those radical right-wing extremists, who would resort to violence once more and open Pandora's box.

III.   Strategy and its Discontents

8. Thoughts on Strategy in the Past and Present: The State of Strategic Muddle*

For those who pause from the lockstep of curriculum to take stock of how contemporary strategy might have changed from, say, the year 2013 until 2016, the debate about power politics imbedded in domestic parliamentary and presidential elections in the western world may lead to some useful insights of a dialectical kind. This hopeful assertion belies the fact that on most levels of war and peace in the democratic powers of the West, the media and professional elite debate about strategy manifests what can only be called a theoretical, but also an applied, catastrophe as concerns level of expertise and the application of sound theory to practice. This generalization applies as much for the voters of western democracies as it does for those in parliaments and think tanks are ever more compelled to the formulation of an efficacious and efficient strategy on a basis of sound democratic civil-military relations. Hidden within the roar of populist indignation and the squeaks and moans of expert opinion about policy and strategy is also a real debate about the modes of strategy in the past and present with theoretically revealing merits. This brief inquiry presents some generalizations about this process in the hope that the quality of strategic reflection might obtain some of its former polish in an earlier time.

The following chapter contains some reflections on these issues bundled into a couple of problems. First, these themes signify a heuristic or epistemological point of view on contemporary events grounded in classical strategy and without the surrender to the suffocating influence of fads, buzz words, and otherwise distractions that have been all too prominent in the last 15 years in the record of war. In the second instance, this inquiry contains some mention of the

* Remarks, Editorial Board of Österreichische Militärzeitschrift, Austrian National Defense Academy, June 2016. Thanks to our colleague Briagdier Dr. Wolfgang Peischel and Hofrat Dr. Günther Fleck of the Austrian National Defense Academy.

baleful impact of personality and fame on the character of the strategist, if not on the subject of strategy generally. Third, and in conclusion, this essay speculates about the impact of a climacteric change in public mood as concerns the making of strategy and its possible implications for those who bear arms and those who think about the higher ends of the bearing arms to some coherent political purpose.

In a phrase, the present state of war and peace and its symbolic interpretation in the struggle to define a coherent strategy constitutes a muddle on a grand scale. This confusion arises out of a cognitive dissonance between two schools of strategy interpreted briefly here. This inquiry is offered by students of continental strategy and security sector in democratic polities in the past and present, who are also well versed in the maritime versus continental schools of strategy. The authors are also alive to the perennial conflict between an annihilationist school of strategy and an attritional school of strategy. These bodies of theory and their proponents are an especially Anglo-Saxon phenomenon, but they have relevance in Europe and Asia as much as they do to the cases of the United States and the United Kingdom in the past and present.

The first of these schools a.) an anti-jihadist and Middle East-focused counterterror school is in 2016 struggling to maintain its interpretative hegemony over contemporary conflict, while another and competing school is thrusting itself into prolonged attention, viz: b.) a geo-political, great-power school in which war between nation-states is not only possible, but ever more likely when one reads the headlines in the years since 2014. Because the authors work for the U.S. Navy, but are also engaged in European security as well as homeland security, we are alive to all these schools and their frictional and loud interaction in democratic statecraft and in theory as found in the advanced classroom.

The Middle Eastern school of strategy has had a near supremacy in thought and deed since the end of 2001, when the Bush-Cheney administration chose to respond to the 11 September attacks with a dual campaign in Afghanistan and Iraq, with the main effort unfolding against the latter nation state with a modified conventional military campaign. The jihadist, profoundly unconventional character of the terror assaults gave the new brooms of strategy in this epoch the breakthrough that had not been possible in the 1990s.

The years from 2002 until about 2006 killed off much of the detritus in strategic thought and programmatic effort in DoD of the 1990s in a contingency that appeared tailor made for special operations echelons of military organization and a grand strategy of counter insurgency. The 1990s school of a revolution of military affairs had already done a great deal to suggest that much customary military thought and practice was obsolete prior to 2001.

Since 2014, however, the startled persons in think tanks, general staffs and among the chattering classes have awoken from the COIN and hybrid war episodes to discover the noisy grinding of the major powers and the revival of geopolitical imperatives in continental and maritime realms of global sweep. This cataclysmic striding-by of God and the fatal choice to do nothing else but to grab hold of the hem of history and geopolitics takes place not in the benighted outposts of Afghan or Iraqi towns or provinces. The center of gravity lies elsewhere.

Despite the blow-by-blow accounts of street fighting in Fallujah or the cave battles in Tora Bora over a period of years, the fate of nations in the world system of states has made only the slightest pause since 11 September. While the American collective strategic mind has been directed to each square kilometer of Anbar Province or Helmand Province or to the vagaries of a forward operating base in the south of said great mythical Northwest Asia land, the exalted machinations of statecraft in the leading chancelleries, ministries, and otherwise high houses of the nation-states have surely not come to a halt. This movement of the wheel of fate in the geopolitical engine of doom has greatly sped up—a phenomenon at the heart of the theoretical assumptions in this essay and forms the point of departure for this inquiry. If this work smashes some very prominent icons of the last 15 years, then it will have succeeded in the sense of Clausewitz in sparking a critical and dialectical reflection on perennial issues of force and statecraft.

Both of these schools well share a trait in common, which is a distrust of democratic civil-military relations, an entirely under appreciated aspect of the whole that is the red thread in this dialectic and which points to the issues contained in the conclusion of this work about the very limits of strategy and its elite hegemony of interpretation in the face of the actual forces of war, which are asserting their rightful place in any scholarly or applied inquiry. This theme constitutes an underlying issue of any examination of contemporary strategy in historical terms and the attempt to provoke reflection through the dialectic employed here with an obeisance to Clausewitz.

The strategic muddle that leads the question here has become so intense since about 2014, that it has spilled into a highly polarized election campaign, which is a kind of referendum on the strategic epoch since 11 September 2001 and might be said also to be referendum on a strategy of annihilation and or a strategy of attrition. The eccentric presidential candidate Donald Trump has exemplified the annihilationist school, hardly a new thing in domestic politics in strategic thought either in his country or in other Atlantic democracies. Hillary Clinton has embraced the attritional strategy exemplified by Barack Obama in his maturity as commander in chief, and in the more sober insights of counter terror and great power strategy as levied against the means and ends, but especially the costs of combating jihadists on a wide scale.

One could also negate the issue with the assertion that no dialectic exists between these two school, as did one informed commentator when the author presented this thesis to the plenum in June 2016, but such a negation cannot hold in the praxis of this issue as it unfolds in the United States and, to some degree, as it unfolds in NATO.

Yet in the face of this *Schmarrn* there also beckons a new epoch of strategy constituted of the second school of strategy, to which these authors more or less subscribe because of serious doubts about the former school of strategy. The divergence between the apparent prominence in the minds of many observers of the character of war and peace in the present of jihadist terrorism as the predominant challenge of the moment and a corresponding view of the globe in which the thrust and parry of great power rivalry of the old model is plainly ascendant. The former issue garners far too much attention among those who profess to understand the making of strategy, while the latter garners too little attention to the peril of all.

COIN versus Geopolitics

The Vienna OeMZ/Europress strategy conference upon which this chapter is based unfolded in June of 2016, more or less a decade and a half after the 11 September 2001 terror attacks on the United States. Without any attempt at being encyclopedic, the following generalizations are in order about the varieties of strategy in the intervening epoch. The jihadist bolt-from-the-blue event ended the strategic debate of the 1990s among several schools of variously strategic thought:

- The Weinberger-Powell Doctrine camp with its outstanding branch in U.S. CENTCOM HQ in the wake of the 1991 war termination exercise in Kuwait and Iraq and its inconclusive aftermath of an air denial zone.

- The technocentric revolution in military affairs, full-spectrum dominance school that arose from these events and was the dominant trope in the 1990s in the JCS, especially.

- Nuclear counterproliferation diplomacy and coercive force in the face of loose Russian nuclear weapons in the hands of terrorists.

- The minoritarian view of continuity through adherence to a wider Euro-Atlantic security zone with the reform of a united Europe/SFOR operation and the start of NATO enlargement in 1995.

- The very assertive and expansionist, in terms of doctrine, counterterror school, hinged upon the new U.S. SOCOM.

The latter presently emerged as dominant, but not immediately after 11 September. All of these schools, as it were, and their institutional interests in DoD had been in conflict with each other for about a decade amid a shrinking force structure, the putative lessons of Vietnam so as to limit most military operations to a political minimum or all out dialectic, as well as the lessons of the Kuwait campaign in 1990–1991, in an epoch of over hopeful dreams of an enduringly peaceful world amid the end of the Cold War.

The opening special operations campaign in Afghanistan in late 2001 aside, the main strategic answer to the terror assault in Washington and London was wrongly to assume that the center of gravity lay in Iraq and its phantom nuclear weapons that were or were not to fill the proverbial suitcase bombs of next dark invader. In response, by the spring of 2003 there unfolded a CENTCOM operational coup de main against Iraq in a neo Jominian school in order to make up for the failed final phase of the 1991 Kuwait campaign and the missing decisive battle on Iraqi soil that had also been reified in think tank and talk show balderdash about the stab in the back in Kuwait.

The offensive put in hand by SECDEF Donald Rumsfeld in 2002–2003 had at least two main goals: to prove that the radical reorganization of the armed forces on a flexible and mobile model would prove strategically effective, i.e. as an example of military transformation campaign on the Tigris and Euphrates to finish what was undone in March 1991; and, on a level of grand strategy, to refute, once and for all, the Weinberger-Powell Doctrine with its six Jomini-like conditions on the use of military force. Despite the initial success of American and coalition arms in the spring of 2003, the American offensive in Iraq bogged down in 2004–2005 into stalemate. The irregular resistance if ruptured Iraqi state revived in a manner that could little surprise anyone familiar with the record of war in the Middle East in the 20th century.

This moment of stalemate and possible defeat offered the new brooms of counter terror with a single geopolitical focus on the Middle East to take the scene. The Rumsfeld codicil of the revolution in military affairs after 2000 had already paved the way for this triumph of special operations and the primacy of irregular war and counter insurgency via the theoretical and symbolic prerogatives of interpretation to have rendered much of the experience of strategy, strategic thought, and military institutions null and void.

In the decade and more since these unhappy events in 2001–2005, the fashion, fad, or dogma of an existential threat from jihadist terrorism to national survival—the aspiration of the murder gangs of ISIS in their Syrian and Iraqi badlands to wipe out world civilization—masks what is really at work, which is a profound geopolitical shift in which rising and or revisionist powers equipped with expansive goals seek a new world order in the 21st century. Part of the reason they can do so, one can suggest, has been from an overemphasis especially in the United States but in NATO generally on COIN. This ballyhoo of ink spots and winning of hearts and minds with classical French and British antecedents of dubious actual merit in democratic civil-military relations that has accompanied the problematic revival of imperial warfare. This process has unfolded despite there being rich evidence sine 2001 that we live in what is manifestly a post-imperial age, and imperial soldiers do not appear to have some new momentum that eluded an earlier generation of imperial soldier in the years between, say, 1899 and about 1960.

The advocates of COIN, rallied by General David Petraeus more or less from the year 2005 when American fortunes in Iraq reached a low ebb, continued the expansive proposition of a military revolution begun in the 1990s. But this revolution was also transformed with new personalities and new weapons in a new counter insurgency battlefield, but with no less cheek as to how all previous military experience and practice, save that of the British and French colonial warfare in the 19th and 20th centuries, had been overturned by Osama bin Laden and his bearded, poem chanting likes of mass murderer. Especially obsolete had become the truths of war in and around Europe in its variety, which was consigned to a particularly dark category of ridicule as being hopelessly out of date, irrelevant, a free rider, Venus-like and decadent.

This rebranding, as it were, was most famously visible in the Icarus-like progress of LTC Dr. John Nagel, the lead author of the so-called *Joint Manual on Counter Insurgency* (2005). The document was, in reality, a less-than-deft recycling of older writings and doctrine from the bush fire, that is, wars of imperial retreat in the 1950s, which had quickly fallen into obscurity in the early 1970s, save for the impassioned guardianship in theory and chronicle of a select few irregular warfare theorists. Nagel and his acolytes emerged as chief advocates of what soon became a grand strategy that, by about the year 2006, promised a way out of the stalemate that ensued from the botched post-campaign phases in both Iraq and Afghanistan. This primacy of COIN and focus on two limited geographical theaters without a unifying and effective strategy on a sound civil-military basis endured only so long as the riposte of the occupied populations remained in abeyance.

The strategic shibboleths put in hand by general staffs and think tanks in the period from about 2004 until 2012 had the self serving attempt to rescue something of strategic merit from the dead end Iraqi and Afghan campaigns. The security-building operations there suffered from crossed purposes of ends and means and the failure to recognize the essential futility of decades long occupations in the face of intractable and energetic national resistance made worse by a parsimony of forces and an uncertainty in the chancelleries and cabinets of the democracies about the long haul. The rise of COIN as a grand strategy was to rescue the prerogatives of bellicose think tanks filled with former lieutenant colonels or to enhance the bureaucratic fortunes of military doctrine assembly lines stuffed to overflowing with rank bloated experts in tactical training.

Freshly returned to the doctrine mills from a stint of insurgent bashing on the Tigris and Eurphrates or the Hindu-Kush, the thousands of benighted persons with red facings and Velcro unit patches strained to understand the character of primordial, anger, hatred, and violence, and resorted to Rudyard Kipling like bromides in the face of insurgent populations who loathed western soldiers in their countries, whether engaged in nation building and or free fire operations.

The great-power system, that is the brace of the leading na-tion states with strategic and global ambitions—all Wolfwitzian Krauthammer-ite unipolar moments, New Pentagon Maps, and Brazil, Russian, India, China, and South Africa (BRICS) and so forth not withstanding—had hardly ceased to exist because of the 11 September terror assault. To think otherwise was a form of insani-ty that has become endemic in the making of national strategy since 2001 and has taken on ever more bizarre forms.

The U.S. over-emphasis upon the Middle East in the decade and more from 2001 until 2013 or so had the inevitable strategic re-sult of imperial overextension made famous by Paul Kennedy in his book of 1987 and then promptly forgotten by most thinkers around the year 1992. Such an evolution was fairly plain to anyone who thought about the wider implications of the flames, smoke, corpses, and rubble that filled the world's imagination in the days after 11 September 2001 and became a standard feature of public life in the decade and a half since.

Since the United States became a world power at the begin-ning of the 20th century, its makers of strategy have perpetually faced the geopolitical dilemma of how to exclude the great powers from its continental sphere of influence in the western hemisphere and, then, to reach well beyond the limits of the Monroe Doctrine and Manifest Destiny, i.e. into Asia and Europe. This process has meant the need to wield American power on multiple fronts is a permanent strategic condition, to which the United States for a significant period devoted the bulk of its effort to peace and security in Europe and Asia from 1945 until the 1970s, and then, gradually assigned growing im-portance to an obsession with the Middle East. The various pivots—the start of the colored war plans in the epoch after 1900, or the Eu-rope first strategy in Plan Dog of the year 1940, or the Marshall Plan in 1947, or Henry Kissinger's Year of Europe in 1973, or the NATO enlargement study in 1995 or the Barack Obama-led "pivot" to Asia in 2011 all mark the record of war and peace from the 1930s onward and testify to this necessity to choose main effort for a geopolitical theater while contending with the neglect of other geographical theaters, a truth that was obscured in the carnage of the years 2001–2003.

With an obeisance to Karl Haushofer and Halford MacKinder, unmentioned then, in contrast to the tendentious vogue for T.E. Lawrence, Dame Gertrude Bell and other British imperialists a century earlier, the terror assaults constituted a grand strategic trap more or less on the model that undid the USSR in Afghanistan in the 1980s, into which the United States was tempted to fall and forfeit its geopolitical preeminence attained by a restrained statecraft in the epoch from 1975 until 1989. This process of falling into a trap and the weakening of the U.S. position in Eurasia took some time to eventuate, but by the second decade of the new century, the revival of geopolitics was complete with the Russian offensive in Georgia in 2008, the ever more assertive Chinese fortification of its maritime littoral, and the advent of the Arctic as a scene of great power competition, to mention several events that constitute an overall strategic trend.

One could also mention here the deliberate stripping of U.S. forces from Europe amid much burden-sharing recrimination as well as declaring NATO in its death throes by certain leading U.S. security figures, all of which must have enlivened the dreams and hopes of the enemies of the western order wherever they were to be found. The collapse of the U.S. defense budget in the year 2013 signified the climax of this development, despite the attempts by the Obama administration to withdraw from both Iraq and Afghanistan and to redirect much of the effort of U.S. security and defense to Asia in the year 2011.

Strategy, the Cult Personality, and the Force of Imponderables

The making of strategy is surely highly linked with the aspects of character and intellect of the military commander, to say nothing of the factors of collective psychology and morale in combatant populations. These insights are as present in the writings of Jomini as they are in Clausewitz, though the American school of strategy assigns high importance to the notoriety of general officers. In the last

15 years, however, this version of character and intellect amid the forces of friction and genius in real war had seen the personage of high ranking soldierly personality has collided with trends in society more generally that cut against the grain of how senior officers wish society to regard them in the glory of combat. The truth of these generalizations has been a constant issue since 11 September and the advent of the global war on terror, in which a small army has borne an outsize burden of the Iraqi and Afghan campaigns, without the general national mobilization that in other times and other places has been the American response in the episodes of total war or in the well known chapters in the story of the American way of war.

Citizenship in its traditional and historical aspect has played a minimal role in U.S. government and society since 2001, being replaced, in a sense, with the idea proffered by right-wing ideologues and militarists in U.S. state and society of so called "savior generals" more or less on the model of Boulanger or Vincent Matoon Scott. That is, the soldiers in the military deserve respect and support of the U.S. population in its entirety, but not so much so that one is obliged to sign up and to become a soldier as in the former times. This generalization notwithstanding, since 11 September a significant fraction of Americans who remain alive to the requirements of citizenship have indeed joined the military, a fact that the authors here salute and celebrate. But this phenomenon in no way detracts from the cult of celebrity among general officers in the present and recent past, and the effect of same on generalship in a global sense.

Rather one can suggest that since 11 September, citizens, as taxpayers and consumers and also as a claque, are obliged to venerate general officers in the sense that Henri de Jomini and all accolytes of the Napoleonic school have venerated flag officers in the midst of the rise of mass politics: as heroes and saviors of the state in wartime. While it is entirely true that such putative "savior generals," i.e. George Washington, or Andrew Jackson, or Ulysses S. Grant, or even Dwight Eisenhower, have played a significant role in the fortunes of war and peace as well as in American government and society, the character of savior general in the 21st century fixed for a period of time on the personality of General David Petraeus, who succeeded General Tommy Franks. The latter had submerged into the murk and chaos of the Iraqi stalemate, in which the failures of strategy and operations in the years 2003–2005 eventually led to the final discomfiture of the U.S. Secretary of Defense in the fall of 2006 and the so-called revolt of the generals in that election campaign.

In the period of the "surge" ca. 2006—in which the United States reinforced its Iraqi occupation forces and suppressed the variegated Iraqi insurgency much local aid and exterior aspects in the fortunes of war, which were then appropriated by the guidance of Petraeus and his lieutenants—this savior general rose to prominence then left the armed forces and became director of the CIA. This career augured even greater glory and fame with the ambitions to further national service at the peak of power, when, in the fall of 2012 an odd and tawdry pile of e-mail spilled into the limelight, depicting the jealous rants among two attractive women associated with the Headquarters, U.S. Central Command in Florida.

At first glance, this episode appeared to an incredulous American public—concerned with the deescalation of the Global War on Terror put in hand by Obama—to be a poor imitation of a "reality" television setup. Then the fall of David Petraeus in 2012 because of gross security violations done in order to promote the fortunes of his beauty queen/athlete soldier/mistress/biographer became shockingly real.

This event signified the onset of what is the usual repulsion in the body politic with wars in American society, even the successful ones. Petraeus and his girlfriend suggested a successful war to the general's think tank and congressional followers, but the American people still adhere to the examples of war in which total victory comes after great national exertion and sacrifice, all claptrap about the altered nature of war in the 21st century notwithstanding. While the story had many laughable elements of farce, the episode meant a profound tragedy especially for the women involved. Paula Broadwell signified the progress of women at arms and in the strategic community versus the earlier biographies of those kept women of the savior generals of the epoch 1941–1951. These mistresses of MacArthur or Eisenhower or Clark had not graduated from West Point nor were capable of singular light athletic feats like Petraeus himself, with his track and field prowess being publically equated to his gifts as a strategist. This savior general was permitted to share highly classified information with an outsider, whereas the average civil servant who mishandles the government's proliferating secrets is threatened each hour with punishment and imprisonment of a kind that would make Colonel Dreyfus or Julius and Ethel Rosenberg blush with shame.

Throughout a picture-book career from the late 1960s onward that, in its sum, sought to duplicate the spirit, if not the deeds, of Douglas MacArthur—but surely not that of Omar Bradley—Petraeus had cultivated a media claque much as imperial soldiers have done since the rise of the mass press and colonial combat in Africa and Asia in the 19th century. In his own advanced study, Petraeus had twisted the record of war and policy with a misinterpretation of the levels of war and policy in the epoch of limited war in the nuclear age. He wrongly reprised in his doctoral dissertation the standard interpretation of MacArthur's no substitute for victory bromides crafted for the right wing in the 1950s and then transformed and inflated COIN into a grand strategy that obscured the fact that the strategic operational ideas that had taken hold since the early 1990s had run into a dead end in Iraq and elsewhere by about 2004.

As part of the corps of civilian adventurer experts, knock-off Rudyard Kipling journalists and Booz Allen Hamilton camp followers that are inveterate in contemporary war as waged by enormous U.S. combatant commands, Broadwell had become a fixture in Petraeus' Afghan headquarters, and, at some point, the general's paramour, whereupon she wrote a treacle laden hagiography of the general. The book lacked analytic punch, but made up for this fact with soppy fawning of a kind that was even embarrassing amid a shelf of similar books produced in recent times by those interested in military affairs and soldierly biography, but without any keen understanding of the fundamentals of soldiering or the truths of combat other than as seen from afar by a voyeuristic public.

Petraeus vanished in a thunderclap of scandal with a swiftness that belied the impact of his fall for the overall question of the efficacy of strategy and the officer corps in wartime at a critical juncture. This event signified the onset of what is the usual repulsion in the body politic with wars in American society, even the successful ones, a process which has accelerated with the geopolitical shifts in Europe and Asia since 2013 as well as the ever more poisoned domestic political explosion in the western democracies evident also in the epoch 2012–2016. Too facile is the assertion that Petraeus was purged by Barack Obama out of the civil-military discord focused on the White House and the ill informed caste of civilian advisors in Obama's inner circle at odds with savior generals. Such an explanation is far too simple, and fails to grasp the impact of this Icarus-like episode for the self-image of the officer as a maker of strategy.

How the politics of American sexual abstinence and feigned public outrage at sexual escapades among the rich and powerful has intersected with the character and intellect of the makers of strategy forms a theme poorly interpreted by most observers. The much noted return of isolationism and critique of perpetual war lodged in the 2016 election campaign of Donald Trump arises in part from the disillusionment with character and intellect in war, and the criticism by the candidate of flag officers, who, in the minds of neoconservatives and neoimperialists have been saviors.

The backlash against the senior military leadership amid the global war on terror might be said to have started with the cult of celebrity at arms crashing into the verities of reality television and the mainlining of pornography as a feature of American popular culture. The fate of women bulks large in the growing cultural and political extremism at the core of the conflict over values, society and politics in the contemporary world, to be sure. The truth in the case of Petraeus, however, derives fundamentally from the blindness that befalls those stricken with too much public notoriety and fawning by think tank war mongers and the omissions by those in Congress who fail in their constitutional role toward the man and woman at arms. Petraeus and his kind dragged the making of strategy too far toward the one pole of a certain kind of war, which plainly is no longer the dominant form of conflict in the year 2016.

That is, the fall of Petraeus amid kiss drenched and email hacked ardor splashed across the blogosphere bespeaks how unserious many in the United States are about the requirements of strategy, about the character of strategists, and about the hidden truths of geopolitics in their most brutal reality in the present. The fall of Petraeus in a reality housewives spasm of passion belies how one kind of war and strategy specific to one place and to one very limited time, and did so with a customary boosterism and spin mongering of a kind that does the truth and the lives of soldiers in a possible future conflict little honor.

This fact is only reinforced in the year 2015 and 2016, when, in view of the deficits of strategy and operations in, say, NATO Europe or U.S. air and land forces in Europe in the face of the Russian threat, lack of anti aircraft artillery in the face of what might be possible Russian air superiority as well as the general inexperience with combat operations at echelons above brigade poses new and shocking challenges to field and company commanders.

9. The Democratic Civil-Military Relations of Austerity*

How do defense institutions adjust to reductions in budgets amid an epoch of upheaval? This process of demobilization and retrenchment takes place amid the intensification of partisan politics in the western democracies made more toxic by an economic crisis all too similar to the 1930s. For young U.S. officers this situation burst forth without precedent. It is a shock for them unlike any in the decade prior of hard service. This chapter regards such shock as a point of departure for deeper reflections about the theme of austerity and military professionalism in the past and present.

There are many examples in the past for this syndrome of shrinking treasure and proliferating military roles and missions amid political upheaval that have receded into forgetfulness in contemporary debate about security and defense policy. The following, firstly, interprets these cases in overview; secondly, the pages below generalize about what unifies these episodes in their political, institutional and professional character, and, thirdly, joins this analysis to some thoughts about the present and future of the mutual aid and self-help of smart defense in the further evolution of NATO and the armed forces of the western democracies in general.

An exploration of these cases of strategy, politics and defense budgets—offered without the customary polemics and gored oxen of political fights about budgets—provides a point of departure for any reflection about best practices and the most efficacious means to surmount such issues today and tomorrow. This interpretation draws some tentative conclusions as to the character and essence of this issue in its context of democratic civil-military relations and to do so in a way that might diverge from the norm of customary defense management and strategic studies.

---

* The original version of this presentation was made at Garmisch-Partenkirchen, Germany, in June 2012 to a group of senior defense and military figures.

The following work introduces ideas of how to address austerity in defense in its essence, with an analysis that aspires to be empty of overheated rhetoric, polemics, and propaganda that always surround the issue of the making of strategy and the evolution of defense and military institutions in times of scarcity.

Precendents

The civil-military record of the maritime democracies (the United Kingdom and the United States), whose strategic and political culture are intertwined in the foundation and character of NATO, suggests that the fight over money in peacetime and economic trial generally takes place as a fight over strategy. That is, while the core issue remains the share of national treasure in the underfunded and abused army or navy budget, this debate masquerades as strategic idealism of one form of strategy as superior to another—Hew Strachan's point in his seminal *Politics of the British Army*.[1] These fights loom central to democratic civil-military relations; they are ingrained in the collective memory of soldiers and defense organizations; they have a glorious past almost like decisive battles, and the past surely suggests that such a fight is at hand amid the strategic character of the present.

In the first instance, these altercations arise from mixture of Anglo-Saxon constitutions and geography within strategic culture. Here the interplay of checks and balances of the power of the purse in parliament with the supreme command of maritime powers (with land forces) erupt in crisis during epochs of budgetary scarcity. Such eruptions are called by partisans a failure of preparedness and a woeful neglect of national defense. The guilty in such legends and myths are usually makers of policy and sometimes colonel blimps in general staffs. This process deeply shapes the military profession and the collective memory that underlines military policy and doctrine.

---

[1] Hew Strachan, *The Politics of the British Army* (Oxford: Oxford Univeristy Press, 1997) pp. 119–162.

This historical memory of austerity and the martyrdom of the military profession is often generalized in the U.S. forces as the legend of "Task Force Smith," an outnumbered augmented battalion of the U.S. Army in June 1950 that was overwhelmed by the North Koreans in the first days of the Korean War.[2] The sacrifice of this troop unit became the symbol of American negligence to arm properly in the Cold War and, in reality, is a canard about the defense budget under Harry Truman. Such rhetoric and myth-making of lack of preparedness has been especially evident since 11 September 2001, but is much, much older. Such legend-making as a tool in the mass persuasion about budgets in a democracy is a natural part of the soldier and austerity.

The 19th Century

This phenomenon of soldiers betrayed by politicians obsessed with thrift extends backward from 1950 well into the 19th century in both the U.S. and British forces. In the wake of the U.S. Civil War, the "dark ages" of the U.S. Army, when it returned to its constabulary—that is, frontier police—role in the Indian wars (1865–1890), the world economic boom that followed the railroads and industrialization collapsed into a depression that began in Vienna in 1873 and lasted more or less for two decades. The president and the Congress embraced the pacifism of the business community and stripped the army of its order of battle. Those who had enjoyed flag rank in the war were reduced to their permanent company grade ranks with little prospect of promotion. For much of the year 1877, the U.S. Army received no pay at all, and its handful of officers in frontier garrisons

---

[2] Roy Flint, "Task Force Smith and the 24th Division: Delay and Withdrawal, 5-19 July 1950," in Charles E. Heller and William A. Strofft, eds. *America's First Battles, 1776-1965* (Lawrence, KS: University Press of Kansas, 1986) pp. 266-299; on the Truman administration, defense policy, and war, see Michael J. Hogan, *A Cross of Iron: Harry S. Truman and Origins of the National Security State, 1945-1954* (Cambridge: Cambridge University Press, 1998); Melvyn P. Leffler, *A Preponderance of Power: National Security, the Truman Administration and the Cold* War (Stanford, CA; Stanford University Press, 1992).

was reduced to living on loans.[3] This humiliation infected the military writings of this generation of officers, who formed the vanguard of the modern American professional soldier and American military thought in the 20th century.

Outstanding was Emory Upton, whose brilliance as a soldier was matched by his energy as a scholar.[4] His experience of wartime command, juxtaposed to peacetime austerity and limited horizons on the closing U.S. frontier, imagined that the U.S. army should duplicate the general staff and order of battle of the recently victorious German army, despite the fact that the United States in the early 1880s faced no strategic situation similar to that of Germany. Upton's writings from his era imparted to his and following generations this resentment of starvation budget and thrift as civilian mismanagement of armies inherent in parliaments, which he saw as inferior to general staffs.

In the late 19th century, the problem of austerity and strategy emerged on a global scale for the British in the climatic epoch of imperialism, navalism, and militarism of the 1880s and the 1890s in the form of over extension amid rising challengers on the imperial stage. The Union Jack spread in Africa and Asia in the face of French and Russian competition without anything like the defense programing, planning and budgeting system of the 1960s and later decades with which we are well familiar. Nonetheless, these imperial forays received ample scrutiny from parliament and the public as to their excessive cost and usefulness as national interest. The result was that soldiers and sailors on distant service in turn felt betrayed at home.

Despite the relative wealth of Britain (which was under pressure from the German Reich and the United States), these fights about treasure and conquest were simultaneously struggles about

---

[3] Russell Weigley, *The History of the United States Army* (New York: Macmillan, 1967), p. 271.
[4] Rusell Weigley, *Towards an American Army: Military Thought from Washington to Marshall* (New York: Macmillan, 1962) pp. 100–126; Emory Upton, *The Military Policy of the United States* (Washington, DC: U.S. Government Printing Office, 1904).

maritime strategy versus land forces.[5] These struggles about the cost of empire unfolded amid the periods of financial chaos that took place from the 1870s until 1890s, and again in the first decade of the new century. The over-commitment to worldwide positions placed a further drain on budgets in the United Kingdom as the naval build-up raced with its stratospheric costs and fear of loss of naval supremacy before the world war.

The Interwar Years, Austerity and Strategy

Austerity in its more extreme form became the dominant experience of the post-1919 epoch in both the U.S. and the UK, where the ill effects of total war repulsed the electorates. Policy in both nations restricted the strength of armed forces amid the rapid technological change of strategy and operations. A generalized pacifism and faith in a liberal world order ushered in a new, even darker, dark age for soldiers and budgets than in the generation from 1870 until 1900.[6] This austerity led to fights about such budgets as strategy in the air and at sea. In the Royal Navy, for instance, the guideline for strategic planning in the 1920s was the infamous Ten Year Rule, in which, in addition to collective security the clauses of the Covenant of the League as well as the arms limitations of the Washington Naval Treaty, to say nothing of the various liberal pacts that had outlawed war altogether, construction of new ships was halted or curtailed amid a public disgust with war. This phenomenon of austerity and arms was made worse by the enduring problems in the international economy by weight of the peace (reparations) especially for the British. The collapse of the boom into depression in 1929 then poisoned relations among the victors as well as encouraged the defeated of 1918 to rearm.

---

[5] Strachan, *Politics of the British Army*, pp. 63ff; W.S. Hamer, *The British Army: Civil Military Relations, 1885–1905* (Oxford: Oxford University Press, 1970).

[6] Strachan, *Politics of the British Army*, pp. 144–162; Paul Kennedy, *Strategy and Diplomacy, 1870-1945: Eight Studies* (London/Boston: HarperCollins, 1983) pp. 87–108.

This new dark age of austerity and military professionalism and the making of strategy in the United States were especially bleak in the U.S. Army and its air corps in the 1920s. This fight about the budget was an existential fight about the efficacy of aviation as the decisive form of strategy, and mechanization generally. In the case of armor in the U.S. Army in the 1920s and 1930s, where parochialism and strategic blindness led into a dead end of motorization and operational forces much in contrast to the Germans and the Soviets. The penury of the budget on the national level in the Republican era of the 1920s was matched by the blinkered conservatism of senior military leaders who did a great deal to extinguish necessary adaptation of air and mechanized forces to the altered face of war.

Noteworthy in this instance is Billy Mitchell as the martyr of air power, a military personality whose skillful use of mass persuasion to politicize soldiers in league with the press and public opinion.[7] Austerity and sparse budgets led to the creation of military personalities in political culture in the era of total war who acted as propagandists for their particular strategic ideal within democratic civil-military relations. Not without merit is the case of the first German Republic, where austerity linked with the deliberate national evasion of the Versailles Treaty caused both a radicalization of younger soldiers, as well as a noteworthy institutional impetus to doctrinal innovation in the shadow of defeat. One might generalize from the interwar experience that such austerity can well be the parent of military innovation, but such an insight stands subordinate the truth that austerity politicizes further soldiers and enflames strategic fights in state and society.

The Cold War and Post-Cold War: Continuities

Such was the case in the wake of the Second World War. The problems of austerity and strategy of the interwar period reemerged

---

[7] William Mitchell, *Winged Defense: The Development and Possibilities of Modern Air Power—Economic and Military* (New York: Putnam, 1925); Michael Sherry, *The Rise of American Air Power: The Creation of Armageddon* (New Haven, CT: Yale University Press, 1987) pp. 22–46.

in the United States and the United Kingdomin a new and more intense form in the pivotal years after 1945. One makes an error to overlook this process whereby the Cold War became a feature in the military posture of the Western democracies in the era 1946–1950 (in which NATO also was born), in which the leading allies stood burdened with the debt of the recent war as well as the imperative to rebuild under the Marshall Plan in 1947. A ceiling on U.S. defense spending prior to June 1950, as well as the need by the British to wrap up their empire while bearing the encumbrances of the Cold War meant a new era of austerity reigned, even as the atomic age propelled further change in the character and size of armed forces. Nuclear weapons appeared to strategists and treasurers as the cheaper, more efficient mode of weapon, but austerity meant no consensus about the posture of forces to use them. The demobilization austerities of the Truman presidency witnessed the creation of the Defense Department and the unification of the armed services as a lesson of Pearl Harbor, which was, in fact, scarcely a unification at all. The reform joined with the unfolding of the atomic era unleashed a bitter fight among the brass and their civilian partisans over the atomic role and general-purpose forces within an austere budget in the years 1947 through 1950. This epoch is essentially forgotten or unknown today, but its legacy endures as it was repeated in turn later in the 1950s, in the 1970s, and again in the 1990s.

The political fight in the creation of the Defense Department in 1947 as a rationalization, efficiency, and revolution in management caused an open breach between the Department of the Navy and the Truman administration in 1949 in a fight over the B-36 bomber and the cancellation of the heavy aircraft carrier. At the same time, the Washington Treaty as the basis of the Atlantic alliance emerged not the least out of the need to pool and share armed forces under the heading of mutual aid and self help for collective defense. The authors of the treaty were led by the insight that no single nation alone could defend itself without such mutual aid in order to avoid national bankruptcy in the age of nuclear war. The creation of the Organization in NATO under Articles, III, IV, V, and IX of the treaty in the years 1949–1954 was guided by the principle of thrift and the equitable sharing of the burden under Article III, in which strictures of economy and savings reigned uppermost even in the attempt to create a NATO battle line for forward collective defense. The Korean War in June 1950 led to a temporary loosening of U.S. defense budgets, as well as the Lisbon force goals by NATO, made however moot by the end of the war in 1953 and the advent of tactical nuclear weapons as well as the thermonuclear bomb. These weapons appeared to render most cost and benefit analyses of policy, war, and alliance orders of battle to be obsolete, adding energy to the ongoing fight about strategy and treasure.

Such a determinant of policy was powerful in the British armed forces of the latter half of the 1950s, especially after the Suez debacle in 1956. The retreat from imperial garrisons amid conflict, which early on, in the face of the weakness of the British economy, led the United Kingdom to cut back its forces and to emphasize nuclear striking power even before this idea became central to U.S. statecraft and defense budgets in the New Look of 1953–1954 in the Dwight Eisenhower presidency.[8] The New Look era of austerity, retrenchment, and massive retaliation with thermonuclear weapons arose from Eisenhower's determination to avoid profligacy in the face of the unending Cold War. The new policy downgraded the army and gave rise to the same inter-service fights as a decade before. Such episodes as the bomber gap and, after Sputnik in 1957, the missile gap showed again with new ferocity that budget fights manifest themselves as strategy conflicts in civil-military relations. The missile gap saw propagandists and mass persuaders in the U.S. Army, the Democratic Party, and the defense industry make Eisenhower's second term into a nightmare of budgets, strategy, topped off by a recession in 1958 and the crisis over Berlin.

---

[8] Glenn Snyder, "The New Look of 1953," in Warner Schilling et al., eds., *Strategy, Politics and Defense Budgets* (New York: Columbia University Press, 1962) pp. 379–524; Lawrence Freedman, *The Evolution of Nuclear Strategy*, 2d ed. (New York:Palgrave Macmillan, 1989) pp. 76–90.

The dictates of thrift and an enduring weak economy in Britain in the era from the 1950s until the 1970s meant in the 1960s that even further defense cuts were made one cabinet after the other.[9] Noteworthy here was the east of Suez withdrawal begun under the Labour government in the late 1960s, in which garrison after garrison from Hong Kong to the Persian Gulf were rolled up in a process of more or less unilateral cuts that led to bitter disputes between the services in Britain. Beginning with the Duncan Sandys White Paper of 1957, in the wake of the Suez debacle the year prior, in which conscription was abandoned, and the size of conventional forces cut back, the years until the early 1970s saw the cancellation of strategic weapons (Bluestreak IRBM); the crisis with the United States over McNamara's cancellation of the Skybolt cruise missile that endangered the force of V bombers; the cancellation of a second generation tactical bomber (TSR-2), and the scrapping of existing blue water aircraft carriers and the refusal to build new ones. The decision in the late 1960s to focus more or less on the NATO role spelt the end of the British forces as a global force, with the culminating point of the Falklands War in 1982 to underscore the extraordinary shrinkage of British forces in the two decades prior.

While the U.S. forces waged war in Indo China in the era 1964–1975, this Asia-first strategy led to a neglect of U.S. commands committed to NATO, which had been downgraded and subjected to a preemptive austerity even in wartime that then became generalized on a world wide basis after 1975. The latter half of the 1970s witnessed the hollowing out of U.S. forces in the retrenchment after the U.S. debacle in Vietnam and the advent of stagflation connected with the two oil crises of the 1970s.[10] This problem particularly affected U.

[9] John Baylis, *British Defense Policy: Striking the Right Balance* (New York: Palgrave Macmillan, 1989); Eric Grove, *Vanguard to Trident: British Naval Policy since World War Two* (Annapolis, MD: Naval Institute Press, 1987); Richard E. Neustadt, *Report to JFK: The Skybolt Crisis in* Perspective (Ithaca, NY: Cornell University Press, 1999).

[10] Andrew Bacevich, *The New American Militarism: How Americans Are Seduced by War* (Oxford: Oxford University Press, 2005) pp. 34–68; Beth Bailey, *America's Army: The Making of the All-Volunteer Force* (Cambridge, MA: Belknap Press, 2009).

S. conventional and naval forces at a time in which the face of combat changed in the 1973 Middle Eastern war, the order of battle of the Warsaw Pact grew rapidly and much of the vessels of the U.S. Navy built in the Second World War came to the end of their operational lives. Also in this era of austerity of the latter half of the 1970s, NATO undertook fitfully to increase defense spending (3-percent goal), as well as to rearm with new nuclear weapons (Neutron Bomb, and Intermediate Nuclear Forces) that provoked something other than orderly consensus among the allies, as the Cold War reappeared after 1979.

The austerity of the 1970s reemerged in the era after 1989 as the peace dividend, the entirely normal political expectation that the end of the Cold War meant that defense budgets would return to a "peacetime level." This hope collided with the revival of war in the international system and the problems of reducing the U.S. forces despite enduring worldwide commitments. The decade of the 1990s, which began in a recession connected with the 1990–1991 Gulf War, was a time of relative austerity, and it, too, saw fights within the U.S. government and defense department over the shape of budget, strategy, and alliance statecraft in the years leading up to 11 September 2001, the end of this chronicle. The economic straits of the late 1970s and the early 1990s made the fights over budgets-as-strategy more intense, and more tangled again in the rhetoric of strategic idealism. Seen from today's nadir of treasure and policy, the problems of money and strategy of these now distant epochs frankly pale in comparison to the present economic situation with its similarities to the 1930s.

Legacy of Austerity as a Source of Strategic Discord

As a preliminary conclusion, the legacies, traditions, legends, and myths of austerity as a weapon in democratic civil-military relations require those who will grapple with this phenomenon to consider the following:

First, austerity has been a constant feature of the lives of cabinets, treasuries, and general staffs—especially in the leading NATO nations—for a very long time in their democratic civil-military relations. It is hardly the exception, but more the norm. Such austerity often stands at the foundation of military doctrine, which, in turn, forms a vital part of the making of strategy often in a negative sense. The altercation that surrounds us in the years to come of scarcity and the formulation of strategy has this rich tradition. But this tradition is a conflicted one, to be sure, for what the parliamentarian and the treasurer see as economy, the soldier sees as austerity and a breach of civil-military faith in the preference for butter over guns.

Second, the maker of policy must be able to extract myth and legend from conflicts over strategy that are, in fact, fights over budget. The latter are natural, normal, and necessary features of form of government in the elite-mass relations in war and peace. Fights over strategy in epochs of austerity are linked to domestic politics, to the tradition of the state, and to the mechanisms of mass persuasion in formation of strategy. They are further linked to the ideals of military professionalism and citizenship as we have seen these since the late 19th century. The biographies of such figures as Duncan Sandys, Robert McNamara, or Donald Rumsfeld embody a warning as to the imperative to de-mystify myth and legend of arms and austerity. The factors of military honor, *esprit de corps*, timeless principles of war as well as partisan politics signify normal features of these fights. There exists no technocratic, technological, or otherwise magical management process to extract, that is, politically neutralize or depoliticize—in the sense of Carl Schmitt—a single piece of the triad of strategy, politics, and defense budgets. This issue cannot easily be made neutral through some management science artifice or rationalization of defense structure borrowed from multi national corporations or the most recent fad in schools of business. For instance, the mixed fortune of the revolution in military affairs of the Donald Rumsfeld epoch suggests the truth of this generalization. The case of Eisenhower's New Look in its time is but another, earlier example of this dilemma.

Third, as a result, those charged in defense ministries, general staffs and elsewhere with leadership in this question are enjoined to understand this dynamic of money and politics in its essence and character within the history, tradition, and character of military and civilian institutions. One must be master, and not its slave. Such an injunction especially applies in the maelstrom of mass persuasion that usually attends these strategy/budget fights. The practices and habits of healthy democratic civil-military relations, as NATO allies have long advocated in these more than two decades, represent a fundamental for the successful formulation of policy and strategy in the face of diminished treasure.

Conclusion: Smart Defense, Austerity, the Need for Statecraft, Policy, and Strategy

This chapter has tried to identify the best practices in the making of policy and strategy and their realization in the face of severe economic and political weakness. Its main goal has been to underscore realism in the making of strategy, without a retreat into fantasy, illusion and buzzwords. The latter has become a more or less constant feature of the making of strategy of the last 20 years, as if an army or a military campaign, in reality, is nothing more than a revamped product from a multinational corporation or an application for a smartphone. The central point has been the making of strategy in an era of austerity has its own metaphysics, its own culture, and its own magic. The comments and insights are guided by Clausewitz as to how we might think about this problem in its historical-political dimension, that is, in its most fundamental and efficacious way.

Smart Defense as outlined by the NATO Secretary General at the Chicago Summit in 2012 plainly indicates the way ahead in the face of diminished treasure and the need to employ mutual aid and self-help for the ends of the Alliance. The willy nilly renationalization of defense without consideration given to the impact on the whole is a familiar problem in NATO, and has existed in one form or the other since 1949. The obvious task ahead is to forestall a panicked and disjointed renationalization of defense at the same time that the international system of states lurches around in crisis of its fundamentals of state, economy, and society.

The pooling and sharing of security, defense, military forces, and weapons symbolizes a plainly urgent and eminently sensible policy. It is the only real way for the future. But this ideal cannot be sold to a skeptical public as a neutralization or detoxification of domestic politics and strategy. NATO undertook to achieve these ends of mutual aid and self help for collective defense in its formative years, and has pushed intermittently in its more than 60 years of history. However, such a noteworthy and laudable initiative as Smart Defense will cleave more or less to the dynamics of strategy, politics, and defense budgets as outlined above (without making pretense of seeing the future as an oracle).

These policy imperatives of efficiency and economy in order to generate strength collided then as it does now with civil-military phenomena that will hardly vanish, and, if anything are intensifying in an alarming way. The sources of friction in the political and economic realm are obvious: the mixed fortunes of multi national and supra national institutions and cooperation in a time of crisis, the revival of nationalism, populism amid the fatigue of the European ideal, the putative U.S. shift of strategy to Asia (despite the bond to Europe as the basis of world power), potential for mischief in the process of demobilization of forces and combat veterans, the proliferation of threats, and security issues.

The size of armed forces will shrink under the reign of the new triad of Special Forces, drones and computer warfare, a subject I shall not explore. The capacity to mount customary military operations of various kinds will diminish in a way that is alarming and quite dangerous since the need for such operations will scarcely disappear even if fatigue with Iraq and Afghanistan is powerful today. The pace of strategic change in connection with new forms of strategy and weapons as they have emerged from the past decade and more of conflict might offer the prospect of more bang for the buck, but such forces and weapons will likely be inappropriate for a further crisis that will unfold six months or three years from now that will make nonsense out of strategic doctrine that looks forward by looking backward.

These dangers of disintegration in the face of austerity and the making of strategy should make the Western nations redouble their efforts to treat the matters at hand for the questions of war and peace, of life and death that they always have been and will remain. Another crisis will emerge presently, or is already here and has yet to become a defense and military problem. Such a crisis will challenge NATO as has happened with regularity in the past. As a point of departure, an understanding of the essential elements and dynamics of past episodes likely provides a better tool for policy than some management-school fad or manifestation of mass persuasion in the 21st century ignorant of the truths of governments and arms. The chronicle offered here teaches no lessons to the present and the future in the form of timeless verities, but should equip the virtues of judgment, character and intellect in those who bear the burden of responsibility in war and peace and must do so with less treasure and fewer forces than has been done in the recent past.

10. The Cycles of Navy Strategy*

The long era of expanding U.S. defense budgets from 2002 until 2010 unfolded with much debate over the best ways to employ Naval forces in the Global War on Terror and in the effort to create stability in Iraq. As the United States emerged from the decade-long campaign to eliminate Osama bin Laden and to crush al-Qaeda, however, Navy leaders discovered that the international and domestic political landscape had changed. Demobilization and austerity, highlighted by sequestration of the Department of Defense budget, now loomed large in American domestic politics. On the international scene, new events—the endurance of international terrorism, the 2011 "pivot to Asia," and the revival of war in Europe in 2014—and such new technological challenges as cyberwarfare, robotics, and a host of more exotic "disruptive technologies" posed a challenge to Naval concepts and operations. Navy leaders agreed that the time was ripe for a renewed emphasis on Naval Strategy. The result was the recent release of the long-awaited revision of the Navy's "Cooperative Strategy for 21st-Century Seapower," a timely and much-needed response to the challenges facing Naval commanders as they contemplate the changing strategic environment.

The creation of this new Naval Strategy was no small accomplishment. Today, Navy strategists find themselves in a rather difficult situation when it comes to devising and explaining the way naval forces contribute to national defense. During the last quarter century, the Office of Secretary of Defense transferred the making of maritime strategy from the OPNAV staff to the combatant commanders who became the center of gravity of U.S. strategy and operations. In the 25 years since the eclipse of the Reagan-Lehman Maritime Strategy, the Navy's strategists found themselves left to defend budget pri-

* Originally published as James Russell et al. eds. *Navy Strategy Development: Strategy in the 21st Century*---Naval Research Program Project #FY14-N3/N5-0001, pp. 24–35. Thanks to Dean James Wirtz of the School of International Studies of the US Naval Postgraduate School.

orities and construction programs. Nevertheless, if the combatant commanders are focused on current operations, OPNAV must not only identify emerging trends and threats, but also find ways to change the course of the Navy to meet the challenges and opportunities of the decades ahead. Naval strategy, as undertaken by the OPNAV staff, is all about the future, and the future Navy. Although Navy strategy must be seen to meet the demands of the day, it will only come to complete fruition when the future force envisioned by today's naval strategists meets some future test in combat.

Newcomers to the process of developing Navy strategy might not realize that Navy strategy runs in cycles characterized by stasis, crisis and reform. Indeed, during pivotal moments in the past, the development of naval and maritime strategy has erupted in inter-service and intra-service fights over the budget and preferred weapons, as well as preferred concepts of combined and joint strategy. These debates usually end when some international crisis tips the balance in one direction or another, as decisions are made to reorient the Navy to meet new operational challenges or international threats. Indeed, these cycles are more or less as old as the Navy itself. The question that comes to mind, however, is exactly where are we when it comes to this pattern of stasis, crisis, and reform?

Four Cycles

Although dividing the history of U.S. Navy strategy into periods is a somewhat arbitrary enterprise, four broad periods of stasis, crisis, and reform can be identified that highlight a pattern in the development of naval strategy and the institution's response to technological, operational or political change. The first cycle occurred between 1812 and 1880, a period that often appears as a dark age of following the growth of the Navy in the Civil War and the rise to prominence of Alfred Thayer Mahan and his works. The second cycle, from 1919 until 1941, begins with the ambiguous role of the new U.S. battle fleet in the First World War through the disarmament and naval limits of the interwar period and ends with the beginning of mobilization that transpired before Pearl Harbor.

The third cycle, from 1946 until about 1960, is characterized by inter-service fights over the role of nuclear weapons in national defense and the part the Navy would play in deterring nuclear war. The fourth cycle, which transpired between 1970 until 1980, illustrates the crisis in naval affairs that led to the Reagan-Lehman 600-ship Navy program that re-coupled the Navy to the general effort to respond to Soviet global ambitions.

The Dark Age, 1865–1880

The phenomenon of cyclic stagnation and rebirth in the formation of naval and maritime strategy is evident in a period that receives little attention from contemporary strategists. Between the War of 1812 and the beginning of the Civil War, the U.S. Navy reflected the constitutional fundamentals that called for the maintenance of a small navy to protect American interests against modest threats on the world stage, and an expansible army based on forts and a militia, all of which matched the demands of the Monroe Doctrine. In this remote era, there existed little capacity within the Navy for the making of strategy. Instead, issues related to the role and size of the U.S. Navy were resolved through discussions between the Secretary of the Navy and Congress. Given that there was neither the political will nor the economic and industrial means to match the navies of the leading European powers of the antebellum era, there was not much interest in doing more than funding a handful of naval vessels to show the U.S. flag along the world's trade routes. The changes that occurred, for instance, the launch of the Yangtze patrol in China in 1854, were not accompanied by a fundamental reassessment of naval strategy.

When war came in the spring of 1861, the United States improvised an emergency fleet suited to win protracted war of attrition on a scale unseen in U.S. history. This feat was made easier by the fact that the Confederacy lacked both a fleet and the industrial base to create a significant naval force. The Confederates cobbled together a fleet commerce raiding cruisers and posed a threat briefly to the commercial North East, complicating the Atlantic trade. The Confederate's strategy also entangled Britain and France in the naval war between the North and South, which raised the prospect of drawing the European great powers into the Civil War. This seemed to be a real possibility at the time as the guerre de course under the Stars and Bars burdened trans-Atlantic relations, especially when U.S. Navy ships fought Confederate vessels in European waters. The use of commerce raiding by the Confederacy made for good headlines, ruined the U.S. merchant fleet and scared the citizens of the Northeast as rumors of Confederate threats circulated among ports. But this effort had no enduring strategic effect. The Union response to this Confederate threat—a blockade strategy—was highly effective and served as the maritime counterpart to the scorched earth campaigns waged against the South by U.S. Grant and Forrest Sherman.

The exigencies of the Civil War transformed the U.S. Navy into a modern fighting force. While the Navy met its need for skilled personnel by pressing merchant sailors into service, newfound roles for steam and iron, and the growing striking power of artillery allowed the Union to catch up and to even briefly to surpass European navies at the height of the Civil War. Advances in technology and industry and the emerging need for individuals capable of manning and maintaining this new naval hardware heralded the impact of the industrial revolution on the U.S. Navy. The new technologies incorporated into warships created a need for shipyards and arsenals along with an industrial policy similar to the ones adopted by contemporary European naval powers. These irresistible forces created a demand for naval strategy, a demand that outpaced the capabilities of the Navy as an institution.

The Civil War effort could not be sustained in peacetime as national priorities returned to westward expansion, the imperatives of isolation, and doubts about the wisdom of sustaining a peacetime military establishment beyond the size or capability of pre-Civil War levels. By the 1880s, the U.S. Navy declined from its wartime strength into obsolescence, strategic misdirection, and civil-military turmoil.

The popular mood at the end of the Civil War was one of exhaustion and vanished appetite for martial glory. The nation had no overseas colonies that demanded defense. Americans did not want to be drawn into Europe's squabbles and feuds. Americans understood that they would never launch a war to conquer another nation so they had no appetite to construct a global Navy; after all, the European state system would prevent the rise of a universal power that could threaten the new world. All these arguments militated against a large navy, which had never existed in peacetime.

The Navy reverted to its peacetime habits. It mothballed or scrapped most of its ships. Focus returned to maintaining overseas squadron stations as the best way to protect U.S. trade and the national interests. Contemplation of strategy was largely confined to the prospect of commerce raiding against a possible European enemy. The rise of steam, however, made even this limited strategic option problematic because of the inherent high cost of forward deploying the steamships of the day. Indeed, discussions of naval strategy only seemed to exacerbate tensions between those who advanced the cause of machine navies and those who resisted this idea not only out of thrift, but because they abhorred the role of machines and the way new technologies demanded the "integration" of people from a variety of social classes into the Navy. Although American interests were gradually becoming more global in nature, debates about Naval strategy were inward looking, focusing on incorporating new technologies and changing personnel requirements.

American politics in aftermath of the civil war also saw the triumph of political and economic interests dead set against free trade, which included opposition to a navy large enough to augment and protect such trade. The struggle by Secretary of the Navy Gideon Welles to reorient the Navy on a sensible basis was suffocated in the political backlash against international engagement and trade that accompanied reconstruction. Many believe that no political or strategic need existed for a stronger, larger, and offensively oriented Navy because the world's oceans formed the best common defense. The life of the Navy was further burdened by claims of graft, corruption and special interests, made worse by the crisis of the U.S. Grant administration. Members of Congress spent their time investigating corruption in the Navy Department rather than providing the political consensus and means to advance anything resembling sea power, an idea that had yet to be born. All of this was topped off in the course of the 1870s by international economic depression. The Navy teetered on the brink of collapse.

The nadir of the 1870s was punctuated by the rise of American sea power, even before Alfred Thayer Mahan gave a name to it with his interpretation of war at sea written in the year 1890. The advent of the age of imperialism in the international system, which more or less coincided with the closing of the American frontier and with it the consolidation of continental expansion in the wake of the Civil War, made Americans think in great-power terms, in which navies figured as means of national power. The great powers increasingly used navies to subjugate areas of Africa and Asia as part of a general struggle for power on a global scale. The internecine squabbling in the U.S. Congress that had precluded reform in the world depression graduated to consensus about the need to repair the neglected Navy. Foreign incidents in which American citizens and commerce were at risk in Latin America and in the Pacific gave energy to those in Congress who had long sought naval reform.

Strategic Muddle, 1919–1941

The forces of decline and rebirth in U.S. naval strategy also reveal themselves in the interwar period. This period has been described by some observers as a golden age of technological innovation, others describe as time of great frustration for naval strategists. The fate of the battle fleet cannot be simply reduced to a story about the foresight and wisdom of Plan Orange that emerged between 1902 and 1941 or a story about how Franklin Delano Roosevelt willfully moved the fleet in 1940 from California to Hawaii without adequate preparation for combat. The story of strategy during this period is less about carefully executed war games, and more about the character of the international system in the first decades of the 20th century, domestic antiwar sentiment and parsimony, and the disjointed nature of Army and Navy strategy in the Pacific.

The record of these issues is more politically complicated and organizationally ambiguous than widely celebrated legend and enduring Mahanian dogma would have it. For most of this period, the Atlantic world and its international political economy held the attention of American diplomacy and policy, which with the onset of the world depression became isolationist and politically accepting of anti-war principles. Imperial Japan only emerged as a focus of diplomacy and statecraft in the late 1930s, when U.S. interest in an anti-Japanese strategy accorded with domestic and international reality. In the years between 1919 and 1935, Imperial Japan took a backseat in U.S. statecraft behind concerns about the fate of Britain or Germany. There was little domestic political agreement over an appropriate response to the growing Japanese threat in the Pacific during most of the interwar period.

U.S. naval strategy in the Pacific in the interwar period also suffered from a series of policy and strategy mismatches created by several developments in international and domestic politics. These impasses and dead ends included the Republican retreat from world power to normalcy in the 1920s, the U.S. Navy's unrealistic and unsustainable fantasies about overtaking the Royal Navy in the number of capital ships deployed following the extension of the 1916 shipbuilding program and the evaporation of international cooperation in the years after 1919.

All of this was made worse by a weak League of Nations that emerged in the wake of the war, especially following the U.S. Senate's decision to abandon the League. The Washington Naval Treaty of 1922 as well as the enduring problems of the international system (the lack of common cause by the victors and the emergence of national rivalries, especially between United States and Japan over the fate of China) created significant strategic problems for U.S. Navy. Naval strategists had a difficult time discerning whether to prepare for naval rivalry with Britain and its Japanese ally or to instead focus on Japan as the enemy. U.S. maritime strategy eventually identified Japan as a likely foe by the end of the 1920s. Nevertheless, this center of effort followed neither national policy, which was pacifist, abolitionist, and commercially oriented, nor a domestic political consensus, which was seized of normalcy and a horror of war. This strategic choice was not supported by a budget that would make this preferred naval strategy completely viable against a rising Japan.

Although the story of interwar naval strategy is often depicted as the fight over technology between battleship conservatives and aircraft revolutionaries, the anti-war stance of the Harding, Coolidge, and Hoover administrations, largely made these debates academic. The domestic politics of normalcy, austerity, and pacifism, which became more acute once FDR became president, made the Navy an afterthought in domestic politics. And isolationism became the order of the day in the face of chaos in Asia and Europe. FDR's decision at the end of the 1930s to undertake a massive build up the U.S. Navy in the face of Japanese aggression hardly ended inter service rivalry about a blue ocean Pacific strategy until months before Pearl Harbor when the Plan Dog and "Germany first" decision was made by the British and American governments. The lessons of Pearl Harbor also imposed a burden on the making of strategy at sea, which became manifest in the 24 months after the unconditional Japanese surrender on 2 September 1945.

Strategic Muddle, 1946–1960

The Second World War brought the U.S. Navy to the pinnacle of sea power and world prominence, but such good fortune could not endure; the pattern of demobilization swiftly reappeared amid postwar strategic confusion. With the victories in Europe and in Japan, national and Congressional focus returned to the lessons of Pearl Harbor as well as to the dictates of economy and peace, which, in turn, portended problems for the making of maritime strategy and the role of the Navy in the atomic age. The way World War II unfolded in the Atlantic and the Pacific had seemed to give validation to Mahan and his acolytes. But postwar strategy was up for grabs. Wartime inter-service bickering over combined and joint operations drove deep divisions between the Army and the Navy. Debate over an emerging need for an "air atomic strategy" revived the strategic and operational outlook of Giullo Douhet and Billy Mitchell. Dogmatic recitation of early–20th-century navalism, based on the assumption that the United States had to maintain a "second-to-none fleet," was greeted with skepticism by a postwar Congress. The search for an affordable peacetime military posture made the lessons of Pearl Harbor more onerous for the Navy in the Presidential and Congressional priorities of 1946.

The Bikini Atoll atomic bomb test explosions of 1946 seemed to validate the position of air power champions, who had prophesied the obsolescence of capital ships. The concentration of naval forces in a future war, as say in the English Channel at Normandy or at the Ulithi Atoll anchorage in the Western Pacific during World War II, would become unfeasible under atomic assault from the air.

To make matters worse, at the height of war as they cleared the world's oceans of all adversaries, Navy leaders apparently failed to consider the looming postwar future. The Navy's sister services were less circumspect. Army revolutionaries had begun to prepare to carry out Mitchell's idea of an independent Air Force and a single defense department, ending the bifurcation of the U.S. defense establishment between a Department of War and a Department of the Navy. This bifurcation was portrayed by Air Force advocates as a key contributor to the catastrophe at Pearl Harbor. With the aid of Walt Disney and the newsreels, the Air Force had also fashioned a "strategic communication campaign" vastly superior to the newsreels that highlighted the Navy's contribution in defeating Germany and Japan. In their view, the "new" Air Force would be the key to America's future defense, not the Navy.

The domestic political austerity and renewed inter-service rivalry that occurred during the battle over service unification brought new organizational miseries to the Navy, whose very existence was called into question by advocates of air power, by Congressional cost-cutters, and by those in the Army incensed over joint operational problems with the USMC in the Pacific campaigns. The nadir of maritime strategy and the role of the U.S. Navy in national defense arrived with the Congressional unification fight that occurred between 1946 and 1949, an episode that was portrayed by a new generation of young critics, fresh from the war, as righting of the wrongs of Pearl Harbor. They also made much of the "guilt of the Admirals," as it was called, who had ignored the role of aviation before the late 1930s and who had neglected the nation's defenses because of Mahanian dogma that no longer fit in the air atomic age.

The leadership of the Navy in 1946—especially leading figures in naval aviation—feared that the new Air Force would sweep up its aircraft and that the Army would absorb the Marine Corps. This fear led to greater partisanship and civil-military insurgency among senior naval aviators in the midst of the legislative reforms of service unification and the creation of the Department of Defense. This battle over the future of ships and planes blinded these men to the realities and requirements of strategy in the pivotal period between the end of the World War II and the Korean War.

Now almost forgotten in the 21st century, this epoch of dramatic change and institutional adjustment thrust Navy Secretary James Forrestal to prominence. As a kind of reincarnation of Mahan, Forrestal became the leading naval strategist of his time, supported in turn by such men as Forrest Sherman, who, together with Lauris Norstad, had been crucial in the creation of the Defense Department and a comprehensive approach to strategy, which quickly fell apart in the face of budgetary restrictions that worsened service parochialism. Forrestal had to fight to preserve the independence of the Navy while forcing its adjustment to the nuclear age.

In the opening encounters of the Cold War in southern Europe and the Persian Gulf of 1946, the Navy played a vital role by showing the flag at hot spots under Soviet pressure. Fateful for the formation of strategy, however, was the brutal demobilization and shrinkage of the fleet. Forrestal's anti-Soviet attitude and his sponsorship of George Kennan's containment strategy little compensated for the political primacy of the long-range bomber, the guided missile, and the atomic weapon. The shift from total war to peace and retrenchment amid service unification led to Forrestal's suicide in 1949, a grim prelude to the inter-service fight over the strategic bomber and decisions about which service would deliver the growing U.S. nuclear arsenal to targets in the Soviet Union.

Civil-military turmoil and technological upheaval led the advocates of capital ships and aircraft to attempt a *coup de main* against the idea of air power in the atomic age and its intercontinental long-range bombers. The aviator admirals sortied in 1949 with the super-carrier, the *USS America*, as the centerpiece of a civil-military revolt against the Harry S. Truman administration and its drive for service unification. This public-relations and legislative gambit against Curtis LeMay and the new Strategic Air Command formed the main focus of Navy strategy until the outbreak of the Korean War.

The decisive encounter in the battle over service unification became known as the Revolt of the Admirals, a berserk approach to the making of naval strategy. The Navy lost this initial legislative fight about strategy, ships, and weapons. Fortune quickly ameliorated this defeat, however, when the Korean War made possible the increase in air, land, and sea forces as set forth in March 1950 by NSC 68. The Korean War forced Truman to overlook the services' incapacity to formulate a coherent strategy and to launch a massive post-World War II military buildup.

The advent of the policy of "massive retaliation" in the years after 1953 gave the U.S. Navy an important opening to compete again for the much-prized nuclear delivery mission. The slow development of Intercontinental Ballistic Missiles helped Arleigh Burke revive naval strategy. His strategic realism as well as his bureaucratic acumen remain exemplary. The Korean War had shown the renewed importance of maritime operations at Inchon, naval strike aviation and sea control. The large aircraft carrier rose from the grave, the size of nuclear weapons shrank, and new jet aircraft emerged to carry such ordnance from the Navy's flight decks. The requirement to wage conventional war against the North Koreans and the Chinese banished the nightmare image of tiny U.S. capital ships under nuclear attack, and gave the Navy a new lease on life. Massive retaliation emerged as a way to deter the Soviets without massive investments in Army manpower.

Massive retaliation contained its own contradictions, which immediately became apparent in the later course of the 1950s in crises in Europe, the Middle East, and East Asia. Such conflicts seemed to call for the limited use of armed forces for the missions of forward defense and crisis management, which allowed Army and Navy strategists to propose alternate strategic concepts at the expense of the Air Force. The new proposals—Maxwell Taylor's flexible response and Arleigh Burke's limited deterrence—were also more in accord with domestic political realities and Soviet threats. These strategic ideas took hold as the United States began to introduce its first intercontinental ballistic missiles and as Hyman Rickover perfected nuclear propulsion in submarines and as centralized operational planning for the use of nuclear weapons in crisis and war—the Single Integrated Operational Plan (SIOP)—became a reality.

These steps enabled the Navy to break the Air Force's decade long nuclear monopoly of the nuclear delivery mission by giving the fleet a weapon that could compete with the strategic bomber: the George Washington class submarine. In the words of Burke, the new submarine would enable Americans to live as human beings—not as a nation submerged in bomb shelters. Burke fought off the attempt by the Air force to seize operational control of the Polaris submarine under the guise of a SIOP, although he was unable to prevent Air Force personnel from participating in the selection of the targets of submarine launched ballistic missiles. Burke's effort helped the Navy solidify its role as part of the "triad" of forces given the nuclear deterrence mission, an outcome that appeared highly in doubt at the outbreak of the Korean War. These ballistic missile submarines gave life to the idea of limited deterrence as an option for nuclear strategy and reinforced the role of the Navy in U.S. security policy at the start of the 1960s.

The Hollow Force, 1970–1980

The fourth epoch of decline and rebirth—marked by the so-called hollow force, of the post-Vietnam and pre-Reagan Navy—is perhaps most easily recognizable from the perspective of 2015. As America's involvement in Southeast Asia began to wind down, Navy leaders confronted a new political and strategic setting: the Cold War now witnessed a new Soviet global assertiveness; new problems emerged in the making of Service strategy following the Vietnam debacle; and the economic concerns loomed large in domestic politics. These issues helped to detach maritime strategy from national policy and strategy, while organizational disputes within the Navy slowed the adjustment to post-Vietnam strategic realities.

The sad story of the nearly derelict Navy that preceded the Reagan defense buildup and the Lehman era of reform comprised the funk of the post-Vietnam retrenchment, the stagflation wrought of the 1973 and 1979 oil crises amid war and revolution in the Middle East, too few ships, and a return to strategic aimlessness in the Navy's evolution. What limited national attention focused on defense concerned itself with the strategic nuclear balance, or "extending deterrence" to the forward defense of Western Europe? Navy leaders faced hard choices because of the rapid decline in the defense budget as U.S. involvement in Vietnam ended.

Soviet ships, meanwhile, grew in number and undertook a more aggressive operational posture each year. The hammer and sickle streamed above sleek new Soviet vessels in such places of the former Pax Britannica as Port Said, the coast of East Africa, and the Indian Ocean. Admiral Gorshkov's rising challenge to U.S. sea power began well before the 1970s, but the rise of Soviet might afloat became inescapable following Soviet naval movements during the October 1973 Middle East War. By contrast, the ships and planes of the U.S. fleet, which shrank in number due to the budgetary demands of the Vietnam War, grew ever more aged in the course of this unhappy decade. This decline was in fact exacerbated by the budget rigors of the middle- and late 1970s and stagflation. The cost of modern capital ships and aircraft soared at the very moment when the Soviets seemed ready to engage in a major naval arms race.

The long episode of stalemated fighting in Southeast Asia and associated frustrations within American society also reverberated on board with racial conflict and a collapse of command and obedience. The same problems of command and discipline that wracked the Army in the matter of race relations and good order generally hardly vanished once the war ended in 1973. The reforms enacted by Elmo Zumwalt in the 1970s remedied many of these problems, but the newest version of the interwar "gun club"—the attack carrier admirals in the school of Arthur Radford—loathed Zumwalt and decried most of the national strategic decisions that unfolded during the rest of the decade to the harm of a capital ship Navy with an offensive strategy.

This friction became highly public in the Pentagon and the halls of Congress in the late 1970s. As a result, the Navy's needs were discounted by those who wrote the budget in an epoch of austerity and stagnation. This internal discord about naval strategy contrasted to the more or less unified purpose found in the post-Vietnam U.S. Army, which embraced the all-volunteer force and modernization of the force to fight and win a Soviet onslaught in Central Europe. The Army benefited from the decision to modernize conventional forces in NATO amid the strategic assumption that the nuclear threshold had to be raised. The belief that any all-out war in the 1970s would be short and sharp, also worked against they Navy. Few believed that a confrontation along the Central Front would stalemate in a long war of attrition that would give the Navy an opportunity to alter the course of a land war through and extended campaign at sea. To many, the Navy would be relegated to convoy duty in a future war with the Soviets.

By the time this lost decade slid to its low points in 1979, which were punctuated by the Iranian hostage, the Desert One disaster, and the Soviet Invasion of Afghanistan, Navy leaders had made the grave error of viewing maritime strategy as nothing more than a chart of red and blue ship diagrams arrayed against one other on the seven seas. That is, strategy was nothing more than force structure and weapons, which, in this case, the authors of naval strategy assumed would be governed by the vagaries of civil-military relations.

The year 1979 witnessed an acute disassociation of means and ends and of the aims of the naval leadership from national policy. Preservation of the carrier construction program became the be all and end all of Navy strategy. The Navy was becoming disconnected from national policy by pushing what appeared to many to be unaffordable weapons, while turning a blind eye to the lack of interest in the body politic that in earlier times had taken a keen interest in sea power and supported the idea and the strategy in American democracy.

Conclusion

It would take a new president and a new secretary of the Navy to reintegrate naval strategy into national strategy. Nevertheless, as this brief survey demonstrates, the fortunes of the Navy, to say nothing of naval strategy, are cyclical. In a sense, changes in the diplomatic, political, economic, and even technological setting outpace the ability of the Navy to adjust to new strategic landscapes. The real irony is that just as the Navy often reaches some pinnacle of operational or technological supremacy, something changes in the external environment to render this supremacy superfluous. Naval officers are then forced to scramble to adjust to new strategic realities, leaving behind preferred strategies and force structures constructed at enormous human effort and great cost. When it comes to navies, planning cycles are indeed long; changes of course rarely occur before crises force a fundamental reassessment of organizational preferences.

There are successes in each of these cycles. These successes were created by visionaries who championed new technologies and operations at the expense of Navy organizational culture and preferences. The fact that the Navy already possessed the aircraft carrier, the successor to the capital ship of the day, before the battleship was rendered virtually obsolete is an observation that should give contemporary strategists pause. Contemporary strategists would also do well to consider that an inability to link force structure to emerging political, economic, and military developments was at the heart of all of the crises surveyed in this chapter.

Admittedly, changes in force structure followed each of these crises, but changes in strategic outlook were necessary officers could find away to link Navy strategy to national preferences and objectives. The trick for strategists today would be to anticipate our changing strategic landscape so that naval strategy, and a more slowly changing Navy force structure, can keep pace with emerging threats and national strategy.

11. Clausewitz: Primordial Violence, Hatred, and Enmity[*]

We find ourselves in a political sphere ever more marked by the reality of political violence for extremist ends—in addition to the jihadist next door, western democracies face the revival of integral, *völkisch* nationalism, as well as enraged middle-class and working-class citizens who are or are not stocking up their personal armories with hand weapons or assault rifles or homemade bombs. The monopoly of the nation-state and the armed forces or the security sector over the limited application of violence to a coherent political end seems thus to be at risk. At the same time, the prospect of great-power war, or hybrid war or irregular war is greater than at any time in the last quarter century, be it in the South China Sea, the Korean Peninsula, the Sawliki Gap, or the Eastern Ukraine.

In the event, this circumstance argues for something other than the insufficient elite-managerial symbolic interpretation of organized violence especially as this practice has manifested itself in the past decade and a half. More relevant—and much more urgent—would be an examination of how the forces of rage, hatred, and primordial violence elude the efforts of commanders in chiefs, defense ministers, general staffs, think tanks, and parliamentary defense committees to rein in such thugs and murders. In the discharge of their duties, the makers of strategic thought should concentrate more on the forces of anger, hatred, and primordial violence in war and in theory without falling into the traps of a skepticism of collective psychology, or cultural pessimism, or contempt for democratic statecraft as has often been the case.

Specifically the categories of anger, hatred, and primordial violence in the final passage of the famous Chapter One of Book One of Clausewitz' work On War deserve a greater pride of place in the

[*] Comments to Editorial Board, *Österreichische Militärzeitschrift*, June 2016. With thanks to Hofrat Dr Guenther Fleck and Brigadier Dr. Wolfgang Peischel of the Austrian National Defense Academy, Vienna, Austria.

analysis of the Prussian theoretician of war as one also reflects on war, policy, strategy, and society today. Such a claim makes no effort at prescription about an efficacious strategy in the year 2016. We live in a time of manifestly ineffective strategy in prolonged irregular warfare and counterterrorism that is simultaneously witness to the domestic political turmoil in the face of great power conflict in Europe and Asia and escalating Islamist atrocities on the continent of Europe itself.

This essay does not wish to overemphasize these particular forces of primordial violence—say, versus the other features of the remarkable trinity, the impact of chance or political purpose—for, as Clausewitz warns us, "... a theory that ... seeks to fix an arbitrary relationship"... to this one tendency of actual war would be "useless." All the same, the tradition of the great theoretician from Burg in the 18th century offers us a different perspective than found in strategic think tanks and irregular warfare journals fixated on the tactical level of war, all of which have come more or less to a dead end. And yet in what purports to be strategic analysis today, Clausewitz is either wholly disregarded or grossly oversimplified, a reduction to the absurd minimum that is so typical of an age of failing intellect in the face of the problems of public life.

For example, no citation of Clausewitz operates in the textbooks and briefings of general staff academies and war colleges today without the obligatory place of the *wunderliche* or *wundersame Dreifaltigkeit*. Thus,

[a]s a total phenomenon its dominant tendencies always make war a remarkable trinity—composed of primordial violence, hatred, and enmity... of the play of chance and probability... and of its element of subordination, as an instrument of policy.

This passage is simplified inevitably by those with a passing familiarity with the topic to the triad of the people, government, and army in the nature of war in theory and practice. Alternately, the relationship among anger, hatred, and primordial violence only gives attention to the last aspect— the army and its relationship to politics and society. Thereby does the force of violence in the U.S. case become locked in a theoretical prison of counterinsurgency doctrine—dogma—and technological determinism (i.e. the 21st-century version of Douhetism visible in the use of remotely piloted bombardment aircraft as the Norden bombsite 2.0).

This promiscuous misreading of Clausewitz's text is doubly problematic as one tries to make sense of the character of war in its historical and contemporary variety and its relationship to classical theory in the present. This issue hinges on the contradictions and imponderables of violence and hatred that appear to play such a central role in contemporary conflict, especially in the aspect of an asymmetry between jihadist combatants and western democratic men and women at arms. This essay reflects on the trajectory of war and strategy in the past and especially the present with reference to Clausewitz' remarkable trinity and its analytic power for our situation.

The Lessons of Vietnam and Forces in Strategy

The interpretation of Clausewitz in the western democracies since the mid- to late 20th century is said by certain contemporary critics to have overemphasized the aspect of rational control of organized violence. This criticism has arisen especially in the protraction of the post-11 September campaigns in Iraq, Afghanistan, and beyond, with a growing blowback of rage and discord in the arenas of the public sphere. This phenomenon especially manifests in western democracies vulnerable to psychological warfare and low-intensity conflict—whoever is waging it.

The misreading of the forces of real war, especially the changing aspect of primordial violence in union with anger and hatred, derives from historical and contemporary attempts by the wizards of military doctrine to uphold the theoretical pristineness of dogma, despite intense civil-military cognitive dissonance in the realms of politics and society. A like phenomenon in a different idiom seized the general staff opponents of 1960s counterinsurgency dogma who wished in the early 1970s to restore conventional military doctrine to its former pride of place in an attempt to re-forge the key tenets of scientific strategy and professional soldiers in a critical democratic polity.

At this fateful moment in which the professional soldier reinterpreted contemporary events in an effort to rescue the soldierly estate from the debacle of Vietnam, the body of Clausewitz's theory in English underwent a renaissance in the English-speaking world. The conjuncture of the end of conscription in the United States, the ignominious withdrawal from South Vietnam, the junking of the small wars/counterinsurgency establishment in the U.S. armed forces and the institutional emphasis on the all-volunteer force in the land services unfolded in less than a decade. The sum of these events meant that the forces of anger, hatred, and primordial violence visible in Clausewitz's own experience of the transition from war in dynastic Europe of the 18th century to the age of revolution and the wars of nation-states in the 18th century receded in its analytic strength. What emerged, instead, was an emphasis, à la the 19th century school of the Swiss Henri de Jomini, on command and military science, which favored the echelons of national command and the formulation of strategy and operations.

The outstanding figure of the 1970s was Colonel Harry Summers, who used Clausewitz to reinterpret the Indochina war, and thus to exonerate the regular soldier of the annihilationist missteps of the epoch of limited war in the atomic age. Himself a soldier in the Korean War as a young man, Summers borrowed from the "never again" school of Douglas MacArthur two decades earlier. (Upon his relief from Asia in 1951, MacArthur had lectured Congress on the imperative of total victory in limited war, an absurdity.)

The American soldier retreated to the political, strategic, and operative principles that would facilitate a revival of ethos from the nadir of Vietnam. This process was aided, in turn, by the election in 1980 of Ronald Reagan, who provided the forces with the treasure and well-publicized presidential esteem needed for this reconstruction.

The reform of the 1970s and 1980s recalled the anti-constitutional, and Prussian-inflected model of Emory Upton's paradigm of command and military institutions in the year 1881, as such looked back to the putative errors of the epoch 1861–1865. In his bitterness over the decades after the civil war of parsimony and strategic muddle, Upton had naïvely believed that a U.S.-equipped copy of the Prussian Army might have won the war in accord with this dogma, if not with contemporary policy goals. The fallacy is the core belief of the professional soldier in the 19th and 20th centuries, when faced with the citizen soldier in the age of total war as seen by Ludendorff, that professional soldiers alone could best determine the strategic effects of the anger and passion (Clausewitz) of the nation in wartime—markedly better than could be said nation's pluralistically elected government.

The crowning event in this process came a decade and a half later in the Persian Gulf War of 1990–1991, where the doubt and sweat of 1976 had been transformed into a brilliant strategic and operational victory against the Iraqi invaders of Kuwait. The reform of a professional army also had restructured the reserve components of National Guard and Army and U.S. Air Force reserves, whereby the leading soldiers could redefine the civil-military relationship in manner more to their liking. The military's masterful management of the media during this conflict—even while such broadcasters as then-newcomer CNN beamed news to the folks at home live and around the clock—was both symptom and cause of this redefined relationship, all of which had the effect of confining violence to a remote realm empty of anger and hatred.

In the process, there has unfolded among professional soldiers attempting to interpret Clausewitz in a contemporary manner the fateful and fatal exclusion of the citizen from providing for his or her own common defense in a manner in accord with constitutional principles and the very best in the record of arms and the state in the past. This story of the elite-institutional disregard for *die moralische Größen* in Clausewitz's ideas illustrates relevant problems in the formation of strategy in its dimension of democratic civil-military relations in the face of counter-terror in the security sector and the geo-political pressure of the Russian and Chinese offensive against American power.

Elite Delusions: Negations and Neutralizations in Theory and Practice

The lack of theoretical and practical attention to the aspect of primordial violence, anger, and hatred in the face of war in the past and present has certain causes unique to the 21st century. The varied political sources of such organized violence today are refracted through an elite lens of professional myopia (articulated as management dogma of quantitative metrics, racist anthropological nostrums, and gauzy nostalgia among inverted establishmentarians inside the neoconservative Washington Beltway for the Raj and Rudyard Kipling) that has formed a problem for far longer.

The tools of war receive far too much attention by professional strategists as the be-all and end-all of strategy and as the dominant force in the evolution of war and warfare, when much evidence suggests that technology may be well beside the point, as was also the case in the guerilla wars of the 1950s and 1960s. U.S. technological superiority in the Iraq and Afghan campaigns has reduced casualties but otherwise does not seem to have led to any strategic good.

On the one hand, just as in the strategic muddle of the immediate post–Cold-War years and its end-of-history euphoria that nourished itself through the 1990–1991 Gulf War, the U.S. military has again taken flight into the realm of fancy in the waging of war with computerized bombardment in a realm more or less invisible to the naked eye with so-called cyber-war. This spasm of electronic bombardment against the critical sites of the global commons reprises all the platitudes and empty phrases of the "Revolution of Military Affairs," which also misread the factors of primordial violence, anger, and hatred in the epoch from the middle-1980s until the early 1990s in the search for some kind of paradigm shift of war—which actually then manifested itself in 11 September jihadist assault on the continental United States.

This prominence of the Islamists, in their variety, on the one hand, mingles with the rise of an enraged, populist integral-nationalist citizenry in the mature western democracies, on the other. Whereas the perennial answer of many U.S. strategic thinkers to the unruly politics of war and the reaction of society in war is to take refuge in science-fiction technological fantasies of some new ultimate weapon, the dialectical response to Islamic State violence as well as Russian irregular warfare with commandos is a kind of *Volksbewaffung* on a scale predicted only by the Second Amendment fanatics in the United States.

The *Volksbewaffnung* phenomenon—in contrast to U.S. Special Operations Command force structure imperatives of a small, highly elite commando organized force via NATO as applied to, say, Afghanistan or some other low-intensity theater of conflict—also is visible in the revival of Finnish total defense doctrine in the Baltics as well as among newly raised Polish citizen militias, the nascent paramilitaries along the Danube, and even the startling reorganization of NATO and/or PfP armies from east to west, with the Austrian, German, and French security sectors all suddenly growing in size after years of steady decline. Here the center of gravity is rather less on computers than on the hearts and minds (*die moralischen Größen* as Clausewitz describes them) of men and women in uniform with weapons that only a few years ago were dismissed as "legacy systems" from a distant and meaningless epoch.

Meanwhile, the face of battle is focused on an elite cadre of imperial police constabularies (exemplified by General William McChrystal's service in Iraq or Afghanistan) in urban ink spots or by courageous men and women astride remote mountaintop outposts under fire from indigenous irregulars. In the proliferation of jihadist mayhem from self-radicalizing murderers and psychopaths in the Parisian suburb slums, or Brussels-Mollenbek, or the depression-ridden Inland Empire of southern California, these battle-hardened constabulary soldiers from Fallujah and Helmand Province return to police the Euro-Atlantic metropole besieged by Syrian refugees or other "dark invaders."

In this connection, while the idea may discomfit some, certain enduring features of the theory of Carl Schmitt in the 1920 and 1930s recommend themselves to a critical examination of the strategic present. Despite this brilliant and dangerous man having been an intractable and long-lived enemy of western democracy, certain of his ideas are useful for the critique of strategy in the present.

Schmitt in his time saw the avalanche of U.S. films, automobiles, corporate methods, and consumer culture unfold in a defeated Central Europe, especially in the brief period from 1924 until 1929 that Germany, if not Austria, seemed headed toward pre-war levels of prosperity and political stability. This brave new world of democracy and prosperity then promptly collapsed from 1929 until 1931, whereupon Schmitt condemned the process as a kind of vast liberal, international, and technological fake that went against the human tendency to political conflict.

The hope and fear of the 1920s in the writings of Schmitt may help one to understand the limits of how computers will fight one another and a hapless citizenry will live in the virtual reality and physical wreckage of massively retaliating cloud-computing data complexes. The citizens of the nation-states waging digital battle will be damned to endure their fate as victims like the benighted citizens of Everytown of Christmas Eve 1940, as imagined in Alexander Korda's film of 1936 of H. G. Wells' *Things to Come*.

On the other hand, another 1940 film—this one by Quentin Reynolds, titled *London Can Take It*—suggests that citizens engaged in such a future conflict may not just simply take it, but they may rise up and fight back in ways that we do not fully comprehend, but cannot in any way exclude. As for today, one needs little imagination to see that even in this son-of-Stuxnet, digital flexible response contingency, human nature in war (as manifest in the *wunderliche Dreifaltigkeit*) is far more resilient—where the positive military energies of citizens are given greater pride of place for a legitimate political end of national survival, which would likely be the case in the present and future.

Perhaps the use of software to sabotage the Iranian version of the Manhattan Project worked perfectly; nonetheless, the strategic efficacy of Iranian force and statecraft in the wake of the operation as visible in the Iranian conquest of parts of Iraq as well as the ongoing operation in devastated Syria plainly suggest the limits of neo-Douhetian technological phantasmagoria versus real war fought with more humble but altogether lethal 20th-century weapons—especially when the morale and will of the western democracies is put under a siege with an unceasing barrage of brilliantly wielded propaganda and the deft use of military force in coercive diplomacy.

The role of anger, hatred, and primordial violence in the formation of ever more military and paramilitary echelons with citizens in uniform in the face of geopolitical upheaval—to say nothing about the manner in which Russian psychological operations has made the morale of central and western Europeans a primary target of their brilliantly orchestrated post-Maidan 2014 offensive against the glacis of the Article VI Area of the Washington Treaty—means that the elite and essentially anti-democratic prerogatives of interpretation of the character of war that have held sway since the 1970s and again in the first decade of this century are in for a shock.

Primordial Violence and the Future of War

Sir Hew Strachan, in his critique of contemporary strategy since 11 September 2001, suggests that western military institutions have become too attached to the epoch of total war and cannot marshal sufficient political direction and military energy to achieve a coherent strategic end. This critique is surely true. The episodes amid Operation Iraqi Freedom of the renewed operational level of war in 2003–2005 was followed by the COIN episode more or less until 2009, without a satisfactory strategic outcome in the Islamic State. The war began again, but this time, with the shock and awe not from U.S. coalition total-spectrum dominance and its vaunted kinetic effects. Rather, the shock and awe unfolded from the ISIS blitzkrieg in the badlands and "ungoverned spaces" of Iraq and Syria.

These phases of contemporary war were modeled on a now-forgotten campaign of the year 1989, when the Bush White House, under the strategic operational delegation of command via then-SECDEF Dick Cheney and SOUTHCOM CINC General Max Thurman, deposed the Panamanian dictator Alfonso Noriega in a coup de main, that, when compared to the campaigns since 2002, was virtually over before it started. This moment vanished from popular memory in the later upheaval of this year in which Cold War ended, but the campaign hardly vanished in the collective mind of Cheney and Rumsfeld, particularly as they peered out over the wreckage of the Pentagon on 11 September 2001.

Such a fairy-book campaign well signified the conceit that somehow the acolytes of the school of Summers and others in 2002 could extract the primordial violence, anger, and hatred from war altogether—and make it so handy and practical as to unfold with the least need of the military energy of democracy and its citizens to protect itself.

Nearly a generation later, a startling gap exists between the political and psychological ends of such conflict, i.e. religious and cultural hegemony through mass murder and acts of random violence (albeit on a comparatively small scale), and the response of western democracies with very limited use of military force (the so-called kinetic effects) nonetheless cloaked in the rhetoric of total war drawn from the 20th century. That is to say, the aspects of anger, hatred, and violence especially emerge in the strategic problems faced today by Western internal security and military figures in which the populations of the Western democracies form a target of terror, especially in the propagandistic and psychological realms of strategy. The citizens of the Western democracies, however, have only at best a passive role in their own defense, which is effectuated by a small cadre of intelligence operatives, a relative handful of professional soldiers in armies organized for the constabulary role and small number of postmodern bombardment aircraft of a type that is equally parsimonious with the lives of citizens and even the lives of its victims in failed states.

Although the goal of jihadist and otherwise semi-criminal and semi-religious nihilists is to transform western civilization into a pseudo-religious charnel house writ large (i.e. those portions of Syria and Iraq in the hands of ISIS thugs and murder gangs since 2012 or so…) All the same, it is not as if Clausewitz has vanished from the brains of armies and from professional military education. Far from it, as the routine citations abound of the remarkable trinity of the people, the government and military in a variety of locales in professional military education and in those parts of state and society professional charged with the making of strategy.

What has vanished, however, is a keen historical understanding of Clausewitz in his time, in detail according the record of the European past. Moreover, what has also quite gone is the experience in the higher aspects of those who plan and wage war today of the citizen soldier in the face of major war. These two disparate things contain a positive insight into those aspects of strategy that might well prove resilient and durable in the face of multiple and increasing threats for which the overly elite and anti-constitutional theory and practice of national security has proved wanting.

Comprised of 11 September 2001, the world economic crisis, the revival of great power conflict in classic geopolitics, and integral nationalist mass politics in the mature democracies in the year 2016, one can easily generalize that our age is one of growing anger and hatred among certain elements of global society. These portions of global state and society have not just been twisted by bin Laden's hymn of hate or by ISIS' head chopping glimpses of hell on the digital screen. They are imbibing the kind of Sorelian exemplification of violence as mythical experience made all the more omnipresent in its political, cultural, and social aspect by the digital age. Their experience jibes today with the phenomenon that Hannah Arendt so well interpreted in the year 1969 about the forms of violence in the mid-20th century, an interpretation with much promise for our own time.

To return to Clausewitz as well as to Schmitt, this essay ends by posing a question for which no simple answer is at hand, and the augurs are all those of incipient catastrophe. The focus of strategy in the present epoch since 11 September has attempted to negate and neutralize the forces of primordial violence, anger, and hatred by an overemphasis on elite control in the facets of misplaced military theory, the use of armed forces drawn from too small a sector of society, and the nostrums of high-tech miracle weapons that in sum are a false neutralization of the forces always and everywhere inherent to politics. This focus on strategy of a kind analyzed here has been especially seized of a wasteful and maniac preoccupation with the pseudo-religious, social, mental and cultural motivations of violent men and women in certain societies that turn to jihadism, whereas Iraqi and Afghan societies do not especially cherish occupation armies. This historical fact requires no institutional effort of hundreds of anthropologists, think-tank war mongers, or latter day knock-offs of Lawrence and Galula to regale us with the timeless verities of counter-insurgency, all the while neutralizing the actual causes of such conflict.

With an eye to what Clausewitz may have had in mind, the transition from the wars of the dynastic estates to the wars of nation-states—a phenomenon in which the forces of primordial violence, anger, and hatred surely can be said to have increased greatly from 1793 until they retreated again after 1815—may be a hint of things to come. In the wake of forever warfare with no tangible strategic outcome of merit, joined with the world economic crisis and the macro-economic phenomena similar to those after 1873 and or 1929, the forces of anger and hatred and primordial hatred are on the rise. Part of the reason for this process arises from errors about Clausewitz's ideas of primordial violence that became manifest a generation ago, and this self-serving prerogative of interpretation in general staffs and think tanks should give way to an absolutely sober realism, which can take much from Clausewitz's original brilliant insights in what may be the escalating phases of either another Thirty Years War or the path from Valmy to Austerlitz in some 21st-century incarnation.

IV.   Civil-Military Relations

12. Soldiers, the Phantom of Conscription, and Political Culture: A Cautionary Tale from the United States of America*

The fate of the citizen in uniform in the 21st century should concern those attentive to the steadfastness of democracy in contemporary conflict. The unsettled nature of the world system in the second decade of the 21st century amid incipient crises across Eurasia makes the fate of the soldier in American democracy and the requirements of military service a theme that is unlikely to disappear soon. While the wars of the present day have been swathed in the rhetoric of total war in the 20th century, they also have engaged a smaller percentage of the U.S. population for what is likely a far more diffuse strategy than the wars of the era 1950–1999. The nature of contemporary war imposes a particularly odious burden on those who must wage it, exacerbated by the perception, founded or not, among U.S. soldiers that civilians fail to understand the nature of their sacrifice in a strategy of attrition and limited violence that runs contrary to national ideals of war in its theoretical and absolute forms.

The posture of the soldier in American political culture is poorly appreciated in these authors' native country, the United States of America, and generally misunderstood in continental Europe. The place of the soldier in democratic political culture in the current crises stands linked to the mixed fortunes of the citizen in uniform, as well as the troubled making of strategy in the extended counterinsurgency campaigns of the past decade. The trend of the last 20 years in both Central Europe and the United States has been to denigrate the citizen in uniform in favor of the professional soldier—or, more lately, to extol the postmodern soldier of fortune/*Landsknecht*. This sentiment resonates with many civilian and military observers alike. It embodies either a traditional civil and civilian skepticism of the military

---

* Revised version of a lecture presented at the Austrian National Defense Academy on 2 February 2010.

class and its political failings or, in neo-liberal circles, a market-dominated ideology; among military professionals, it stems from a sense of caste undergirded by exaggerated ideals of military discipline versus the laxity of civilian society.

Those interested in democratic civil-military relations and the citizen-soldier in U.S. political culture do well to remain focused on the knotted themes of political institutions, ideas, and strategic culture where the ghost of the long-departed wartime draft of the 20th-century United States represents a greater political force than many concede. The U.S. armed forces abandoned conscription nearly 40 years ago amid the termination of the Vietnam War and the concomitant turmoil in and of U.S. political culture. The neo-liberal policy of the early 1970s had twin facets: first, to nullify the worst effects of the southeast Asian conflict on domestic politics by downgrading military service as a pillar of citizenship; and second, to achieve a re-professionalization of the U.S. armed forces in the era of limited war in the nuclear age through a reduction in the size of the force and an overemphasis on the operational level of war. Such policies belong to a vanished world, and one can well ask about the meaning of the all-volunteer force in the democratic civil-military relations dominated by irregular warfare, violent religious extremism, domestic terrorism, and prolonged expeditionary campaigns with U.S. and allied/partner ground forces that are overstretched and exhausted. In the United States, the civil-military reality is marked further by the inequitably shared burdens of security and defense in contemporary state and society, which context lends the issue increasing urgency in the ever more partisan, contentious, and bitter political environment. The upshot is the troubling phenomenon of U.S. politicians wielding the symbols of soldiers and war in the increasingly polarized domestic politics. What effects has this specific development had on politics at large, on the role of the soldier in the state, and on the political attitudes in civil society about military institutions and soldiers?

This chapter examines the place of the soldier in state and society and the collective political memory—or phantom—of conscription in U.S. public life. The goal of this paper is to link this political phantom to the strategic reality of present. The lines that follow treat the reform of military institutions in the past and contemporary U.S. political culture in which soldiers figure prominently.

Conscription in Recent Memory—and Politics

The history of conscription in the United States occupies a central role in this analysis, rendered in periods from the origins of the republic until the era of total and Cold War. The measures of the late 1960s that led to the phase-out of conscription are followed, in turn, by significant civil-military events in the era 1969–1991 that this paper sets out at greater detail below.

The "victory of the all-volunteer force" in the Iraqi campaign of 1990–1991 appeared to bestow the laurels of triumph on the reforms of 20 years prior. The *fata morgana* of limited war with high-tech arsenals in the 1990s (the so-called revolution in military affairs) became a fixture of foreign policy in the wake of the Persian Gulf victory, with a reprise in the middle-1990s Balkan campaign that ended with the air bombardment of Serbia in 1999. These events added to the prestige of the military in society and state. As a result, the 1990s witnessed a civil-military gap in U.S. political culture made more significant by the growing self-confidence of soldiers in political life, as well as the transformed domestic politics of increasingly bitter red-versus-blue partisanship. The long-term effects of the absence of conscription meant that the number of citizens and especially members of the elites had ever less direct experience of military affairs, be it from the making of strategy in the general staff to the painting of rocks in garrison life. This state of affairs boosted the fatuous claims of those well versed in tactics as the trump of strategy, augmented the caste mentality of men and women in uniform, and otherwise cowed civilians overwhelmed by PowerPoint briefings filled with military acronyms of levels of command and operational maneuver.

Then came the 11 September 2001 terror assault on the continental United States, which presently confronted the 1970s defense reforms and their legacy with a new strategic reality in which the absence of conscription loomed as an ever greater national weakness. The fantasy of certain general staff and think-tank savants that war could be robbed of its union of chance, anger, and violence through brilliant munitions and supernatural command and control vanished in the ashes and twisted steel of four downed airliners. Instead, what followed in American political life was rather the opposite of a united home front in wartime or an end of partisan political rancor in the face of the al Qaeda threat. Instead, the public ill feeling of the contested 2000 election let the demons out of the harness in party politics, while the chimera of quick victory in Afghanistan and Iraq presently gave way to strategic blunders of the worst kind.

In the first years of the new decade of the long war or Global War on Terror, the George W. Bush administration dispatched soldiers—and former soldiers among the chattering classes—in roles that augmented their missions at the fighting front and in the highest counsels of state in wartime. Yet the same administration also did much to debase the professional standing of soldiers, for example, through the congressional humiliation of Army Chief of Staff Eric Shinseki and later the public *coup de grace* of the Secretary of State, former General Colin Powell, in the Security Council—Powell being the most vocal proponent of the "never again" school of military hyper-professionalization. The result was the politicization of soldiers in a manner unseen perhaps at any time in the last century or so of U.S. history.

The Barack Obama administration in 2009 flirted with the ghost of conscription in U.S. political life with the decision to escalate the Afghan campaign in order ultimately to withdraw U.S. forces. The need to redouble national energy in an exceptionally difficult theater of war unfolded in the shadow of the global economic crisis and war-weariness at home. Obama's revival of the duties of citizenship and the civic idealism of a generation of young people otherwise unengaged in politics or national service soon collided with the necessity to liquidate the Iraqi theater of operations and to escalate the Afghan campaign. Obama did not reinstate the draft because of the promise of strategic and operational reform that emerged in the latter phases of the Iraq campaign. Counterinsurgency doctrine makes little allowance for the citizen in uniform, with its emphasis on the traditions and operational code of special-operations forces amid the legacy of 19th- and 20th-century imperial warfare.

Political Culture, Citizenship, Neo-Conservatism, and Their Critics

But 21st-century military doctrine is neither the end nor the beginning point of this inquiry. One must also consider the ideas that have been at the core of current policy and the reaction to these ideas in practice by those who embody the ideal of the citizen-soldier. The neo-conservative inhabitants of think tanks and universities signify a theme of historical inquiry in their own right, which exceeds the bounds of this work. (For continental Europeans, the role of the neo-conservatives as the alibi of a nation to explain the bellicose, even militarist, character of U.S. political culture in the 1990s represents a caricature—at best.) One cannot assert seriously that these figures have militarized American statecraft and society by their own deeds. The phenomenon is more complex and nuanced.

The thought and deeds of the neo-conservatives in the blast of war in 2002–2003, however, do form a useful point of departure because of the failure of such policy in practice and the critique that such policy summoned among thoughtful observers in the course of the decade. Indeed, the smoke of the terror assaults had barely cleared above Manhattan and northern Virginia as the pundits embraced Robert Kagan's tendentious ideas on the respective martial and feminine traits of U.S. and European societies at the moment; meanwhile Deputy Secretary of Defense Paul Wolfowitz laid out his grand strategy for the democratization of the Arab world by force of arms under the able operational command of Tommy Franks. Aided by the neo-Gaullist troika of Gerhard Schroeder, Jacques Chirac, and Vladimir Putin in 2001–2002, Kagan had his moment in the limelight, only then to lose his bearings amid the Iraqi insurgency and the atrocities at the Abu Ghraib prison. Like his fellow anti-European denizens of the right-wing Washington intellectual stratum in their number, he poorly foresaw that Venusian Europe, in the guise of France under Nicolas Sarkozy, later in the decade would rejoin the integrated military structure of NATO and deploy significant combat power to the Afghan theater, fighting alongside the United States in the most difficult conditions.

A West Point career officer and Vietnam veteran, Andrew Bacevich has emerged as the most ardent and persuasive critic of the neo-conservatives. His more recent work has analyzed the pitfalls of U.S. statecraft generally. Here Bacevich associates himself with a tradition of soldiers who later became dissident in U.S. policy—for example, Marine Corps commandant David Shoup—and who decried U.S. policies in the cold-war era, especially during the Vietnam war. Shoup wrote a book on U.S. militarism in 1970, a term that Bacevich has reframed with notable fluency as part of a more generalized attempt to promote ideal conservative values in society that derive in part from Bacevich's Catholicism, as well as from the conservative soldierly ethos idealized more problematically by Samuel Huntington in The Soldier and the State. Bacevich also maintains the classical republican and noninterventionist tradition of constitutional imperatives of the 19th and early 20th centuries.

In such works as *American Militarism* and *The Limits of Power*, Bacevich interprets the evolution of the U.S. armed forces as an institution in government, society, and the public mind. His work on militarism in the contemporary United States embodies a more generalized *Gesellschaftskritik* of U.S. civilization that has strayed greatly from Main Street values of anti-militarism, thrift, modesty, and citizenship as depicted by Alexis de Tocqueville or Booth Tarkington. Bacevich especially condemns the transformation of civil-military relations and the growing romance of war in the popular mind that has unfolded since the 1980s—that is, the noteworthy change in elite and popular values and attitudes from the period in which military service was a generalized institution of U.S. citizenship in the age of total war until the postmodern present.

The service of the citizen-soldier in the age of total war enshrined a noble tradition handed down from Greek and Roman states to English constitutional practice, extolled in turn by Machiavelli, and made a force of remarkable power by the French Revolution: the citizen in uniform, that is, the soldier as citizen and political subject, enfranchised to defend his rights and freedoms of the nation-state by the duty at arms. This tradition seemed corrupted by the student protests of the Vietnam War and was undone as an institution of national defense in the United States of the 1970s. The deferment from military service for college—the right of the middle and upper-middle classes in the era 1948–1972—was extended generally when the draft was put into mothballs until the unlikely outbreak of World War III.

In the postmodern civil-military relations of the 21st century, according to Bacevich, soldiers reflect an age of consumption, celebrity, and profligacy, in which political violence has become omnipresent. Actual combat remains the purview of a small group in U.S. society generally, whose sense of caste and social exclusivity has grown as the wars they have fought have stretched out over the past two decades (and narrowed in the actual scope of violence when compared to war in the 20th century).

At the same time, the chief military activity of the U.S. population consists of the consumption of images of past and present military hagiography and various manifestations of weapons technology that are ever harder to distinguish from Hollywood sci-fi thrillers. A film about ordnance-disposal experts in Iraq has won the Oscar in 2010, while a television series by Steven Spielberg on the U.S. Pacific campaign in World War II has enjoyed a White House screening. The citizens of the United States also have been rendered as a passive audience for what in the Bush/Rumsfeld administration had been exceptionally blinkered strategic analysis offered by former flag officer propagandists on cable news networks, whose corruption and venality later was revealed by a press that too late responded to its constitutional role.

But overwhelmingly the chief activity of the U.S. citizen as concerns military service in the last decade has been a sense of guilt expressed in yellow-ribbon decals affixed to the back of sports utility vehicles, as well as a sense of weariness at the sight of yet more faces of the fallen, packaged for one-stop memorials on the glossy pages of *People Magazine* every month or so. Bacevich argues that soldiers and their legends, doctrines, arsenals, and prerogatives have outsized political and symbolic roles in a society in which men and women at arms (especially professional soldiers in the senior ranks) nonetheless constitute a tiny fraction of the population as a whole.

The period from the close of the 1960s until the recent past has transformed the armed forces and their relation to American society in a highly worrisome manner that is somehow fitted within the more generalized mutation of the political and social realms in the United States. This relationship has gone from the traditional roles of the citizen-soldier, with the attendant nationalization and socialization in the profession of arms, to the passive consumer of symbols and images as in so many other facets of society. The American citizen experiences war through the media—television, newspapers, the internet, and films, in which the lionization of military celebrities and the damnation of those who are too critical of strategic imperatives loom large over with the ceaseless images of gunfire and explosions (now oddly called "kinetic effects" in an especially Orwellian turn of phrase) that unfold in inhospitable desert and mountain locations in which neither corpses of the enemy, nor the innocent civilians, nor our own troops, nor any other human consequences of conflict sometimes—or ever—appear. At least the dreary sensationalism of the Vietnam-era casualty counts, appearing to the accompaniment of CBS TV News reporter Walter Cronkite's sonorous recaps of the recent action, still averred to the human component of fighting and dying in the service of the nation.

Soldier Statesman/-woman versus Militarist/Military Desperado/Military Entrepreneur

How has the increasingly prominent role of soldiers in domestic political life manifested itself in the national politics of the present even though the absence of the draft assures that really very few Americans have much real experience of actual war? The war ethos of the Bush administration as well as the civil-military frictions of the opening years of the Global War on Terror politicized soldiers and especially senior officers in an alarming way. Defense Secretary Rumsfeld's ham-fisted propaganda campaign circa 2004–2006, filled with select former general officers on the boards of aerospace and defense firms as media experts of total spectrum dominance, damaged constitutional traditions of civilian control, while it debased professional neutrality of soldiers in the realms of policy and domestic politics.

The poor relations between Rumsfeld and his Office of Secretary of Defense senior staffers, on the one side, and the senior officer corps, on the other, represented another source of civil-military stress and weakness for the long haul. All sides—civil and military—shared a measure of guilt for the strategic misfortunes of the nation, but the men and women in uniform soon deployed the stab-in-the-back legend against Rumsfeld, regardless of the merits of the issue, to assign chief blame to him. This phenomenon followed the pattern of demonization by senior officers of Robert McNamara in the 1960s and borrowed from 19th- and 20th-century European practice.

While the Iraqi campaign bogged down in the insurgency in the years 2003–2005, the shadow of the man on horseback loomed in the 2006 election campaign, marked by the baleful and tendentious "revolt of the generals" mounted against Rumsfeld by certain impolitic, media-hungry ex-flag officers who had previously enjoyed his favor. While Rumsfeld surely deserved the political oblivion into which he tumbled after the midterm election that year, the too-little and too-late protests in mid-2006 of these television generals and colonels (versus their conspicuous silence in 2003 at the martyrdom of Shinseki and Powell) offered no laurels to the soldierly calling.

Despite a record lacking almost any interactions with the armed forces, Barack Obama secured military professionals as advisors, who depart from the quasi-praetorian mores of 2006. Thus the politicization of senior officers in the second Bush administration contrasts sharply with the civil-military record of 2008–2009. The misfortunes of the McCain camp in the 2008 election, with its diminishing appeal of the Vietnam War legacy in the hearts and minds of 18-year-olds, forms one aspect of this semi-demilitarization of national life, as does the sound stewardship of the Defense Department by Robert Gates and Chairman of the Joint Chiefs Admiral Michael Mullen, who have ably returned military life to its non-partisan principles that maintain the tradition of George Marshall.

But how does militarism, if it exists, manifest itself on the level of local politics, where generals are less likely to be found? In order to examine the politicization of soldiers in the present, one can raise the question of the soldierly biography in domestic politics then and now. That is, has the tradition of the citizen-soldier been so perverted in the present that such should cause alarm among those alert to the health of U.S. democracy in wartime?

Katherine Jenrette is a young Republican woman running for Congress in the midterm election year 2010. Jenrette has unfolded a fairly noteworthy presence on the Internet to advance her political fortunes. Bowing to the Zeitgeist, her election material contains no written proclamations, but instead an illustrative series of contrasting photos: one sees an attractive smiling woman in T-shirt, bare feet with lacquered toes, counterpoised to her persona in a blue suit, her steady hand placed on a volume of South Carolina history (the locale whence began the U.S. civil war)—because in addition to her role in local business and athletics, the candidate describes herself as an adjunct history professor. We find Ms. Jenrette in evening wear, a nod to her pageant days, and also dressed like any other suburban mother (though she is clambering into a Dodge pickup, rather than a minivan.) Still, the website is topped by an image of Jenrette in combat uniform, hefting an M-16 rifle. The soldierly references dominate the page, and distract from her girlish toes. While one can infer that Ms. Jenrette has had a conventional career in South Carolina politics, whatever "conventional" may be in the beleaguered Palmetto State, and made her way within the Republican Party as do many of her professional political colleagues, her military biography is the most striking aspect of her self-promotion. Her roles as an athlete, mother, political staffer to a U.S. congressman, and driver of a pickup truck stand subordinate to her military service in the 1990–1991 Gulf War and her subsequent progress through the ranks of the U.S. Army Reserves.

In American life before the 1960s, such a biography would have been unremarkable, at least for a man. The citizen-soldier as political personage has a rich history in the United States as it does in Great Britain and France, though without the sulfurous odor of grapeshot or other Bonapartist flourishes. But granted the militarism that Bacevich so well interprets, especially the variety that underlay the recent Bush presidency, then one is uncertain of how to assess the respective elements of Ms. Jenrette's career. Can she be seen in the lineage of George Washington, Ulysses S. Grant, Theodore Roosevelt, and Harry Truman—soldiers and citizen-soldiers who embraced democratic political culture and succeeded in elective office while upholding the constitution?

On the other hand, there lurks a darker, more troubling codex in Ms. Jenrette's campaign message that accords with the Bacevich's thesis of militarism, namely that soldiers are politically superior to civilians by dint of the virtues of duty, honor, and service to country. One is reminded here of a 2009 *Wall Street Journal* article on higher education, in which certain opinion-makers propagate the similar (and related) idea that the U.S. Military Academy (USMA) is a finer university than Harvard, Princeton, or Yale because of the imperatives of combat, character, and self-sacrifice. Put another way, students in the Stanford Graduate School of Business have little need to keep tabs of the casualty lists of their fellow class members as they prepare for a life of innovative investment banking, which now seems less than noble since the world financial crisis of 2008. Losing one's position at Lehman's is somehow not quite the same as losing limbs to an improvised explosive device (IED). The article concludes, in essence, that West Point cadets are superior to civilians because the former must reckon with the baptism of fire and the effect this duty and

235

honor have for the formation of their character as young men and women.

In fact, these martial virtues are denied to U.S. citizens in elite universities or elsewhere in wartime because of the suspension of the draft more than a generation ago. Further, the mixed fortunes of the reserve officer training program, gutted by old hippies in tenured positions, plays a role in this issue, as does the ever greater reliance on high-tech weaponry as a tactical substitute for grand strategy and the tradition of national mobilization in crisis and war. The newspaper-men or -women overawed by the appearance of the thin grey line at USMA fail to add these civil-military facts to their otherwise warrant-ed praise of the exemplary character of USMA cadets and their maintenance of a sense of honor that otherwise seems little in evi-dence in such places as TV reality shows, Hollywood studios, New York investment banks, and the white-collar prisons for the criminal figures of the recent economic crisis. Nor do the journalists enam-ored of kepis and spit-and-polish see that their arguments when car-ried to their logical end swerve quite close to those of Ernst Jünger or even Ernst Röhm, in whose youth such cultural pessimism and ro-mantic nihilism joined, in turn, with militarism was standard fair—to vastly less edifying ends.

The message here goes further, at least at the implied level: soldiers are also superior to those in the bourgeois professions be-cause of the merits of command and obedience. That is, the nature of pluralistic politics should somehow be reorganized to the needs of a military hierarchy, and that the ideals of soldierly virtue handed down by what is, in fact, a tiny minority in U.S. society are to be preferred to the workings of the three branches of government in the U.S. tra-dition and especially to the decadence, materialism, sexual perversions, and notoriously limited and changeable attention span of civil society.

One can wonder: Had the Bush administration in the wake of the 11 September assaults introduced conscription as well as higher taxes—that is, had it asked for an equitable sharing of the burdens of its wartime policies—would such assertions about the superiority of soldiers to politicians be as viable a campaign slogan as it seems to be among many right-of-center citizens today? This cosmos of ideas derives in part from the consumption of images of military virtue and a fatigue with the ills of civilian society seen by all—whether or not the observers have any direct experience with the battlefield or even the parade grounds. The trope, as it were, says more about the political anxieties and dreams of civilians that it does about the reality of military life and its respective vices and virtues.

Now to return to the election in South Carolina once more, this negative interpretation of Ms. Jenrette's campaign is perhaps unwarranted and unfair, but it is not out of the realm of the possible granted the state of U.S. political and strategic culture in the present in the wake of nearly a decade of conflict. The inevitable civil-military burdens of protracted irregular warfare and civil-military fusion that is the byproduct of counterinsurgency in the record of western democracies—exacerbated in the current U.S. case by the Bush administration's interventions with soldiers in domestic politics—form ideal conditions for the rise of militarism and praetorianism.

Such mutation in U.S. strategic culture and national life has arisen in part because of the neo-liberal dogma and the doctrine of outsourcing in economic affairs as applied to military matters in the recent past. This phenomenon of the market as the dominant force in warfare and military institutions is joined, in turn, with the collateral damage of the failure of the 1990s revolution in military affairs, the rise of counter insurgency doctrine, and the improvised tactic of strikes by winged robot assassins of al Qaeda hideouts and encampments. The sum of these developments has further nullified citizenship at arms, save for those unlucky enough in the National Guard and U.S. Army and U.S. Air Force Reserves to have been compelled to serve against their will, especially in the first years of warfare in Afghanistan and Iraq.

The Citizen-Soldier and Conscription in the Past and Present

The problems of arms and society interpreted cannot obscure the history and tradition of conscription and the necessary role of the citizen in uniform for U.S. democracy—even in the present. From the foundation of the republic until the latter part of the 20th century, the ideal of military service as a feature of citizenship and the citizen in uniform served the United States well. This institution assured the endurance of U.S. constitutional values and struck the balance between the needs of civil society and the requirements of national defense in the appropriate epoch, even in the Cold War.

The framers of the constitution provided chiefly for a militia system on the medieval British model, which relied on an armed citizenry, with a small army and navy. (The reflexive American abhorrence—at least in theory, if not in practice—of "large standing armies" derives from the period of the English Civil War and the Glorious Revolution, when men in uniform marauded through the land. Both the context and the theory fail utterly to fit U.S. circumstances, but Americans cling to the instinct, right down to the Second Amendment of the U.S. Constitution.) In the early 19th century, the leaders of the U.S. embraced the principle of the expansible army, which relied on volunteers in wartime to reach its fighting strength. This institution subsequently imitated its European prototypes with conscription during the U.S.Civil War. The expansible army (and navy and later air forces) was perfected further in the age of total war into the 20th century.

While conscription in the American Civil War was far from a popular institution, compulsory military service meshed with superior political, economic, and social cohesion of the northern states to secure triumph versus the limited capacity for total war had in the Confederacy. This victory was more than merely the task of a handful of well known general officers, but the sacrifice of citizen-soldiers in their millions. An important institution of the citizen in uniform, the Reserve Officer Training Corps in the land grant colleges of the Midwest and the West, arose in the years after the Civil War. (Meanwhile, the size of European armies grew in the militarism of the late 19th century while the United States otherwise reduced sharply the size of its military and naval services.)

Conscription was instituted again in World War I by the Selective Service act of 1917, in the attempt to match the fighting power of the Central Powers. The effort tipped the balance in the favor of the Entente in the summer of 1918. This law offered the basis for subsequent military reform legislation after the war for the ideal of an armed citizenry on the Swiss model in the national defense act of 1920. Although there was no peacetime draft in the 1920s, the military reform law embraced various forms of citizen-soldier roles and missions (Civilian Military Training Corps) in spite of the generalized demobilization and anti-war sentiment of the 1920s and 1930s and the world economic crisis.

The greatest moment for the conscription of the U.S. citizen-soldier occurred in World War II. The reinstitution of the draft actually preceded Pearl Harbor by 13 months. The isolationism and anti-military attitudes of the 1930s gave way to an upwelling of national purpose without precedent. While the United States never mobilized as many troops as its planners had originally hoped in 1941–1942, the memory of this event as seen through the lens of conscription-based mobilization endures in the minds of the 21st century. This collective memory bulks as a more powerful force today in the United States than the historical reality of the Second World War, which conflict, having begun in the infamous small countries far away, caught much of its soon-to-be rank and file unawares and unengaged. In the event, the American side of World War II was filled with complexities and facts that are difficult for the present generation to comprehend because of the illusions worked by popular film accounts the computer depictions of aerial combat. The memory of national purpose that relied upon conscription and the citizen in uniform thus contrasts with the diminishing national effort of the present and its inflated rhetoric.

Whatever latter-day fudging of the spirit leading up to the United States entering World War II, the perfection of weapons technology seemed to nullify the need for large standing armies in the wake of the atomic bombings of Japan. The draftees of 1940–1946 returned home to civilian life and expected to partake in the postwar boom. Nonetheless, the United States instituted a peacetime draft in 1948, after makers of policy rejected a national militia with universal military training as had been considered in the 1920s. Strategic air power allowed the United States to burden American society less than the mass armies of Central and Eastern Europe under the hammer and sickle weighed upon subject peoples. This aspect of what can be called the cold-war compromise in U.S. civil-military relations under escutcheon of the citizen-soldier and conscription held steady for two decades. Such compromise was then undone in part by the burdens of irregular warfare and the disequilibrium between military professionals and the citizen-soldier in the 1960s.

From the Citizen-Soldier to Postmodern Soldier Caste: Vietnam to the First Iraq War

The course of conscription in the Cold War included in two wars in Asia, to say nothing of the nuclear confrontation in central Europe and the Caribbean that avoided the outbreak of a shooting war because of the sobering effect of atomic weapons. The Korean War (1950–1953) and especially the war in Indochina (1959–1975) relied on conscripts in the ground forces, as well as the stalwarts of air and sea power on an exceptional scale. The use of ships and planes in the latter conflict could not turn the tide in Vietnam, and draftees were made the scapegoat and alibi of a nation for the failings of the senior political leader and the top generals and admirals to devise a coherent policy and effective strategy.

Moreover, the Vietnam War dragged out across three decades at the same time that U.S. society underwent noteworthy changes at the expense of old hierarchies that undercut the ideal of the citizen in uniform. These forces in the domestic scene made conscription for limited war in Asia in the nuclear age a source of political upheaval. The pacifist sentiment that had long existed in American society reasserted itself especially in such places as college campuses and local churches, just as racial conflict connected with the further enfranchisement of black Americans manifested itself. Social and political groups critical of U.S. society and foreign policy in the 1960s reviled Selective Service as the central pillar of American imperialism and warmaking. Resistance to draft registration, demonization of local draft boards, and boycotts of and violence against Reserve Officer Training Corps programs became the norm at many colleges and universities.

The climax in this process came in the year 1968–1969, when campus turmoil connected with the worsening of the war in Vietnam as well as racial unrest in leading cities combined with political and celebrity murders. These events elected Richard Nixon, whose policy was to escalate the Vietnam War to end it, along with a force and statecraft of detente with the USSR amid regularized diplomacy with the Chinese. He also sought to de-escalate the war on universities first by the abolition of student deferments in Selective Service and then the phase-out of wartime conscription altogether in 1972–1973. The shock waves of this uproar presently collapsed Nixon's presidency in the Watergate affair, but the military reforms of the era took hold in the decade that followed.

These reforms based on the all-professional force reorganized the reserve and active components of the U.S. military so as to force a national mobilization in the event of war on the pattern of the expansible army of tradition. In the tendentious retrospective of 1975, the failure to mount a national mobilization in 1964 stood as a stark warning to the future. In conflicts to come, the doctrine of never-again suggested that senior officers could best determine how to engage the sense of political purpose, anger, and hatred which contemporaries in uniform—a role for which constitutional safeguard as well as the record of the past suggested that it was ill-suited and inappropriate.

These "lessons of Vietnam" emerged in the decade after war's end and consolidated in the presidency of Ronald Reagan. Filled with the total-war ideas and rhetoric of, say, 1943–1944 as applied to the strategic situation of 1981–1982, Reagan gave the soldier back his sense of honor by way of a large defense budget, for which conscription nonetheless played no role any longer. The doctrine of the lessons of Vietnam suggested that, at the operational and tactical level, the United States had never suffered a defeat. This theory somehow made nonsense out of the reality of strategy and pushed all guilt onto others as concerns the real nature of the war and its implications for state, society, and military institutions. This self-serving reading of the immediate past aligned the drugged-out draftee with the long-haired flower-power pacifist as the allies of the Viet Cong.

The era since the end of conscription in the United States in the early 1970s saw the ascendancy of the doctrine of free enterprise and the reduction of the state in national life, especially in its economic dimension—a distinct contrast to the first half of the 20th century, when the era of total war strengthened collectivist tendencies in state, economy, and society and fostered state building in the United States until the 1970s. But in the first decade of the new century this otherwise sensible idea of lowering taxes has hardened into dogma in the midst of the globalization of modern markets and intruded too far into military affairs with destructive effects.

One surely goes too far to make Milton Friedman the godfather of Eric Prince and the founder of Blackwater Corporation, even if the Nobel laureate did play a role in the Nixon administration's decision to junk Selective Service. (Prince and the private military contractors grew notorious in the past decade as the epitome of a military-industrial complex gone haywire—or a kind of shadow state within a state in the midst of the Global War on Terror.) Similarly, the apparent dominance of military contractors—and those who rotate out of uniform and into the defense industry and its many offshoots—in senior levels of government and in recent combat and security-building operations under the Bush administration owes rather more to less intelligent and more rapine personages who have profited from the lopsided U.S. civil-military system of the immediate past.

The absence of conscription joined with the increasing role of market dogma in the waging of war summons to mind, especially for a European audience, historical exemplars of a worrisome kind. That is, the failure of western nation-states generally to engage the military power of its citizens in the realm of anger, hatred, and political effect appears instead to take U.S. military institutions somehow backwards to that realm before the rise of the standing army in the European experience and to open the vista to war in the early modern epoch. Military free-booters and soldiers of fortune then represented the dominant source of combat power for profit in early modern Europe. The world of the Landsknechte and of such military entrepreneurs as Wallenstein in the Thirty Years War somehow seem much more contemporary in the last decade than they did 25 years ago with the nuclear anxieties of the times.

Recent history has also seen the rise of military desperados who grew into independent political forces at the head of paramilitary organizations that slipped free from the constraints of the rule of law and western statecraft. These military desperados and their business ventures treated organized political violence as a commercial activity within warfare. One thinks in this connection of the trajectory from Ernst Röhm to Heinrich Himmler, and how the cigarette factories, which had co-financed the Sturmabeilung (SA) in the period before 1933, a decade later had mutated into the vast economic enterprises of the Schutzstaffel (SS) Wirtschafts- und Verwaltungshauptamt (WHVA). Ultimately, the authority for the Nazi concentration camp system, as well as a few of the death camps, fell to the WVHA, with its model based on the booty of ethnically cleansed populations of the European continent and the labor of huge slave work force.

The 1990s witnessed the consolidation of such trends with a particular misreading of the "lessons of Iraq" especially on the tactical and operational level in the so-called revolution in military affairs. This trademark phrase for U.S. military superiority in perpetuity also denigrated the role of ground forces drawn possibly from conscription, and signaled a cult of strategic idealism in the war colleges and the board rooms of defense contractors, which soon spread to the halls of the legislative and into society generally. This doctrine further separated the military from American society and in turn infected the latter with romantic ideas about war that have seldom worked out well.

Such romanticism should have been abruptly shattered by the Somalia operation of 1992–1993, where gunmen and pistoleros nullified U.S. advantages in arms and equipment. But strategic autism on the U.S. side took hold anyway, and the shock and awe of precision strike (manifestly a thing that obviated the need for conscripts and even democratic civil-military relations at all) was free to mutate into an end in itself, as it had under Guilo Douhet and Billy Mitchell in the 1920s. In the later version, the strategic idealism of U.S. power in the revolution of military affairs mingled with the cultural pessimism of the American right wing, with its "culture wars" to undo the 1960s in the present. Moreover, this phenomenon fed on the civil-military gap carved in part by the long-term effects of the absence of conscription, that is, the growing political homogeneity and caste mentality of the officer corps versus society generally. This phenomenon worsened in the early 1990s with the presidency of Bill Clinton and the issue of homosexuals in the armed forces. In the eyes of his critics, Clinton, an intellectual and a "draft-dodger," manifested repugnant character traits and thereby had a checkered relationship with the officer corps.

General officers had emerged in a grandiose yet skittish mood from the victories in the Cold War and the Iraq campaign, thus to nurture an ever more praetorian set of mind. This mentality arose from several sources: the Weinberger-Powell Doctrine of either all-out war or no use of military force whatsoever, in the vein of the "never again" school; the technological cult of the "revolution in military affairs"; and the siren-song of easy, swift victory in 1991—and the legends of war termination and thwarted decisive victory proffered by those observers who misunderstood the limited war aims of the first Gulf War. This jumble of doctrines, dogmas, and credos looked backward to the 20th century—and not always to its finer hours. Its authors ignored the changing face of political violence in reality (i.e. the Somalian expedition) and made the United States more vulnerable to the actual conflict in those parts of the world most plagued by warfare.

Outstanding in this national vulnerability was the unwillingness in the Bush administration in late 2001 and early 2002 to mount a general mobilization with conscription in the Global War on Terror. This policy derived in no small part from the false historical conclusions about conscription as well as a latent anti-democratic attitude among certain makers of policy, whose admixture of strategic idealism and cultural pessimism infected them with the same skepticism of popular will in wartime that proved the undoing of more worthy personalities in the past. The promiscuous abuse of total-war rhetoric in the Bush administration remained unmatched by deeds. The campaigns in Afghanistan and Iraq became protracted and attritional far more quickly than the right-wing think tanks, the savants of the joint staff, or the research wings of aerospace firms predicted in 2002. The dream of the decisive battle and total spectrum dominance with the single sweep of the information-age sickle proved a farce by the summer of 2003 as Iraq descended into chaos and the tactical and operational advantage in Afghanistan began to fade away.

The short-sighted choice by Rumsfeld to rely on the "army you have"—that is, to eschew any large-scale mobilization that could provide sufficient forces for the long haul—meant that overstretched reserve forces stumbled into roles and missions for which they were ill suited. The cardinal error of 12 September 2001, namely the choice to use regular military forces to fight the terrorist bandits—fell on the shoulders of too few troops. In the event, the under-numbered regular units of the ground forces faced repeated tours of duty in exceptionally grueling conditions of counterinsurgency and the occupation of hostile territory. Their marathon of sacrifice put them in further disequilibrium to a U.S. society that busily played casino with real estate in California and Florida.

Conclusion: The Ghost of Conscription, Civil-Military Fusion, Politicization of Soldiers, and Damage to Democratic Political Culture

The failure in the first decade of this century to achieve some kind of national mobilization with the principle of the citizen in uniform has damaged the military profession, undercut American democratic civil-military relations, and destabilized the international system of states. The legacy of the Bush-Cheney-Rumsfeld years has been to worsen the polarized and partisan bitterness of U.S. politics and society while simultaneously fostering the rise of new military institutions and doctrines that are pernicious to the endurance of American democratic customs and traditions.

The strategic and operational failures of the era 2001–2006 led to the revival of counterinsurgency doctrine in the U.S. military. In the French, British, and Israeli experience this strategy and operational concept has led to civil-military fusion, that is, to the primacy of the operational-tactical principles as superior to the making of policy on democratic principles. Such always harms democracy. Worse, this civil-military fusion, clad in the ideals and esprit de corps of elite special-operations units, has become generalized beyond the armed forces in an era of homeland security and irregular threats to national defense. The result has been a higher degree of the politicization of soldiers in U.S. life than ever before in modern memory.

These distressing phenomena took hold fairly quickly after the bogging down of U.S. military operations in Iraq. The ghost of conscription appeared in the election campaign of 2004 in the political assassination of John Kerry by the so-called Swift Boat Veterans, a right-wing group of media thugs who defamed the candidate's naval service in Indochina with innuendos about inflated claims to medals of valor. (Out of context and surely out of the comprehension of most, the small combat engagements of the final phase of the Vietnam War were unfurled in domestic politics amid a pernicious stab-in-the-back rhetoric.) In other words soldierly bravery in the past era of conscription and the present of a professional force was misused by a small group in domestic politics for selfish ends—and spun to a citizenry has not borne arms in the past generation and thus had no sense of the realities of combat.

The rise of the counterinsurgency doctrine in 2005–2006 increased the fortunes of general David Petraeus, a politically astute officer not without the shine of praetorianism to his shoulder boards. Such civil-military fusion arose because the uniformed advocates of counterinsurgency (who had otherwise spent a long exile after the Vietnam War) now marched out to the think tanks and the Sunday-morning political talk shows from their redoubts at West Point and Fort Leavenworth. The election campaign of 2008 tried once more to make military valor in the Indochina war the arbiter of presidential bona fides the better part of a half-century later. Barack Obama symbolized a particularly unmilitary personality, not least because he came of age in the era of the consolidated all-volunteer force and thus never was subject to the draft (which in an earlier era had made many seek a reserve commission). The military role he faced in 2009 was especially daunting granted the campaign promise to wrap up the Iraqi campaign and to escalate the Afghan campaign through the counterinsurgency strategy that had unfolded since 2006 in Iraq. To be sure, this grand strategy has embraced a conservative approach to an exceptionally difficult situation that has not made use of conscription, even though one might have imagined a reconstituted military draft for the occasion; Obama better manifests a tradition of citizen and service than did his notoriously uncivil predecessors.

An exit strategy even from the Afghan campaign was announced in early 2010, a circumstance that allows one to ask: What are the likely long-term effects of the themes analyzed here for young American citizens in uniform and civilian dress? That is, how can one explain to those who will be most affected by the ghost of conscription the evolution and character of U.S. strategic culture in the wake of the unevenly shared burdens of war and citizenship? The end of the draft in the 1970s, however, has promoted a military romanticism in political culture that interacts with cultural pessimism in domestic politics and untenable strategic goals in security policy. The lack of the draft harms a vital link between the energy of democracy and the imperatives of national defense, which can never be entrusted to a warrior caste or soldiers of fortune. The political misuse of the legacy and heritage of the citizen-soldier in domestic politics—as a kind of emotional catharsis for those who do nothing for the soldier other than rhetoric and pathos connected with the entertainment industry—have also damaged the profession of the soldier and the efficacy of U.S. arms in the long run.

Already there are calls from those who have served at the front for years of multiple combat tours in Iraq and Afghanistan for a return to the draft. These soundings represent much more than the frustration of a few cranky reservists who would like to return to their regularly scheduled lifestyles. A real strategic aspect attends the proposal: The outbreak of a serious and unexpected passage of arms, with U.S. interests clearly at risk, will lay bare the overextension of U.S. forces in a shocking way. But the real issue here is the sharing of the burden of the nation's defense and the damage that inequalities in this burden do to the health of U.S. democratic institutions. Even the rhetorical distinction between "them" and "us," American civilians and the U.S. military, enshrines a fundamental inequality that, as this paper has shown, has an inglorious past, to say nothing of its clouded future.

Un-exorcised or simply unexamined, the ghost of conscription will continue to be a force in political life, especially in the case of those who have summoned it for selfish and partisan purposes. Thus do they damage the fundamentals of U.S. democratic civil-military institutions, which ultimately reflect the society and its most cherished norms ... for which, of course, the military fights in the first place.

13. Strain on Honor: Aspects of Soldierly Ethics in the Past and Present[*]

After more than a decade at war, American society, perhaps not surprisingly, has assigned more prominence to military commanders and high-ranking officers—sometimes as public officials but rather more often as celebrities. A fair few of these figures, including flag officers still serving in uniform, embrace their star status and the publicity that goes with it, as has occurred periodically since the foundation of the Republic in the 18th century. But of late, the top brass has not always shone as brightly in the spotlight as anyone might hope. Instead, a tide of tabloid scandal that has suffused life in Hollywood, Wall Street, Capitol Hill, and sometimes even the White House has risen to engulf the senior ranks of defense ministries and general staffs.

Ten or more years ago, one might have attributed such high-profile flame-outs to the unfamiliarity that serious senior officers were presumed to have with the public-relations machinery and social-media niceties of this digitalized age of the unending news cycle. But these officers have the steepest part of this learning curve well behind them by now. The real issue, then, lies rather deeper in the essence, ethos, and ethical experience of the 21st-century rock-star general—in the strength of discipline and honor in democratic civil-military relations as well as the military customs of command, obedience, morale, education, and training in their higher aspects.

This curious development unfolded in the wake of the war termination phase of the global war on terror, the endurance of the global depression, and the generalized discomfiture of hierarchies and elites. The most dramatic episodes of scandal and discredit unfolded at the same time that steep cuts to defense budgets in NATO countries, and especially in the United States took hold, boding a dim fu-

---

[*] Revised version of a presentation at the Austrian National Defense Academy on 14 November 2012.

ture for the many soldiers who had stood to arms in the decade of combat in the wake of 11 September 2001.

The period of conflict that began in late September 2001 has left its mark on a generation of young men and women whose enthusiasm for soldierly ideals of duty, honor and country, as well as their willingness to bear the burdens of irregular combat and constabulary service, have been exemplary. But this example of martial bearing has a contested political and ethical meaning especially now amid the stock-taking that must unfold in the dawn of what is more or less peace of an ambiguous kind. The story of these men and women who have stayed out of the limelight is the one that matters the most, all lurid headlines about general officers in extremis notwithstanding.

This model soldiering in its variety awaits its full honor in the military as well as in society in the realm of war and memory in a way that departs from perverted voyeurism of military life and the face of battle—a stylized and unhelpful view with particular currency for civilians who see war as a big-screen adventure and who glorify the battlefield and barracks square (which they have never really seen or endured other than in a movie or imbedded propaganda) as a corrective to the messiness of pluralistic society that has strayed into the perdition of diversity and wide-horizon gender choices that strike horror in the hearts of certain white men of advanced age.

This hard service at arms, without the heaps of lucre and prestigious lectureships on "leadership," forms one vital part of the strain on honor, that is, the professional and thereby ethical failures among senior officers. One is reminded of Erich Ludendorff's generalization about the British Army in 1914–1918 ("an army of lions led by donkeys") might well apply in the contemporary example, as well—particularly amid the diminished and distant civilian insight into/oversight of military affairs that prefers celebrity to leadership. The following lines analyze the cause and effect of this phenomenon and speculate about its place in American statecraft, the self-image and ethos of soldiers, and the efforts made by all for the common defense.

* * * *

On both sides of the Atlantic, these core features of military life have come under stresses that can well be circumscribed under the heading of Morris Janowitz's work on the professional soldier of more than a half century ago: the strain on honor. (In Germany, the strain on honor has plagued not so much serving generals as their civilian bosses.) In his magisterial—and entirely un-plagiarized—sociological analysis of the soldierly profession in the age of total war, Janowitz highlighted the need to adapt central principles of martial ethos—essentially pre-modern, estate-based, and feudal conceptions of honor and discipline as well as the ethical demands of combat—to the managerial, technological paradigm of western state and society in the mid-20th century. The tensions inherent in this situation gave rise to particular strains on the professional self-image of the soldier as well as the theory and practice of military leadership and civil-military relations.

This strain, in Janowitz's view, was especially intense in the mid–20th-century United States and was prominent in the biography of such figures as MacArthur, himself one of a cohort of more or less 19th-century men at arms who began their military lives in the early 20th century and found themselves plunked into the epoch of limited war in the atomic age, the managerial maelstrom of the postwar corporate regime, the jet and space age, and the new national security state of the early Cold War.

The serial disgrace of senior generals and the growing strain on the honor of soldiers in public life in recent memory might be said to have begun with the demonstrative break with the Weinberger-Powell Doctrine in 2002–2003, an event symbolized by the ill-fated statement on weapons of mass destruction by Colin Powell, co-namesake of this program of last-resort and lowest-impact armed force and co-claimant of the operational brilliance of the Kuwaiti campaign 1991, when the former general had briefed the air and ground phases of the operation with the rout of Saddam Hussein's forces. Now in February 2003, as secretary of State, Powell was dispatched to the U.N. Security Council to present the WMD story touted by Vice President Dick Cheney and Deputy Secretary of Defense Paul Wolfowitz as a pretext for the Iraqi invasion. This event destroyed Powell's reputation with the dishonor of either willful or negligent strategic deception at the highest levels of command. Powell's ignominious downfall was only to be followed by further episodes of the political and strategic failure of senior officers in the Iraqi and Afghan campaigns until 2006, when the Bush administration changed its mantra from "mission accomplished" to "hearts and minds" à la counterinsurgency (COIN)—and a succession of superstar commanders stepped up to lend these grand tactics a face and a carefully managed persona.

In the year 2013, this predicament is entangled in the role of soldierly celebrity in public life in a period of rapid change in state, society, and armed conflict. Then there is added the dimension of democratic civil-military relations in irregular warfare on a protracted scale. In turn, this dimension includes the element of the temper of the crowd as it shows itself in social networks in the broadest sense— what conventionally might be called public opinion or even morale. "Morale" is often a source of the deepest anxieties of soldiers who make frequent mention of their honor in connection with morale and organized violence for whatever political ends in the present. The last question borrows something from Clausewitz's categories of anger and hatred as phenomena of war in reality versus war in theory. This element of classical military theory about the inner lives of soldiers might help to illuminate the political discomfiture of senior defense civilians and senior officers that has become legion in the past few years.

* * * * *

And a bit of classical theory would have gone a long way in the recent episodes in this story of the soldier and his or her honor— "brass gone wild," or gone off the rails, or at least sorely scuffed with an off-color glint that reflects something less noble than the glean of fine metals of the field marshal's baton in the sunlight. Take, for example, the bold, maverick, new-broom theater commander, Stanley A. McChrystal, himself the son of a general, noted for his ascetic capacity to elude sleep and ward off body fat, who took command of the Afghan campaign in 2009, a promotion that came with a fourth star. There, he set about trying to box in the President of the United States with a lopsided operational plan—an old trick of the Joint Chiefs of Staff going back at least a half century to the beginning of the Vietnam War.

And why not? He had already convinced the same Senate that confirmed this appointment to overlook his purposeful dissembling about the friendly-fire death in Afghanistan of pro football star-turned-Army Ranger Pat Tillman in 2004, when McChrystal was commander of Joint Special Forces Command (JSOC). He also successfully sidestepped the allegations that the outfit that he rode to fame in 2006, when it called in the airstrike that led to the death of al Qaeda leader Abu Musab al-Zarqawi in Iraq, made a regular practice of abusing detainees at Camp Nama. While nearly three dozen of his subordinates were disciplined for these actions, McChrystal himself went on to bigger and even more exalted things.

In the event, he courted the press in a reckless manner akin to a sports, finance, or music celebrity; and he openly scorned the national command (particularly Vice President Joseph Biden) and senior defense civilians in a way that resembled the most egregious outbursts of Douglas MacArthur in the years from 1935 until 1951. This swashbuckling behavior properly resulted in McChrystal's abrupt and forcible early retirement, though he retained his fourth star—an unwarranted act of largesse by those civilians whom he and his inner circle had demeaned in print.

The deformation of civil-military relations at the heart of the matter continued unabated. No sooner had Stanley McChrystal's general officer regalia been consigned to some vitrine in the West Point alumni pantheon, he strutted into a fine career as a lecturer in an Ivy League classroom—where his students were barred from taking notes on his teachings about "leadership," which amounted to collections of his bizarre aphorisms of COIN and special forces dogma. This light-infantry ethos deployed into the lives of aspiring young elite students marks a flourish of pure militarism in the middle of the most liberal collegiate bastions and a nail in the heart, if not the coffin, of sensible democratic civil-military relations.

The treasure and status imparted to the ex-general by the adoring but ill-informed claque of readers of the *Wall Street Journal*, war-monger neo-conservative grandees in right-of-center (and right-of-right) think tanks, and the Yale University Board of Directors in the 21st-century power elite symbolize the strains on the honor of the soldier that end in corruption and substantial harm to the veracity and authority of the higher echelons of command and thus to the inner structure of armies. Instead of a legacy of opprobrium for insubordination, if not outright praetorianism, vis-à-vis his civilian leadership, McChrystal been flattered with five-figure speaking honoraria, invitations to sit on corporate boards, and scads of consulting gigs, all of which, per public appearance, net him well in excess of the average American worker's salary in this unhappy epoch of recession.

McChrystal's cornucopia contrasts particularly starkly with the slim pickings of subsistence wages that reward many veterans of the Iraqi and Afghan campaigns newly entrapped in the basement of civilian life. Their lives unfold far from Yale and are plagued by the baleful effects on body, soul, and loved ones of too many combat deployments in irregular warfare in reality. Their lives are damaged by the rigors of demobilization and force reductions as well as delayed promotion boards and by illness—physical and mental. Meanwhile, their one-time commander continues, unapologetically, to ply his disdain for the basic rules of democracy, transparency, accountability, and perhaps even human rights in a period of fame and fortune that has, by now, stretched well beyond its Warholian 15-minute limit, to say nothing of the bounds of honor. In 2017, the ex general—now a Linked In-vetted expert on leadership in a global sense as renumerated in the Ivy League and other academies for the aspiring 1-percenters—took his editorial pen in hand to defend the

U.S. National Public Broadcast Service and its children's program, "Sesame Street," as being central to the needs of children on the path to citizenship.

* * * * *

As if the McChrystal episode were not enough of a tarnished-brass story to jolt contemporary civil-military relations back to some sense of purpose, in the fall of 2012, a raft of hormone-drenched emails between two women jealous of each other for their place in the ever-growing entourage of ex-General David Petraeus, once the four-star commander of the International Security Assistance Force (ISAF) and U.S. Central Command (CENTCOM) and then director of the U.S. Central Intelligence Agency (CIA), emerged amid a state police investigation laden with political intrigue and sexual tension. What seemed for all the world at first telling as nothing more than the script of a reality television episode in camouflage, in fact, signified a stranger-than-fiction bimbo eruption on the strategic level—replete with widely reported breaches of data security—that meant the doom of the generation's most famous soldier. A central European of a certain age could not help but be reminded of the Hitler/Fritsch/von Blomberg scandal in 1938, but the full bodied Paula Broadwell and Jill Kelley were far more riveting than Erna Gruhn, who, of course, neither wrote books, ran marathons, nor threatened other shapely women in the Berlin demi-monde with poison-pen letters.

The Petraeus scandal—which went from bad to worse and from tragedy (the affair also threatened the career of the U.S. and ISAF theater commander, Marine General John R. Allen, who had been headed from the rigors of irregular war in southern Asia to the just reward of the NATO operational headquarters at Mons before the Petraeus scandal broke) to farce as the U.S. presidential campaign seemed to chug along on an almost entirely separate track—suggests even more rot at the top of a structure that ultimately directs the U.S. national defense ... while holding its senior-most personalities to rather different standards of conduct than apply to civilian leaders or to mid-career and mid-level officers of the U.S. armed forces.

Petraeus can hardly claim to have been back-footed by the media as his scandal unfolded—not when he staked so much of his later career on his ability to shape his media profile to maximum advantage. Presumably Petraeus, who attained the rank of lieutenant colonel during the first Gulf War, learned from observation then how well-scripted military leaders could set the tone for media coverage in the post-Vietnam and post–Cold-War epoch and, thus, for the discourse back home, especially in Washington, amid the growing public acceptance of semi-censored military affairs and sub-rosa conduct of lightning war. When Petraeus finally took to the battlefield for the first time in 2003, as a major general in Iraq, he had some ideas on how to wage the campaign for American hearts and minds; this sense ripened into his rediscovered principles of counterinsurgency, with its strong component of mass persuasion in pluralistic domestic politics. Thus, characteristic of the Petraeus approach was his deftly wielded information operations offensive at the core of the doctrine of counterinsurgency and the much-trumpeted Iraqi surge.

In the course of this project, Petraeus added into his ISAF and CENTCOM headquarters a young woman whose bona fides included USMA graduate, reserve officer, athlete, fashion model draped atop machine guns, trophy wife, doctoral student, and defense-intellectual camp follower, and with whom he presently began a sexual liaison. Meanwhile, she published a breathless account of his ring-knocking career from the thin gray line to the pinnacle of wartime command. The American custom of hagiography of generals notwithstanding, this book embodied celebrity schlock of the most pedestrian kind, with every platitude included in the hyperventilating prose about the savior-general mashed together with the strategic fad of COIN and its utility for a variety of things beyond the battlefield.

Paula Broadwell was at once similar to the storied paramours and kept women maintained by such luminaries as Douglas MacArthur, Dwight D. Eisenhower, and Mark Clark or even the fictitious Miss Scott, the va-va-voom secretary/mistress of General Buck Turgidson in Stanley Kubrick's film "Dr. Strangelove"—but radically different in how she embodied 21st-century gender roles and women at arms. She aspired to be a female version of Petraeus himself, at junior rank, as warrior and soldier-scholar as well as mother and woman of malicious animal magnetism. Thus, she could break the bonds of her sex with the West Point Class ring as well as endless, uphill marathon runs—at least so long as her secret passion in the shadow of the command banner remained, well, secret.

Such discretion, however, was beyond Broadwell, since the ardor that surely was the partner to her physical energy led her to send threatening emails to yet another woman in the trace of the command group, the dark, radiant, and buxom Jill Kelley. Beset by Broadwell's poison-pen e-mails and seething jealousy about Kelley's apparent closeness to "Peaches," Kelley (along with her twin sister)—the confidante and, in contravention of the normal staffing in CO-COM headquarters, the de facto social secretary of more than one general in Tampa, Florida, and HQ CENTCOM—in turn, appealed to a politically motivated FBI agent for help against Broadwell's cyber-stalking. This man, in turn, apparently nourished his own lust for Kelley with six-pack–centric selfies sexted to less-than-anonymous and clearly insecure cell phones. (This FBI agent also made a little putsch of his own in betraying the love triangle to members of Congress intent on damaging Barack Obama by any means and modality.)

Once the scandal of the "real housewives" of the supreme command in Kabul and Tampa broke in the fall of 2012, the images of two women solidified the public perception of this profoundly odd affair of the generals. The soldier-scholar/-triathlete's going-steady pose, pink cheeks, athlete's physique, and superior smirk, well practiced on her book tour and television appearances, contrasted with the bespectacled expression of quiet rage on the rather more maternal face of the general's West Point sweetheart (in the long-gone year of 1974, Hollister "Holly" Knowlton was the daughter of the USMA commandant), now wife wronged so publically after nearly four decades of building his four-star career. Holly Petraeus managed to lend a certain no-nonsense dignity to the task of standing by her man amid a top-of-the-news-day humiliation, nowadays a dreary stock performance in public life. Broadwell instead emanated the female aesthetic of the postmodern age made grand by another busty woman with a gun, Sarah Palin, whose mixture of celebrity, rapid-fire weapons, and political affect hinted at the mainstreaming of pornographic archetypes within the 21st-century manifestation of the paranoid style in the American body politic.

If anything, one might lament the relative naivety of the civilians who, since about 2003 or so, who have blindly anointed Petraues the single-handed hero of the so-called long war, the reincarnation of Lawrence—while never suspecting that the general knew enough about shared Yahoo! accounts to evade the prying eyes of even the CIA's security people (for a while, anyway). His coterie of 1-percenters, who read the *Wall Street Journal*, fill the coffers of the Heritage Foundation and AIPAC, and openly toy with forms of government devoid of legislatures, courts, and a public, awoke in the fall of 2012 to find that their hero of duty, honor, and country had waded into the muck of adultery—a crime under the Uniform Code of Military Justice for which the general's former military subordinates routinely have their careers foreshortened. But the civilian leadership and the chattering classes that so often call its tune sought out this unreflected civil-military blurring—and have no right to be surprised at how the story eventuated. The penchant for taking the top brass at its word—without any follow-on scrutiny or quality control as required by democratic civil-military relations and oversight of the armed forces and its leadership—bespeaks a very serious problem in the business-as-usual of the Global War on Terror, a failure on both the civilian and the military side of the COIN.

How the corps of young company grade officers, NCOs, and volunteers after 11 September 2001, who have endured the deprivations of war and service in irregular combat since early 2002, might have registered their disappointment with the ideals of honor and service was more or less lost in the hysteria of the tabloids and the roar of the crowd in the blogs and tweets. Nowhere in this scene could one see the broken bond of trust between the general and his soldiers with their sense of betrayal by those who led them. And yet, there is the real strain on honor—just beyond the glare of the photo flashes.

* * * * *

But the Petraeus/Allen scandal seemed only to open the floodgates as more scandals of tarnished brass followed—while the civil-military fusion acquired even stranger partisan charges. Yet another U.S. theater commander, General "Kip" Ward, carried American strategic influence into Africa with the newly formed African Command (located, curiously enough, in southern Germany), not least to fight the terrorists there, but also partook in the lavish balms of international security affairs along with his large retinue and expensive office furniture. These excesses sparked the ire of the guardians of the public treasure, whereupon his civilian bosses relieved him of his duties.

Ward was followed as AFRICOM commander in March 2011 by General Carter Ham, who spent a year and half overcoming Ward's tendentious leadership and solidifying the command's role in U.S. strategy in Africa. A year and a half later, the Secretary of Defense rather abruptly announced the nomination of General David M. Rodriguez as Ham's replacement, which may or may not have coincided with Ham's regularly scheduled rotation. In the overheated political blogosphere, particularly among inside-the-Beltway pundits, the story circulated that General Carter Ham really lost his position when he undertook to send some kind of armed assistance to the U.S. diplomatic mission in Benghazi, Libya, when it was attacked on the night of 11 September 2012. The assault claimed four lives, including U.S. Ambassador J. Christopher Stevens—and promptly acceded to full-on the stab-in-the-back status among conspiracy theorists and Obama-bashers when the administration sought to pin the unrest primarily on localized reaction to an ugly, if rather obscure, anti-Muslim video.

In the circles that insist that the president purposefully left Americans in harm's way in Benghazi, neither coincidence nor Army detailing could suffice to explain the commander's sudden departure. (The plot—and the invective—only thickened when, in late October 2012, the U.S. Navy, amid an inspector general's investigation, reassigned Rear Admiral Charles Gaouette, who had been commander of the *USS John C. Stennis* strike group deployed in the Middle East.) The suggestion that the president should be more deferential, if not reverential, to his generals is at least as troubling here as any White House spin-control efforts, which at least comport with one well-established, if controversial, school of thought on the constitutional exercise of executive authority in matters of national security and foreign affairs. Indeed, the fact that the same partisan hecklers who tend to proclaim the necessity of a muscular and presumably civilian presidency (as long as their guy is in office) also advocate a retreat from, if not an inversion of, the principle of civilian control of the military is an irony that seems to have eluded every last pundit who weighed in.

* * * *

The issue of what ails the top brass is significant, because the respective downfalls of these men beg sufficient explanation other than the stab-in-the-back (McChrystal) and beyond the sadly normal over-sexed powerful public figure (Petraeus) as part of the transformation of the armed forces and the officer corps within American state and society from the last century into the present. There is a need here to get the story right, and to preclude the inevitable ravages of the tales told by the terrible simplifiers, who want a man on horseback to fix the rotten state and society. These personages will soon seize on the scandalized and otherwise politicized general officer in the extended crisis of state, society, and economy as some kind of Georges Ernest Boulanger, Smedly Butler, or Paul von Hindenburg; or Vincent Matoon Scott, the general officer intent on a putsch in "Seven Days in May"; or the disaffected French officers in the OAS intent on the murder of De Gaulle in the war termination phase of the Algerian war and memorialized in the work, the "Day of the Jackal."

The voice of common sense as concerns whatever misshapen ideas and practices might obtain in the high command that constitute the strain on honor emerged ca. 2007 in an at first obscure essay within military circles by a young U.S. Army armor officer, Lt. Colonel Paul Yingling. He gave voice to the perspectives of a younger generation of officers from the front who had been left cold by the political shenanigans of such figures as Tommy Franks and John Abizaid, whom he damned for their incapacity to adjust ends to means in the downward spiral of the Iraqi conflict from 2003 until 2006, and the handful of officers in the entourage of then-Defense Secretary Donald Rumfeld, who opportunistically tried their putsch-lite on Secretary of Defense Rumsfeld in the infamous "revolt of the generals" in the latter part of 2006.

Taking exception to the official heroic saga told by many of the post-Vietnam all-volunteer force, Yingling, the son of a general himself and a combat veteran with a fine record, interpreted how the professional and ethical failure of general officers as far back as the 1970s had led to American defeat in both Vietnam in 1975 and the strategic setbacks in Iraq around 2005–2006. Most significantly, Yingling's ideas showed none of the militarist influence of MacArthur and his acolytes as has come down to McMaster, McChrystal, and Petraeus and which strains to the breaking point the ethical fundamentals of the officer corps within the frame of the U.S. constitution and the more or less western experience of officer-ship and war. From Yingling's view, the deficiency in the heart and brains does not implicate some technical deficiency in the operational level of command or an individual failing here and there that damns the specific person and leaves the institution of high command untouched. Instead, he has proclaimed a crisis in American generalship, as an institution, that derives from the "intellectual and moral failures common to America's general officer corps in Vietnam and Iraq."

This ethical decay manifests most clearly as a consistent retreat into fantasies of "military culture," that is, a sense of wronged and wounded honor—what Elliot Cohen in the mid-1990s called "Upton's Ghost"—with a disdain for civilians and democracy. This attitude among military leaders culminates in failures to provide the civilian overseers with accurate or honest insights into the battlefield with a corresponding sense of policy in a democracy. It begins with an uncertain sense of how officers must address the higher aspects of war and the making of policy without MacArthur-tinged bromides that no longer fit within the ranks of the military—and how they ought to do it on a sound professional basis that includes ethics, though perhaps rather less prime-time television coverage, as a part of democratic civil-military relations.

* * * * *

Yingling's argument was taken up in 2009 by a defense civilian and academic, Richard H. Kohn, a scholarly authority on the ethos of soldiers in the American state with significant military experience of his own. In these issues, Kohn discerns a crisis, a decline in professionalism in the fundamentals of the U.S. armed forces that has struck its officer corps, among other ways, in its ethical failings in the midst of strategic tribulations for which strategy and operations have proffered something less than total victory. The imperatives of the new Spartans to mass overwhelming force at the decisive point and to accept no substitute for victory remain the most profound ideas in U.S. strategic culture and practice. Kohn notes that the "overuse and under-strength" of the U.S. military that begins to explain the halting progress toward genuine independence and democracy in either Iraq or Afghanistan.

The key weakness, in the estimation of the former Air Force chief historian, has been not weapons and materiel after a decade and more of fulsome defense budgets, which lately have begun to collapse. Instead the declining capability of command that Kohn detects around him owes to infirmities ingrained in what might be called the brains, heart, and soul of the American military establishment—three interconnected challenges to healthy military professionalism. First, and most pressing as concerns the brain and heart, is the neglect by the highest echelons of strategy in its classical sense as a central focus of the leadership of the armed forces. On this point, Kohn agrees with Yingling about both cause and effect: "Discovering the so-called operational level of war in the 1970s, the Army seemed to lose interest in strategy."

In this connection, the Army went back to Moltke's trap about the separation of politics and war—a core article of faith for disappointed officers the world over. All four armed services have demonstrated this disengagement from the strategic level, according to Kohn. As a direct consequence, "Iraq has become the metaphor for an absence of strategy"—a point also made by Hew Strachan at the beginning of the war. This gap was then filled with the series of improvisations from 2005 onward, in which Petraeus took the lead with the counterinsurgency doctrine amid the baleful effects of perpetual war at home and abroad on democracy and society.

A second challenge, as concerns the soul, arises in the rapid increase of politicization in and of the American officer corps. General McChrystal's case certainly calls up the specter of the uniformed military seeking to manipulate the political decision-making process as well as the explicit (and frequently expletive-laden) lack of regard for his civilian leadership that he tolerated among his subordinate officers, if the Rolling Stone article represents at all accurately the days-in-the-life experience of McChrystal's headquarters. While the politicization among certain of the higher-ranked officers in the U.S. armed forces can be said to have begun as early as the 1950s if not earlier, this phenomenon has gained strength particularly as the generals' stars became dull in the Iraqi insurgency of the last decade. The vitriol in domestic politics in the past 15 years, and especially since the election of Barack Obama has worsened this trend, which was already fully and unhappily developed in the Clinton administration in the early 1990s.

Kohn identifies the third of his tripartite challenges to military professionalism today as careerism, which concerns the soul and strikes at the heart of ethics at arms as it really exists in practice—in contrast to the theory of instruction in academies and defense colleges, which begets "risk aversion and sometimes to cover-ups, avoidance of responsibility, and other behaviors that harm the ability of the armed forces to succeed in battle." Yingling similarly laments the "powerful pressures for conformity" and the devastating effects of officers going along to get ahead. Thus, we hardly can be surprised to find instances of spectacularly questionable military leadership occurring regularly in the past quarter century or so that has done little for or with ethics at arms. As Yingling notes, "[t]he system that produces our generals does little to reward creativity and moral courage."

Worse still, both Yingling and Kohn agree, the system seems to do even less to punish moral or ethical failings other than to pillory the lowest-ranking person in a manner that for a while absolves the higher-ups of responsibility, but which has the final effect of compromising all concerned. Observers who tend toward neither cynicism nor conspiracy theories may still see in McChrystal's promotion to four-star and his gentle tumble from presidential favor as evidence of a phoned-in slap on the wrist for an escalating pattern of professional and ethical disregard for the classical codex of the American officer as disciplined and obedient to constitutional safeguards.

Ethical instruction at all levels of command aside, of the question remains: what flaws and defects operate in the ethical inner structure of leadership, command, morale, obedience, and ethos in the U.S. armed forces, as Yingling and Kohn have properly pointed out, and which have lately been so obvious in the downfall of Petraeus?

* * * * *

No sooner have Petraeus' stars been consigned to the murk than a new man with shoulder boards has risen to prominence and celebrity in the wake of the Snowden defection to Russia and his revelation of NSA's Prism all-horizons intelligence operation. The commanding General of the National Security Agency (NSA), General Keith Alexander, dressed in his faux Winfield Scott or Ulysses S.

Grant full dress blue uniform, tells Congress that he cannot reveal classified issues in the face of global outrage to the PRISM operation. Conversely, a few weeks later in the summer of 2013, he admonishes his hecklers at a Las Vegas convention of "black hat" hackers and technicians of the brave new world of digital bedlam and challenges them to read the constitution and also meekly to submit to a militarized worldwide signal intelligence operation in which the citizens of the globe are all potential insurgents.

This posture and the posturing shows the real reason for the scandal of the generals and the downfall of such figures as McChrystal, Petraeus, and no doubt others: strategic overreach born out of uncontrolled escalation in the dimension of anger and hatred and a blindness to the balance of ends and means for the common defense, that is the imposition of some coherent political limit on organized violence. Is Alexander in his own mind a latter day Winfield Scott or Joseph Totten, bravely erecting a series of computer bastions astride the global commons to ward off the dark invaders of cyber war on the vital infrastructure, as the Third System of fortresses of the first half of the 19th century built a series of coastal bastions to protect a young America from a European invasion in the age of the Monroe Doctrine? Or, more likely and more ominously, is Alexander in fact a cyber version of Curtis LeMay or even of General Jack D. Ripper in "Dr. Strangelove," albeit bereft of propellers and jet engines, but with the ultimate weapon of a really big whiz-bang constituted of first-strike digital death from above (or below, or from inside à la Stuxnet in Iran recently)?

The rise of U.S. Cyber Command continues the process that began with Petraeus's overhyped, if under-considered, rediscovery of counterinsurgency but carries it forth with other, more irresistible means native to the digital age. Will cyber war become the new Massive Retaliation and the huge NSA complex in the Utah uplands as the 21st-century iteration of the storied Panopticon, the equivalent of SAC headquarters of this epoch, wielding a cyber cudgel to mass overwhelming digital force at the decisive point? Will this process thus empower the rigors of the battlefield and the garrison square further to be applied abroad and at home with neither real civilian oversight nor legal recourse available, despite the uptick in public appearances and ham-fisted attempts by senior brass at mass persuasion? Winfield Scott's fortresses were defenses, connected to the civil-military fundamentals of the early 19th century Republic—the constitution, the citizen soldier and the military engineer as Thomas Jefferson's ideal of nation builder. This generalization can hardly be said to apply to NSA in its new role in the 21st century.

The strain on honor arises from the manner in which contemporary war fought with special forces, drones, and now cyber megaton bombs has knocked down the old borders of war and spread to a battlefield without a horizon in three dimensions and in which everyone is a combatant or potential combatant in a manner that makes even the thermonuclear war of, say, 1958, seem somehow limited in its scope. Irregular warfare with a religious inflection and its escalation of counterinsurgency causes civil-military fusion in which operational tactical imperatives of security as seen by constabulary soldiers, neck-deep in a combination of counterinsurgency and internal security operations, finally poison domestic politics and collapses the limits of discipline in generalized violence and the escalating hunt for enemies within and insurgents at all points of the compass. That is, all ills in society are seen by an ever more constabulary but also deeply unsettled military burdened with the strain on honor as an insurgency of one kind or another and, thus, must be suppressed more or less by the same organized violence.

In this escalation and transformation of anger and hatred in war as understood by Clausewitz, the generals, especially the household names, at the head of the armed forces are losing the loyalty and obedience of his or her own troops with this fussy over-focus on the cult of celebrity and the temptations of power out of their fear of a collapse of morale that are classical. Worse, the distractions of fame and its aftermath exacerbate the incapacity to limit this violence to a coherent political end that can be sustained by a democratic nation.

The scandals of generals arise from the professional rupture of the ideals of command and long-nurtured principles of war in more or less the conventional sense, a process that unfolded from 1945 through 11 September 2001. Some wrongly portrayed this development as a strategic revolution or a revolution in military affairs; in reality, it was the violent reaction of the weak and dispossessed certain parts of the world to the leading role of the United States in the Middle East, the high-water mark of this power and its culmination point of power then to shift and the fresh tendency toward violence that is the hallmark of this epoch. This rupture in the fundamentals of command has, since 11 September 2001, created a panic at home and abroad about the efficacy of conventional military power and national defense as such traditions of professional competence are swept away by the dynamics of violence and the forces in state and society that lead to the state of emergency—which is the most lethal trap for the professional soldier and his or her ethical fundamentals.

The case of ex-Lieutenant General Michael Flynn in the 2016 election campaign lies outside the space of this inquiry (originally from the year 2012), but his discomfiture and likely role as an agent of Russian influence in an American presidential election signifies how the strain on honor and the civil-military effects of the soldierly profession of prolonged anti-jihadist war and geopolitical rupture demand the attention of scholarly inquiry as well as the interest of American citizens concerned with their own survival.

The core of the problem of the strain on honor lies in the contempt for human dignity and professional codex of irregular war and internal security that has infected the armed forces in its constabulary role and that in no way recognizes the more fundamental ethical challenge of command in the war on terror to resist the ever seductive temptation of state terror that arises from civil-military fusion. In its failure to achieve its own strategic objectives in either Iraq or Afghanistan, the war—and its superstar warriors—those who speak the most of the soldier's honor have gradually begun to cripple democracy already roiled by crises. Meanwhile, these new elites and the horde of deltas and epsilons would impose authoritarian, if not totalitarian, practices on state and society with concentration camps, torture, and all-horizons worldwide surveillance, all of which corrupt the moral essentials of generals and soldiers alike.

14. Ethics and the U.S. Armed Forces: Some Reflections amid the Turbulence*

An inquiry into the character of ethics as a feature of the U.S. armed forces in the year 2010–2011 must survey the past ten years in American state, society, and economy in wartime. Such a discussion also must take into account the ethical evolution of the U.S. armed forces in what might be described as their classical form in the 18th, 19th, and even 20th centuries—clearly as part of the development of society at large.

Especially today, one must undertake such an analysis free of the polemics about the profession of soldiers in a pluralist society that operates on both sides of the Atlantic in the minds and words of those who know little of the world of soldiers but nonetheless disdain it. On the other hand, those who are so unfamiliar with soldiers and their ethos and ethics—other than perhaps what appears in films and at antique military regalia fairs—as well as those who seek to replicate this misbegotten "way of the warrior" in civilian institutions and society for dubious political or cultural reasons do figure into this article, at least as warnings and worst cases. Such misconceptions and misuses of military professionalism often harm the ethical fundamentals of soldiers.

In contrast, this inquiry arises from an abiding theoretical and practical concern for the professional durability and ethical horizon of men and women in uniform, many of whom are colleagues and students of the present authors not only in the setting of a defense university but in the echelons of strategic and operational command and at the front amid multiple conflicts. In the authors' experience, such soldiers, sailors, and airmen/-women are, almost without exception, persons of the highest professional and ethical standards. The

* Originally published as Donald Abenheim and Carolyn Halladay, "Ethics and the Armed Forces: Some Reflections Amid the Turbulence," in Uwe Hartmann et al., eds. *Jahrbuch Innere Fuehrung 2011: Ethik als Geistige Ruestung* (Berlin: Miles Verlag, 2013), pp. 282–303.

authors of this essay are themselves defense civilians, and they have devoted their professional lives to public service in the company of soldiers and have taken a keen interest in the military profession not the least as a sublime aspect of citizenship in a democratic state. While many ideas and issues here have emerged before—and have been well analyzed by others as concerns the ethical and professional code of men and women at arms—our effort here derives from our young colleagues in uniform, who regularly confront us with these same questions about the deeper meaning of their profession in our daily teaching, research, and consultancy duties, after more than a few superior officers in their intermediate chain of command have answered these questions with dogma and polemics taken from the television screen or the blogosphere. Our question and theirs, essentially, is whether soldierly ethics reflect and advance the civil-military health of this democracy.

Ethics in the sense of a professional code in course of the working day of the soldier and sailor—as in "Do not sexually harass subordinates" and "Refrain from cheating on the travel claim for the latest trip to northern Virginia"—forms a secondary area of inquiry in this analysis. These routine and, one might also say, civilian aspects of ethics in the U.S. armed forces stand more or less in the same state of health as they do in any large American corporation or the California state university system—for better and worse, as we note below. The center of gravity in ethics and soldier here concerns the role of ethics as symbolized in command, obedience, morale, and discipline in the extreme case of conflict, war, and combat, and especially the role of ethics in the higher echelons of command as these manifest themselves in the body of the armed forces in protracted conflict.

For example, in the year 2010, one of the influential figures in the brains of the U.S. military as it has emerged after this decade of conflict, H.R. McMaster, lectured young soldiers on the shape of war in the 21st century and the links between a classical understanding of ethical education and training and contemporary military doctrine. McMaster's reputation relies on his recent war record on various fronts and his role in the redrafting of operational doctrine toward the needs of counterinsurgency and security building. Most important, however, has been his earlier retelling of an old tale in the vein of Emory Upton, nearly but not quite forgotten, that is, of the U.S. professional soldier's unease with pluralistic state and society in the face of the requirements of modern war.

This redrafting of the Uptonian professional credo emerged in a historical monograph of the 1990s on the political failures of the Joint Chiefs of Staff in the 1960s vis-à-vis their civilian masters at the time of the Vietnam War. McMaster's lecture on ethics proceeds from the primacy of operational doctrine as subordinating ethics and professional conceptions of soldierly honor, a hierarchy that itself perhaps best illustrates the challenges of soldierly honor and self-image in the realms of ethics and ethos that are interpreted below. Despite his plea for historical understanding of the soldier's task, his ahistorical and institutionally self-serving gloss on counterinsurgency leads to a curious juxtaposition of ethical simplifications and strategic ambiguity in the face of conflict in the early 21st century.

Values and ethics imbedded in democratic state and society surely should precede the strategic/operational or tactical formulation of the use of armed forces as doctrine—and not the other way around, as McMaster advocates, and has happened before in the experience of small wars and counterinsurgency in modern history. The abandonment of the strategy in favor of generalized violence as it breaks loose from the political culture of a democratic state, as the primary focus of effort of the brains of an army that blunders into the half-baked role of internal security organization, carries its own set of ethical consequences, which cannot be overcome by tweaking operational jargon.

The Problem Today

A tour of the internet websites of the armed forces, as well as the places of advanced learning and training where soldierly ethics are cultivated and refined, seems to offer reassurance that, despite whatever effects of more than ten years of irregular combat and security building in Iraq and Afghanistan might suggest, the ethics and the ethos of the American soldier stand in good order because the service academies and the places of professional military education offer primary and advanced instruction in ethics. The service academies, which take as their mission the cultivation of officers "of character," devote particular energy online and in their curricula to such efforts, and even in the senior echelons of advanced defense education, ethical instruction enjoys a certain pride of place. An entire scholarly publication—the *Journal of Military Ethics*—exists as a forum for the exchange of views on the topic.

And, as we must note again, the overwhelming majority of uniformed Americans in the armed service of this state and society comport themselves consistently in a principled, disciplined, ethical manner. But then there are the disturbingly frequent and highly public displays of abject ethical collapse in the midst of conflict. Perhaps most famously, there was the 2004 torture scandal at Abu Ghraib, then a U.S.-military-run prison in the early phases of occupied Iraq. The same year, Pat Tillman, a former professional football player who became an Army Ranger following the 11 September 2001 terror attacks on the United States, died in an ambush in Afghanistan; investigations by both the U.S. Congress and the U.S. Department of Defense later showed that Tillman was killed by friendly fire, quite a different account than the heroic treatment that the Army originally gave of the incident. (The Tillman story represented but one instance of the U.S. military desperately seeking unequivocal heroes on the pattern of Hollywood films in the early part of its Global War on Terrorism. By 2007, former PFC Jessica Lynch, in her testimony before Congress, corrected the original official record of the circumstances that, in the U.S. offensive into Iraq of 2003, led her to become the first U.S. woman to become a prisoner of war and then to be liberated in a *coup de main* of U.S. forces.)

By 2010, the center of gravity in the question of ethics at arms had lurched toward the ranks of general officers at the front, where it combined, if not collided, with the core of democratic civil-military relations in wartime. The media sizzled with the dismissive and often profane remarks by General Stanley McChrystal, then commander of the NATO International Security Assistance Force (ISAF), lambasting everyone from his civilian political oversight to major allies. Had the driven Special Forces officer perhaps been tricked into such unguarded utterances by a wily embedded journalist with an eye for sensationalism? More likely, McChrystal knew exactly how to handle the press by the time the Rolling Stone reporter began collecting heroic details (for example, that the ascetic general with the Ranger Patch ran seven miles a day, slept four hours a night, and read voraciously in a manner that sets him apart from other Americans) for the profile piece.

When the war in Iraq began, McChrystal—at the time, he served as the vice director of operations in the Joint Staff in the Pentagon—provided the public face for Department of Defense briefings. Then-Lieutenant General McChrystal had been prominent in the Tillman cover-up, approving the young man's posthumous Silver Star in part to promote the Army's first, touched-up version of the incident. Undaunted, McChrystal pinned on his fourth star when he took command of U.S. and NATO ISAF forces in Afghanistan. One of his earliest acts as U.S. commander in Afghanistan was to leak to the media his own report to Secretary of Defense Robert Gates, requesting 40,000 additional troops, a move that struck many observers as a praetorian flirtation with the making of strategy in an unsound tradition that reaches back to the Truman-MacArthur controversy during the Korean War.

In many alarming ways, the record of McChrystal stands for the ethical question marks that have appeared above certain of the top-most levels of U.S. military and defense leadership—but one must note, not above all of them. In a provocatively titled article—"A Failure of Generalship"—from 2007, Lt. Colonel Paul Yingling profiles a long generation of general officers whose abdications of their moral and ethical duties led to American defeat in both Vietnam in 1975 and the strategic setbacks in Iraq, circa 2005–2006. Nowhere to be seen in Yingling's ideas is any praetorian ethos on the model of MacArthur and his acolytes as has come down to McMaster and

McChrystal and which pollutes the ethical fundamentals of the officer corps. From Yingling's perspective—as an armor officer with several combat tours behind him—the problem does not implicate some technical deficiency in the operational level of command or an individual failing here and there that damns the person and leaves the institution of the soldier untouched. Instead, he has proclaimed a crisis in American generalship, as an institution, that derives from the "intellectual and moral failures common to America's general officer corps in Vietnam and Iraq." This ethical decay manifests most clearly as consistent failures to provide their civilian oversight with accurate or honest insights into the battlefield, but it begins with a faulty sense of what officers ought to do within the ranks of the military—and how they ought to do it on a sound professional basis that includes ethics.

Similarly, Richard H. Kohn, a scholarly authority on the ethos of soldiers in the American state, has noted a crisis in the fundamentals of the U.S. armed forces that has struck its officer corps, among other ways, in its ethical failings in the midst of strategic challenges for which strategy and operations have proffered something less than the total victory that remains the most profound idea in U.S. strategic culture and practice. Kohn suggests that the "overuse and under-strength" of the U.S. military that begins to explain the halting progress toward genuine independence and democracy in either Iraq of Afghanistan. The key weakness, in the estimation of the former Air Force chief historian, is not weapons and materiel after a decade of fulsome defense budgets. Instead the declining capability that Kohn sees in motion owes to infirmities ingrained in what might be called the brains, heart, and soul of the American military establishment—three interconnected challenges to healthy military professionalism.

First, and most pressing as concerns the brain and heart, is the neglect of strategy in its classical sense as a central focus of the leadership of the armed forces. On this point, Kohn agrees with Yingling about both cause and effect: "Discovering the so-called operational level of war in the 1970s, the Army seemed to lose interest in strategy." All four armed services demonstrate this disengagement from the strategic level, according to Kohn. As a direct consequence, "Iraq has become the metaphor for an absence of strategy." This gap lately has been filled with the series of improvisations constituted of a counterinsurgency doctrine, the ethical implications of which have yet to be fully recognized, but about which the European and even American past have some troubling things to say for the ethics and ethos of soldiers in protracted conflict.

Alternately, when in early 2011 the U.S. Navy removed from duty Captain Owen Honors, the commanding officer of the nuclear carrier, *USS Enterprise*, for approving and even appearing in crude and inappropriate onboard videos back when he was the ship's executive officer, much of the public and insider reaction amounted to shock that such a sanction was imposed. At issue, then, isn't how an individual Navy captain might have come to believe that ribald, sexualized skits on the ship's video system exemplified sound leadership and morale-building. The conjuncture of the events of the past ten years, ethical instruction at all levels of command notwithstanding, poses the question of what flaws and defects operate in the ethical inner structure of leadership, command, morale, obedience, and ethos in the U.S. armed forces, as Yingling and Kohn have properly pointed out?

Honor and Ethics

Contemporary generalizations about ethics at arms must still rely on Morris Janowitz's analysis of the professional U.S. soldier, released in 1960 and re-released in 1971 amid changing civil-military circumstances in the Vietnam War era. From his vantage more than half a century ago, Janowitz noted that the advent of the Cold-War peacetime military establishment in state and society of a size and complexity unknown in the American past "…had produced a strain on traditional military self-image and concepts of honor." Janowitz thereby called into question the discrete and separate military professional honor and soldierly ethics in U.S. society of the 1950s, which had seen the rise of soldiers as a partisan interest group since the lost era of a small army in a civic culture devoted to trade as a higher virtue.

Honor, for Janowitz, forms the basis of the military belief system and an indispensible aspect of ethics at arms in a modern democracy. In its essence an institution of the European estates of the old regime transplanted to the New World via the U.S. Military Academy and similar establishments, the idea and ideal of honor, as translated to the U.S. military, redefines and reprioritizes—but does not add or remove—the main components of honor among those who bear arms for the state: gentlemanly (and now gentlewomanly) conduct, personal fealty, brotherhood, and pursuit of glory. These values persist in the self-perception of the armed forces today, of course, but, as Janowitz noted, they were at the time of his writing increasingly unable to "resolve the strains within the [military] profession." The "strain" on concepts of military honor and thereby on ethics that arise from the challenges to military institutions in combat and in state and society has, if anything, increased greatly since 1959 and especially since the rise of the anti-terror campaign in the wake of 11 September 2001, not the least because in the era of a conscription military whatever positive experience of this institution of honor at arms had affected more American citizens in uniform in a direct sense than has more recently been the case.

Janowitz wrote—perhaps in a more aspirational than declarative tone: "In a democratic society, it is highly inappropriate for honor to be the sole, or even the dominant, value of the professional military cadre. Honor comes to be combined with and dependent upon public prestige and popular recognition." This reflexive nature of honor, in an epoch in which the all-volunteer, professional military has marched into a crisis in part of its own making, as analyzed by Yingling and Kohn, means first that military ethics must reflect the values of contemporary society in the best sense, while, at the same time, upholding the requirements of command, control, obedience, and discipline in the armed professions within the framework of constitutional values of checks and balances and the assurance of human dignity.

Second, the military may only understand itself in the context of the state and society that it serves, despite all claims by those in military academies, in staff colleges, and among right-wing editorial boards with little soldierly experience, to adhere to some "timeless soldierly virtues" which, in reality, arose in the 19th century and which, in context, may not be so virtuous. Indeed, Janowitz concerned himself more with the martial self-image, at the time rather shaky in the post–Korean-war and thermonuclear age, that he ascribed to professional soldiers in the grey flannel thrust and jab of the late 1950s U.S. society, economy, and culture (versus the prettified memory of it among some middle-aged persons today) amid the ambiguities of honor on atomic or third-world battlefields.

This generalization applies particularly in its older-fashioned and less democratic iterations, and armed service (by citizens) in a modern democracy. But even more problematic circumstances today as concerns the place of the soldier in state and society also lead to a rather overstated sense of martial self among some military personnel—the problem of moral superiority, wrought of the increasing separation of the military from civilian society as well as the state of being upended that has struck many social and political elites in the midst of the early 21st century. Where Janowitz could write that "[f]ew officers, including those of the highest rank, with the exception of an occasional isolated maverick, accept the self-image of a standard bearer without some degree of uneasiness," in the present we have McChrystal's aide sniffing at the general's first meeting with President Barack Obama some four months after the latter took office: "'It was a ten-minute photo op. Obama clearly didn't know anything about him, who he was. Here's the guy who's going to run his f-cking war, but he didn't seem very engaged. The Boss was pretty disappointed.'" Presumably, the aide had the praetorian and constitutionally troubling substance, if not the exact wording, of this gripe directly from the general, who made no secret of his disdain for his civilian leadership.

McChrystal's farcical resurrection of the Truman-MacArthur controversy followed in the wake of worst setbacks of the U.S. campaign in Iraq and the so-called revolt of the generals in mid-2006, which constituted a kind of putsch-lite against Secretary of Defense Donald Rumsfeld in the midst of that year's election campaigning. A number of retired flag officers, some of whom had been protégées of Rumsfeld, engaged in partisan politics in an unprecedented fashion, violating traditional codes of ethics to undermine the constitutional authority of national supreme command in favor of the "timeless principles of war" and the "way of the warrior" and similar flourishes of latter-day uptonianism that brought no honor to the men who advanced them.

This collapse of soldierly honor and ethics in the 2006 election campaign was made even more problematic in 2008 (prior to the McChrystal event), when the press learned that many of the retired officers who had provided PowerPoint-heavy strategic commentary on television had, in fact, been paid agents of propaganda employed by the Office of Secretary of Defense in the years 2002–2006 to counteract defeatism in the media. In very short order, then, the United States was treated to the one-two spectacle of military officers mixing heavily in politics and then being revealed at the start of the war as having offered stage-managed "advice" to the American public and policymakers. Neither development bespeaks a functional military ethos.

Where Have All the Civilians Gone?

These seismic rumblings in the American military ethos rightly lead one to consider the state of ethics and arms as anchored in civic and political culture in the United States in the past and present. To no small degree, in fact, civilian America today encourages the distance between the armed forces and the rest of society, including its attachment to ethical standards that can withstand the baptism of fire in crisis. The widest-spread popular response to the sight of uniformed personnel in public places—increasingly common in U.S. airports and other transit hubs since the post-11 September 2001 campaigns began—has been a sentimental and often slightly guilty effusiveness of "support" for "our troops." Therewith is the public obligation to the military absolved, in the minds of the supporters. Few of these fans have the slightest idea of what goes on in a soldier's or sailor's life in or out of combat.

A commonplace of civil-military scholarship holds that the gap between the civilian realm and military service has only gotten worse since the United States abolished conscription in 1973. While this measure responded to the popular distaste for all things martial in the wake of the Vietnam War, ultimately it also moved the armed forces much further from the main stream of culture and society, the tendency that most alarmed Janowitz.

This divide had been building for some time earlier, in fact. Perhaps as veterans returned uneasily from the Korean War—amid economic downturn and public disinterest in the ambiguous conflict—the sense took hold that the thermonuclear "New Look," with its emphasis on megatons as the ultima ratio, should curtail the need for such wars. With little left of its old calling of honor amid maneuver and fire for decisive battles on the pattern of 1918 or 1944, the military of even World War II seemed old-fashioned and a out of step with the forces of innovation and chrome-plated peace that arose from economy, society and science. This period of popular culture saw such characters as the malevolently inept Captain Queeg (played by Humphrey Bogart in 1954's "The Caine Mutiny") or even the chicken-shit disciplinarian, Captain Morton ("Mr. Roberts," 1955), who contrasted in the question of ethics so starkly with his humane and honorable executive officer, Lt. Douglas Roberts (Henry Fonda). Surely the new-fangled nuclear Navy of the 1950s would be a different kind of institution?

Ten years later, the mainstream media overflowed with dishonorable and unethical figures in uniform. Sterling Hayden's General Jack D. Ripper in "Dr. Strangelove" (1964) brought the world to the brink of a nuclear war through his manic bellicosity. ("They're fighting in the war room!") More subtly sinister was Air Force General James Mattoon Scott, played by Burt Lancaster, plotting to overthrow the commander-in-chief—the U.S. president, played by Frederick March—for signing a disarmament treaty with the Soviets ("Seven Days in May," 1964).

The war in Vietnam began in earnest at this time, during which both the advent of a particularly rebellious youth and anti-war culture seized on such events as the release of the so-called Pentagon Papers in 1971 to render ever larger segments of American society skeptical of authority in general and the military and its core ideal of duty, honor, and country in particular. At least in the first decade or so of the all-volunteer period, this suspicion—whether warranted or exaggerated—about the motives and methods of the fighting forces was answered by the professional soldier retreating into staff colleges and to troop training areas empty of draftees to reformulate the principles of war and the soldierly ethos in a yet more refined form, while society confronted the diminished horizons of limited oil and economic upheaval. Popular culture had little good to reflect in its interpretation of soldierly honor and military ethics. One searches in vain for an unswervingly upright character in, say, "Apocalypse Now" or "Full Metal Jacket" (a self-conscious throwback from 1987 to this age and genre)—or even TV's much toned-down "M*A*S*H*" series.

The Zeitgeist shifted in the 1980s, however, with the election of Ronald Reagan more or less as the process of professional repair of soldierly ideals and practice had consolidated in the all-volunteer force. Films like "Blue Thunder" or "Top Gun" of the mid 1980s glorified the new armories of the Reagan-era and the fresh generation of men and women at arms who stood to the colors. For the most part, Americans stopped worrying about their armed forces, especially with the victory in 1991 against Iraq over the Kuwait invasion.

By 1998, the smash hit of the year was the soldier's saga in the mawkish mode of Steven Spielberg (a notorious non-soldier with an interest in the pathos of classical U.S. war movies as a lens of soldierly honor and ethics), "Saving Private Ryan." Most fans of the movie make particular note the graphic battle scenes with which "Saving Private Ryan" opens, depicting the Omaha Beach landing in 1944. Half a century later, such experiences as service under fire or even armed service to the nation were sufficiently remote to so much of

American society, other than CNN's video coverage from the 1990–1991 Gulf War, that the public sat transfixed by the Dolby sound and special-effects graphics of Wehrmacht MG 34 machine fire against U.S. infantry on the open strand. The movie inspired a tidal wave of nostalgia for World War II, culminating in the construction of the National World War II Memorial in Washington, D.C., the visitors to which, in the main, if they are under the age of 50, likely have had no military service and no direct experience of ethics at arms other than in some symbolic medium. Few reflected any further on such themes as the mass wartime call-ups that would have led to Private Ryan's unfortunate family circumstances (he had to be "saved" from the fighting that has already claimed the lives of his other three brothers) or to the ethos of the men and women who served at the time. The point, for the filmmaker and the clamoring audiences alike, was to engage in cathartic and stylized sentimentality, set in the seemingly straightforward moral context of the mid-20th century that was ever more remote from the reality of the actual wartime lives of persons in the era 1939–1945.

As seen from the distance of a decade of conflict and more since the film's premiere—soon thereafter the terror assaults took place—in which no comparable mobilization occurred at all, this fit of pathos has only fortified the civil-military divide, suggesting that the honor that inhered in the "greatest generation" is somehow out of reach of today's society—and thus, perhaps, its military.

Concomitantly with the falling away of popular engagement of soldiering as an idea and a practice in the lives of U.S. citizens, the legal and political structure of the United States changed in ways that exacerbated the civil-military divide and have harmed ethics at arms. As Diane Mazur writes, starting about 1974 at the end of the Nixon administration, a series of decisions by the U.S. Supreme Court systematically distinguished military service and the rules that govern it from the body of law that sustains the rest of American society, thereby imbalancing the core relationship of a democratic state to its armed forces, namely democratic civilian control and oversight. Indeed, in the first of these cases, *Parker v. Levy*—in which an unhappily drafted dermatologist, Captain Howard Levy, sought to overturn his conviction by court-martial for urging his subordinates to shirk their military duties as a protest against the Vietnam War—Justice William Rehnquist asserted that the Supreme Court has "long recognized" that the military is "a society apart from civilian society." Neither assertion comports with constitutional theory or practice, but both reflected the nature of soldierly honor as standing above civil society and its laws, as had operated in the military estates of the European past.

To be sure, Rehnquist's further point in *Parker v. Levy* read: "The fundamental necessity for obedience, and the consequent necessity for the imposition of discipline, may render permissible in the military that which would be constitutionally impermissible outside it." On its face, this point seems uncontroversial—a restatement of the truism repeated in every Bluejacket's Manual and Field Manual about the special requirements of military discipline on the citizen in uniform. However, Rehnquist's opinion goes much further toward ensconcing the military in praetorian isolation from society; it sets apart military jurisprudence, and thereby ethics in the military, from civilian scrutiny except under the most unusual circumstances. Mazur writes that the future chief justice of the United States repeated and, indeed, advanced this idea in later decisions, establishing a constitutionally clad alibi for subsequent courts and even Congress, where (as in the case of gender equality) its members so desired, to retreat from their oversight of the armed forces in the name of "deference" to military motives and requirements that echoed the ideas of Erich Ludendorff and his dictates of total war.

Wrong Answers All Around

As Colonel Yingling points out, this excessive deference presents exactly the wrong response, particularly by members of the U.S. Congress, who remain guardians of the professional ethos of the soldier, along with the President of the United States as the commander in chief. Where "the tendency of the executive branch to seek out mild-mannered team players to serve as senior generals is part of the problem" of poor generalship, Yingling writes, Congress should step in, as it has done in the past, with the full effect of its legal powers of oversight of the military. Professor Kohn still believes that the U.S. military can right itself with a reformulation of its professional and ethical principles, or at least set itself up to weather successfully the necessary legislative review that he believes is forthcoming. Both writers advocate the kind of thoroughgoing overhaul on the basis of the ethical principles that underlie U.S. democracy in its best sense (versus the wrongheaded constitutional fundamentalism and 18th-century atavism as operates on the fringes of American political culture today) that finally would overcome the moral torpor and ethical rot that plagues the few prominent figures of ethical trouble brewing in some parts of the American armed forces in the wake of the "long war."

For its part, the leadership of the U.S. military, especially Secretary of Defense Robert Gates and Chairman of the Joint Chiefs Admiral William Mullen, appears to have accepted this sense that its morals are askew at least as far as the creation of all the ethics courses and institutes noted above. In this regard, however, the armed forces have arrived at a different wrong answer in pinning their hopes more and more to the civilian model of professional ethics, as one might encounter in, say, business school or the legal profession, complete with all the coursework the educational and training institutions can muster on the topic.

The argument runs, on the one hand, that the airless, if timeless, Philosophy 101-style debates about the ethics of soldiering do not generate enough useful material for a military man or woman, particularly in a combat situation, to parse into real-world advice. While the military ethicists (and certain anti-democratic and culturally pessimistic historians) retain their penchant for the Greek classics on all occasions, Socrates himself reports being a poor excuse for a soldier; perhaps better examples should be found in other sources? On the other hand, one interpretation of the "post-honor" U.S. armed forces suggests that military officers form but one of the several professions. As such, an ethical codex ought to suffice that compares with the standards of surgeons or attorneys or corporate executives.

The first problem with this reasoning is that ethical practice among the classical civilian professions does not really suffice for the ethical needs of men and women at arms, not the least because many of these professions in the United States in the year 2010 find themselves in pretty bad professional shape at the moment. To be sure, professional ethics preoccupy lawyers sufficiently that one's license to practice in most jurisdictions requires a specialized ethics test in addition to (and separate from) the bar exam. Most law schools offer variously intensive preparatory courses for this exam as well as for the ethical challenges of legal practice. However, for the most part, official lawyerly ethics refer to the fiduciary relationship that attorneys often occupy vis-à-vis clients, and most of the rules and requirements pertain to the proper handling of client funds, with confidentiality and accurate recordkeeping coming in as a consequence. Certainly very little other than abusing others' money will get an attorney disbarred, in practical reality—a rather narrow subset of possible ethical discrepancies in the wider range of lawyerly activities.

All other questions that might implicate professional ethics in the law are subject to much follow-on discussion and, perhaps out of habit and proximity, litigation. For example, the Constitution, the highest law of the land, provides for representation by legal counsel in criminal cases; subsequent Supreme Court decisions have established the requirement that this counsel be effective. (Arguably, the lawyers who brought these cases already knew they should make their best professional efforts; these rulings clarify just what rights the criminally accused have under the Sixth and Fourteenth Amendments.) But further formal guidance has been needed to determine just what effective assistance entails. Thus, Congress, like most U.S. states, has enacted a rape-shield law, barring a defense attorney from impugning the sexual history of a rape victim. On the other end of the vigorous-defense spectrum, the Supreme Court tells us that a defense attorney who sleeps through whole sections of a capital murder trial has not necessarily denied his or her client effective representation.

As a model of professional ethics, then, the law has little to offer the military. The actual area of practice in which attorneys deign to self-regulate leaves out too much, while the methods of clarification and enforcement are slow, cumbersome, highly procedural, and impractical for a military that must make ethical decisions in rapidly developing situations. While living and lived ethics demand a thoughtful exchange of ideas to establish the boundaries of proper and improper conduct, one can hardly imagine an effective fighting force gripped with appeals to the highest authorities for clarification of, say, the mens rea required to establish ineffective leadership.

A more alluring model seems to arise in the realm of business ethics. Even amid the various big-business scandals that precipitated the latest U.S. (and world) severe economic downturn, business methods and motives continue to enjoy an instinctive reverence in American society and have long formed a part of the ethics system in advanced military education because of the various intellectual links between war colleges and business schools over the past century. Certainly the leading minds in management theory have borrowed heavily from the sources and lexicon of the military and vice versa in ways that are not sufficiently interpreted in works of scholarship and theory. Perhaps business can return the favor lending its ethical practices to the armed forces? In the event, professional business ethics present a field of inquiry at least as unclear as the legal variety did. The principal issue for business ethicists in a capitalist economy is the problem of the bottom line or profitability in the market place, which is the universal measure of all things in state and society—and morality.

Put bluntly: A business decision may or may not be good in the moral sense, but all the benefits that may flow from it derive more or less exclusively from whether it makes for "good business." For example, in early 2011, the *New York Times* reported on its front page that Libya's Col. Muammar el-Qaddafi in 2009 shook down several major foreign oil executives, specifically demanding that their companies come up with the $1.5 billion that Libya owed as part of its settlement with the families of the victims of the bombing of Pan Am Flight 103 over Lockerbie, Scotland, in 1988. Some of the companies that agreed to pay up rather than face any "serious reper-cussions" to their drilling are based in the United States. In other words, U.S. companies agreed to cover Libya's liability for killing scores of Americans (and citizens of allied states).

In the event, no particular public outrage over blood money or corporate misdeeds followed the publication of this story, but any top-level manager who agreed to the arrangement surely felt sure that the stockholders to whom he or she reports would agree that protect-ing the profits from the Libyan branch of the oil business was more important than claiming the notoriously petroleum-poor moral high ground in this matter. The shareholders would have their dividends and the executive at issue would have his or her bonus, and neither would worry about the ethical implications of this clearly win-win business decision. The same basic moral calculus applies when com-panies shift production offshore or "outsource" labor to get around contract or other obligations to long-time permanent employees. With the imperative of maximum profits at the apex of corporate priorities, business ethics, such that they are, necessarily remain sec-ondary at best in all decisions. Again, this model does not hold much promise for the armed forces, which may not consider, say, strategy as something utterly separate from military ethics.

One simply must reflect for a moment on the difficulty of finding one physician to testify against another in a malpractice trial to see the mismatch of professional ethics as practiced by the civilian realm today and the ethical needs of the U.S. military. (If soldiers were more like civilian doctors in this regard, courts-martial would hardly ever convene, let alone convict anyone!) Like any other profes-sion, the military requires ethical standards that really do help the armed forces in their particular missions and activities every day; in this endeavor, the ethical conventions of other professions offer pre-cious little usable precedent. At the same time, the military may not devise its ethical code in a praetorian vacuum. As we have noted, the civilian oversight must weigh in on the subject. And, of course, the citizen soldier remains the chief arbiter of ethics at arms and the focal point of the civil-military balance.

Conclusion

The statement "I am a soldier, a leader of character, a servant of the nation, and member of the profession of arms" cannot suffice in the present as the measure of all things in military ethics. Lists of secondary virtues that seek to uphold the inner cohesion of a specific organization as its primary goal (with little regard for universal values that underlie state and society in general) frequently become a means of abuse, as the past so frequently suggests to those who seriously consider the subject. The strain on military honor which Morris Janowitz found at the end of the 1950s is today vastly greater on the fundamentals of character, the purpose of the nation in conflict, and the durability of ideals of the profession amid the proliferation of organized violence among non-professionals—terrorists, guerillas, soldiers of fortune, men and women at arms, and even unseen, anonymous figures behind a computer screen who are able to upend bank databases or just hack someone's Facebook page.

While the majority of soldiers and sailors have adhered more or less without trespass to sound ethical principles, certain noteworthy figures in the senior echelons of command have not. Their few but famous examples lead, as Professor Kohn has mentioned, to "moral deficiencies" seen by subordinates as much as by those whom one decries as being "anti-military" and hence disloyal Americans. Perhaps nowhere is the professional and ethical damage wrought by the "global war on terror" as evident as in H.R. McMaster's placing a moral and ethical codex on its head and subordinating ethics to operational doctrine for the creation of internal security in foreign wars and maybe even domestic political conflict. Here stands the imperative of the moment for soldiers and civilians together to remedy the "moral deficiencies" in the professional core of the armed forces so well analyzed by Yingling and Kohn. The still-current cases of military tribunals for the trial of al-Qaeda terrorists as well as the disclosure of U.S. Siprnet secret documents by a disgruntled U.S. soldier to Julian Assange of WikiLeaks only add further urgency to this central issue of the military ethos in a democracy.

The foregoing suggests that the fundamentals of the ethics of soldiers in the midst of what has been longest armed conflict in modern U.S. history defy analysis solely by the means and by the measures of military organization and soldierly figures on their own, though these institutions and personalities remain compelling and revealing for the subject at hand and are analyzed here in an interpretative manner. To be sure, the state of ethics in the armed forces, especially where such has deviated from time honored concepts of ethics and honor, does nothing more than reflect the state of ethics in such other leading institutions of elite politics and society as universities, banks, and the houses of the legislative at a time of shocking turmoil and worrisome developments in what had seemed until very recently powerful and stable institutions of state and society. At the same, the public perception of the ethical foundations of the armed forces when contrasted to state and society at large portrays a separate world led by the catchwords of "duty, honor and country," which slogan for some in the civilian world has become nothing more than an excuse to apply these soldierly terms in pluralistic politics to suffocate pluralism in society.

This fact should be a cause for concern not only in those thoughtful and indeed ethically motivated figures in the armed forces, but among those civilians charged with the constitutional imperative to watch over the professional principles and practices of soldiers in an army in a democracy. In this latter aspect, particularly, the authors wish to contend, civilians have failed in their own role as citizens to maintain the professional and ethical codex of military service. Such a failure is unworthy of those in the American past who did better with citizenship at arms when the times demanded it. Such a civil-military failure should also warn those in Central Europe who will read this article to adhere to their ethical code of soldierly honor anchored in the constitution and the primacy of the legislative, rather than dump it in a paroxysm of absentmindedness like some outdated and no longer desirable set of wheels, as might presently be happening along the Rhine, Spree, and Oder.

V.   Education

15. Globalization, Defense Institution Building and Officer Education: Competing Paradigms as *Ideengeschichte**

The international education of officers in policy, strategy, and security and defense institutions represents a facet of the globalization of the world capitalist economy and its effects on leading societies in the past two decades. How the globalization of state, society, economy, and culture have challenged traditional elites (in our own case, defense civilians, military officers and university researchers and professors) and their self-image through the institutions of higher defense education on an international scale in the present and future occupies me here today. Is the transformation of officer education in the midst of the reform of defense institutions to be achieved in the same manner as the reorganization of a global corporation, that is, identical to the reform of General Motors undertaken at the direction of the U.S. government in the past two years? That is, should internationalized defense education derive its central practical guide for action on a global scale in the face of transnational threats from the research and teaching of chiefly graduates schools of business, where an application of knowledge to the needs of the market reigns sovereign? How does the case of a revived General Motors compare to other examples of contemporary defense reform in which internationalized defense education plays a role, say, the creation of the higher levels of command of the Afghan National Army, which consume the energy of many of us at this moment?

The evidence has been universal with the double shocks of the global blast of Islamicist terror and the near collapse of the neoliberal economic regime in North America and Europe. In this connection, the spread of knowledge with little regard for hierarchy surely has an impact on traditional elites, with particular implications for

---

* Expanded and revised version of lecture at Austrian National Defense Academy on 18 November 2010.

the principles of military command, obedience, morale, education, and training, which always have occupied this series of seminars.

How do the brains of national armies adjust to a circumstance in which the application of military power unfolds ever more in a combined and joint context? The armies of the world are no longer sufficiently strong to apply military force to the ends of policy in the traditional manner as the ultima-ratio of a single nation state. Echelons of command are ever more international, indeed, globalized, if one looks at the organizations charts of the high commands of such security and defense organizations as the UN, Organization for Security and Co-operation Europe (OSCE), EU, and NATO. This process of integration and standardization among the armies, navies and air forces of the Western-oriented democracies is plainly somehow linked to globalization, but how does the latter affect the brains of armies for which we are responsible in their formation and perfection, that is, advanced education?

To be sure, I live in Silicon Valley, in the shadow of the Google campus and the Headquarters of Facebook, but I am not of Silicon Valley, because I got my PhD at Stanford in European history rather than electrical engineering. The impact of Sputnik on me in the years after 1957 was to drive me toward the humanities where I have stayed in the half century since. What I have to say to you here today does not borrow from such figures as Terman, Hewlett, Packard, Kerouac, Jobs, and Zuckerberg, but more reflects a willful mixture of Herder (the role of culture and language), de Maistre (skepticism of the Enlightenment and opposition to the French Revolution in favor of tradition), Clausewitz (critic of the pseudoscientific approach to war and able to join the forces of politics and psychology in a theory war), Schopenhauer (the metaphysical pessimist of the age of reaction), Burckhardt (a skeptic of the mass movements of the 19th century), Le Bon (the theorist of the crowd and mass politics), Spengler (the cultural pessimist), and Isaiah Berlin, as he has interpreted these observers of the forces of change in European state, society, culture, and economy. Such arcane names are but poorly known among the pioneers of technological change in the information and knowledge society much celebrated in Palo Alto and Cupertino, California, who care nothing for what we think here and who poorly have an answer for the security and defense problems of the present other than more technology with likely Orwellian impact on pluralistic society.

Such ignorance is obvious to me, because such persons as the founders of Apple Computer and others along Sand Hill Road in Menlo Park, California, have been contemporaries of mine, but never colleagues; nor did I invest in their start up capital offerings to strike it rich in the 1980s and 1990s; nor do I celebrate their accomplishment in the manner that is doctrine and dogma in my country and within globalized society in the writings of Francis Fukuyama, Thomas Friedman, and the editorialists of the *Wall Street Journal*. Thus, I can well share some of the informed skepticism about the ill effects of globalization on liberal, pluralistic Western or universal values.

What do I mean with my *Ahnengallerie* above as regards a skeptical view of rapid political, social, and economic change and how such a list of ancestors in the history of ideas has any meaning in the present question? Isaiah Berlin has interpreted the skeptics of the Age of Reason and the French Revolution with particular skill, as befits a public intellectual driven from his native Baltic to the Atlantic civilization of the era of the world wars and the Cold War. He reminds us that the skeptics of progress and the triumph of reason and the application of the natural sciences to the politics of the old regime in the 18th and 19th centuries had also hinted at the problems that beset the 19th and 20th centuries. Berlin taught me about many of these skeptics and critics of the Age of Reason and the French Revolution more than 30 years ago, certain of whom are politically incorrect in our world, to be sure, but whose critique retains its validity. This knowledge has been especially helpful to me for the purposes of context and perspective in the past 20 years, amid so much change and upheaval since the fall of 1989 in which the victory of liberal values and institutions seemed once so assured and now is in such doubt. An educated officer should know the work of Berlin's skeptics and critics in order to make sense of the present and future. The humanistic knowledge of Berlin and of his subjects in the 18th and 19th centuries forms a vital portion of what an officer must know today in order to master the challenges of policy and strategy, to say nothing of the use of education as a means of defense institution building to exclude the sources of political violence as it manifests itself today.

I am outspoken on this score, because I have been an agent of the internationalization of military education in the Euro-Atlantic sphere quite without having ever planned such a thing. Many of us have not anticipated such a thing in 1989 and 1990, but have stepped into these roles with hope and promise, in my case, despite being a historian of 20th-century Germany. This experience has made me work with people of other disciplines and professions in which it has often been a challenge to me to find common ground. The Institute of Human Sciences and Humanities of the Austrian Defense Academy is a highly agreeable, inter disciplinary undertaking in this connection and shows that such an effort can be highly successful.

My own experience of the internationalization of defense education amid defense institution building in the last two decades has been joined with the skepticism that operates in Central Europe in the face of the *Zeitgeist* of the last ten years amid the so called Global War on Terror and its attendant effects on U.S. and NATO defense and military institutions. This skepticism might offer a point of departure for a more informed and acute analysis and set of generalizations about a humanist versus a pseudoscientific, neo-Taylorite paradigm in the internationalization of officer education. This skepticism on my part has only increased greatly in the past decade since 11 September 2001. What might have worked in defense education and institution building, say, in the reform of the Polish Ministry of Defense in 1995 strikes me as far less effective today in the construction of an Iraqi or Afghan Ministry of Defense in 2010. I do not wish to say that Poles are better than Iraqis or Afghans. Far from it. My argument is more subtle and nuanced.

I do suggest, though, a perhaps willful and even contrived thesis and counter thesis, namely that the role of the Bundeswehr in

German unity within the eventual enlargement of NATO (which I describe as based on values and indeed European humanism) can be joined to the U.S. and coalition campaigns in Iraq and Afghanistan (based on the pseudoscientific and neo-Taylorite paradigm) to comprise a generalized phenomenon filled with many contradictions, but also certain commonalities of merit that demand a more skeptical analysis.

Thus, I want to examine these theoretical and practical facets of the phenomenon of the internationalization of defense and military education and to end with a warning about contemporary trends in international military education in the face of globalization that worry me and which surely fit into the themes of this seminar. Here, I wish to present these two paradigms, or, thesis and antithesis, in more detail than above, concerned with the globalization of security, defense, and military education on an international scale. This dichotomy, however, flawed and incomplete it might be, has grown manifest to me in my work for the U.S. Department of Defense and research on civil-military relations and the character of armies in the past and present. Finally, I want to conclude with a critical examination of counter insurgency doctrine, whose theoretical and practical place in the theme of globalization requires a more critical and thorough going analysis than unfolds in my native country or in Germany, your neighbor, and the other place in Europe with which I am most familiar. Let us take the case of Germany, then, that we first turn and in the second instance to the United States and to some degree to NATO.

Before I do, however, a word of explanation that I do not merely mean here that all things German as regards the mind and spirit as conceived by the traditional university are good and all things that apply to such principles as American pragmatism and economic and social organization for the broadest possible material benefit via mass education are perhaps all bad. Not at all. Indeed, there are elements of humanism and the celebration of Enlightenment values in the U.S. system, and the neo-Taylorite, pseudoscientific and cult-of-the-manager approach can also be found in the Bundeswehr, to be sure. Nonetheless, in the explanation of these two cases before you now I hope to make my ideas more clear.

The First Paradigm and its Tradition:
Central European Humanism, Values, and the Universality
of Education in the Face of Political and Social Change

Two hundred years ago, the newly created University of Berlin opened its doors according to the path breaking idea of citizenship and knowledge offered in the shadow of Napoleon's challenge to the old order by the Prussian Minister Alexander von Humboldt. The newly founded war academy adjacent to the university offered courses for officers of the reformed Prussian Army in the art and craft of war in a union of German idealism and national awakening across the estates in society. Among its faculty was Clausewitz. Next to the abolition of serfdom in Prussia, the establishment of the university and Kriegsakademie on the Linden represented the most remarkable reform of state, society, and the army amid the European response to the political and military revolution that arose first in France and spread across Europe. The men and women of the enlightened nobility and the bourgeoisie who reformed the Prussian army and fashioned its brains in the face of the Napoleonic threat remain astonishing even today for their intelligence, character, and culture. The *Bildungsbürger*-at-arms and the enlightened, educated member of the nobility who embraced the liberating dimension of education in the officer corps, established a Central European tradition that receives too little attention in my own country and in other NATO countries; or which, as I shall describe later, is perverted from its original and most fundamental meaning of universal values and humanism toward a narrow professionalism obsessed with the technological and the tactical on a purported scientific basis as understood in American practice of military education and training.

This perversion is worsened greatly today amid the intellectual ennui in the west confronted with ideological extremism of the present. The former is exacerbated by a renewed emphasis on relevance, functionality, and cost cutting in higher education at the expense of all that seems somehow to be an antiquated luxury of an irrelevant past: the humanities and its classical disciplines. For some of you this phenomenon has been present in the Bologna reforms in the European Union and its intrusion of market forces into the traditional university; for us in North America, such has been especially virulent with the economic crash since 2008 and its impact on colleges and universities and the attendant cuts to programs, especially in the humanities.

Rather than being a luxury, the humanistic paradigm of officer education with its roots in German idealism and the era of bourgeois awakening in the face of the French revolution, has a particular urgency in our own time of accelerated political and social change. The historical roots of this paradigm of humanistic education need no extended retelling in a central European venue, but can be sketched as follows: the point of departure has been political and the military revolution in France, with the eclipse of the world of estates which led violently to the world of nation states and classes via the liberalization of society via education in the face of the Napoleonic challenge especially in Central Europe. The need to respond to this crisis joined professors and soldiers in a way that had not been possible before because of the deep hostility to learning native especially to the Prussian Junkers-at-arms. The reform of university education to join research and instruction, and the liberalization of estate based training of the sons of the nobility to careers of military talent with less regard for social background complemented one another.

While in the case of Germany, this original impulse went afoul later in the 19th century as university and officer higher education and training diverged because of the durability of military estate in its transition to a military profession at odds, in turn, with mass politics. This process of militarism and professionalism at odds with human rights gone wrong contributed to two world wars.

But the aftermath of the second war worked out far better than contemporaries expected at the time. Pluralism, democracy, and humanistic values of knowledge fared far better in central Europe after 1945 than in the era from 1890 until 1918. Those heirs to the civil and military figures of the Enlightenment in the period of awakening against Napoleonic Europe degraded by 1914 into a technocratic professionalism, which eventually collapsed by 1918 into military desperados and was undone by ex soldiers in mass politics whose embrace of racist nationalism made a mockery of the legacy of humanism of more than a century earlier. This process also debased military professionalism by 1941, whose decline into an over preoccupation with tactics and ignorance of politics debased its claims to professional excellence via advanced education and training.

The West German (and the Austrian) response to this era of total war led to a revival of the original idea of humanistic ideals and education for soldiers in its mid–20th-century form as *Innere Führung* in the West German Bundeswehr. This institution represented one of the great accomplishments in the tradition of the Prussian reformers and really of all figures in the German-speaking world who have joined the virtues of learning in a free setting with the needs of military discipline in what is otherwise an improbable, if not impossible combination. Outstanding in *Innere Führung* has been the rebirth of *Führung mit Auftrag,* i.e. *Auftragstaktik* whereby the combination of intellect and character (naturally reinforced by a high degree of education and training) reasserted itself as a guiding principle of what German speakers mean with the term: Führung, which English speakers can never fully comprehend.

Not by accident in the ten years between war's end and the armament of the Federal Republic of Germany did certain leading former general staff officers, later central to the conception and success of *Innere Führung,* embark on such unmilitary lives as sheet music salesman (Ulrich de Maiziere), publisher (Johann Graf von Kielmansegg), and even artist-sculptor (Wolf Graf von Baudissin), to say nothing of so many former Wehrmacht soldiers who went to university in the late 1940s and early 1950s to pursue advanced study in humanistic disciplines (Dr. Eberhard Wagemann). This experience at odds with a traditional conception of a general staff officer either before or since nonetheless embodied a fundamental principle of a humanistic approach to advanced education for soldiers.

Among the signal accomplishments of *Innere Führung* has been the introduction in the early 1970s of the Bundeswehr universities. These universities in Hamburg and Munich were established in 1973 amid a crisis of the self-image and political and social role of the Bundeswehr, and were greeted with great skepticism by many in the officer corps and in civil society at a time when German universities were scenes of social revolution and contempt for military virtues. The Bundeswehr universities have become anything other than a military state within a state, cut off from the requirements of civilian advanced education, but were integrated into civilian state and society in an exemplary fashion. More so has this German civil-military integration succeeded, in fact, than is the case with certain institutions of higher military education in my native country about which I have something to say later.

To be sure, the Bundeswehr universities embodied a kind of Americanization in one sense of the 1960s (a university education had been a prerequisite of an officer's career in the United States long before such was the case in the FRG), which was nonetheless carried out by acquaintances of mine in a uniquely West German manner to best effect in the further development of the Bundeswehr in German state and society in the decades since. The Bundeswehr universities as well as such institutions as Zentrum Innere Führung in Koblenz /Berlin, the Militärgeschichtliches Forschungsamt in Freiburg and later Potsdam, and the Sociological Institute of the Bundeswehr in Munich/Strausberg manifest the humanistic and civil ideals of advanced research and education in the German experience with a signal meaning for the internationalization of advanced military education.

Subjected to intense criticism in its early phases, *Innere Führung*—as an enlightened ideal of command, obedience, morale, leadership, and education based on the ideals of the Prussian reforms— found, however, its greatest test of the humanistic paradigm of the internationalization of officer education in the challenge of German unity in the years 1989–1995. The army of unity further shows the essential soundness of *Innere Führung* and its adaptation of the educated citizen as officer. The peaceful integration of the soldiers of the former East German National People's Army set a standard in the political revolution of the 1990s.

This event stands in contrast to the collapse of armies in such failing states as Yugoslavia, Iraq, and Afghanistan, which damaged the international system of states. The problems of state building and armed forces in post conflict reconstruction in Afghanistan add yet other examples to this list, which I wish to interpret below, where the imbalanced relationship between misconceived, pseudoscientific ideals of international defense and military education have produced strategically damaging results that go far beyond the military places of learning. The case of *Innere Führung* and German unity within NATO enlargement and the subsequent is unknown especially in my country, mostly because its success camouflaged its theoretical value, while the other examples are more well known—but their theoretical and practical importance is jumbled by intense boosterism by the pseudoscientists of the Taylorite/Huntington school and for lack of informed criticism especially in the present.

While many factors beyond the confines of the military and even universities surely played a role in this positive outcome in the unity of Germany, by no accident have many of the men and women who made this success possible on the German side been associated with *Innere Führung* and with its realization in higher education in the German forces for two decades prior to unification. The role of the integration of the former East Germans into the Bundeswehr also set an example in NATO enlargement in the 1990s and into the recent past, which theory and practice has failed to honor sufficiently. That is, the army of a failed state was absorbed by a pluralistic state and society, and by an army in a democracy with an educated officer corps, integrated, itself, into this society in a durable and sustainable manner. The Bundeswehr universities embody the ideal of the citizen in uniform in the republic of the learned in a pluralist state and society. To what degree this tradition from Humboldt reforms in Napoleonic Europe to the fall of the Berlin Wall can be applied in a general sense in other instances I leave to the reder, but I offer this humanist paradigm here mostly as a contrast to the second element of my theory that I wish to examine next.

Namely I mean the pseudoscientific, neo-Taylorite/quasi-Hutingtonian paradigm of institutional insularity in defense education in defense institution building from pluralistic values, humanism and society. Whereas Taylor constructed a doctrine of industrial efficiency through a pseudoscience, which underlay American management techniques through much of the 20th century, Huntington's work of 1957 reified the USMA in the context of U.S. society of the era with its ideals of military virtue, conservatism, public service, and the posture of citizenship in the face of the era of total war in the atomic age. The odd mixture of Taylor and Huntington that lies often at the center of the internationalized enterprises of U.S. and NATO officer education has created a very mixed legacy, which, I believe, stands in contrast to the Humboldtian-*Innere Führung*-values paradigm at the start of this inquiry.

The citizen in uniform as an ideal of officer education in Central Europe also has manifested itself in NATO's comprehensive concept, as well as the common foreign and security policy of the European Union all of which have taken account of the altered strategic reality in the 21st century. Here one sees in the wake of the set backs of the U.S. campaign in Iraq and Afghanistan in the years 2003–2006, where combat at the tactical and operational level in the traditional sense has had only a limited political utility, and must be augmented and complemented by other means of statecraft suited to post conflict reconstruction. An understanding of the structures of society and the needs of postwar state building and reinforcement of civil society cannot be achieved solely through the pseudoscientific paradigm in defense education.

The problems of political violence and the reinforcement of state, society and economy to preclude the failure of states and the spread of violent mass movements or guerillas/terrorists directed against the western order of pluralism and democracy on a capitalist basis constitutes something other than a problem of siege craft, nuclear physics, or Taylorite scientific management. At this point, our inquiry takes us to what I see as this opposite paradigm, or the antithesis of the humanistic ideal, which is not really so much its opposite, as its misapplied *Doppelgänger* mutated into a dominant force that seems to me, at least, to have outlived its usefulness.

The Pseudoscientific School of Big Defense Management and Military Transformation: Military Science of Samuel Huntington Meets Frederick Winslow Taylor at the University of Phoenix

What then do I mean by the second part of my theory here, which I have described above in polemical terms as the Taylorite/Huntingtonian pseudo-scientific paradigm? Why would I join Frederick Winslow Taylor, the early–20th-century mechanical engineer turned innovator of industrial motions studies and prototype management consultant with Samuel Huntington, the political scientist and theorist of democratic society and culture especially in a military context? One need only add that Huntington ended his life somewhat in the vein of Schopenhauer and Spengler with a deep pessimism about U.S. society and democracy in the 21st century, whereas Taylor believed that his applied mechanical engineering to industrial organization in mass society could eradicate class conflict and neutralize such alien ideologies as Marxism and socialism. These two men were civilians, after all, not soldiers, and two very different civilians (mechanical engineer and political scientist) to be sure, although Taylor became a professor in a business school while Huntington spent his life at Harvard.

In the question of military education and its ideals, most Americans would seize on Douglas MacArthur or David Petraeus as examples of soldierly professionalism of the U.S. Military Academy or Colin Powell as a citizen soldier via the Reserve Officer Training Corps. In the biographies of these men, their military education occupies a not unimportant role, but such goes unremarked in a theoretical way especially for our purposes. Neither Taylor nor Huntington appear in any tangible form in such popular biographies of great military men and their battles found by the linear foot in Border's bookstore or elsewhere. The lives of generals are generally seen in process of humble beginnings, young accomplishment in the sporting male life, some setbacks normal for young men that are then somehow overcome, and then in a meteoric rise of battlefield glory and an accumulation of stars well earned.

Thereby one gives little reflection to the impact of these military exemplars on the armies of the world and security institutions generally, other than Petraeus, got a Ph.D. at Princeton. MacArthur and Petraeus were graduates of the U.S. Military Academy, a place which today for reasons that I have explored in other talks here each fall for the past several years, exerts an outsized fascination on an American public that has little to do with soldiers and their places of learning and knows little and cares less about the themes I am exploring with you now. Few Americans other than a tiny number of experts outside of the mainstream of political life today could explain the relation of Taylor and Huntington to such generals past and present who are otherwise widely celebrated in popular culture today and in the halls of government.

But my point is this: the modern day successors of General Douglas MacArthur in the service of General David Petraeus, who are actively globalizing officer education especially in the Middle East and Southern Asia, have taken more than a page from the works of Taylor and Huntington—maybe also the wrong pages without even knowing it. Might I assert that there exists a central idea that in turn spreads through a large bureaucracy with its own self interests and mutates into doctrine, which in turn has become a leading force in the internationalization and indeed globalization of military education. We must ask now whether the central idea and its doctrine apply at all in a given national context. How this process functions is something that takes more or less the following steps.

There unfolds in this pseudoscientific paradigm of defense and military education best exemplified by the core instruction at the

U.S. Military Academy—especially its Social Sciences Department (but in other places, as well)—an emphasis on rigorous efficiency based on mechanical engineering and its offshoot management science (à la Taylor) joined with traditional military science of its 19th-century variant: the application of the natural sciences to the needs of siege craft, fortress construction, and artillery.

One recalls that instruction in tactics (and later in strategy) at West Point in the 19th century grew out of this instruction in military engineering and its associated disciplines with a French origin. Such stood very much at odds with the central European tradition that I described at the outset. This dogma is imbedded, in turn, in an elite self-image of the officer and his or her pseudoscientific doctrine (à la Jomini via Huntington), which is at odds with democratic state and society. A dearth of humanism poisons this dogma. The prerogatives of a defense managerial-military elite derived from socially and politically exclusive institutions of higher defense and military education share little with the figure of Graf Baudissin, nor the reformers of the Bundeswehr University or the *Innere Führer* who assumed leadership of the remnants of the East German army. There is no place for freedom in obedience and *Auftragstaktik* here, either.

In places of higher education in the U.S. military, which are then engaged in a more international role, the amalgam of these Taylor and Huntington's ideas has been transmitted on a global scale with renewed energy in the past ten years. In the earlier epochs, this process of the transfer of U.S. principles of defense management and military professionalism in the context of the mid-20th-century U.S. security assistance worked to better effect. One example is the U.S. role in the recreation of the West German Air Force in the 1950s and 1960s, which has worked out over time rather well as a case of defense institution building especially in historical terms. At the same time, U.S. officers schooled in Taylor and imbued with Huntington's elitism help build the Austrian Bundesheer from the remnants of the Wehrmacht, though one does not want to overstate this case here since the U.S. role was less prominent here than in West Germany. The greatest example of the pseudoscientific approach has been the

U.S. experience of industrial mobilization and mass armies for total war in World War II that graduated to U.S. nuclear strategy in NATO in its heyday of the 1940s through the 1980s. Here the union of elements expressed itself in the doctrine of nuclear deterrence, which nonetheless worked far better in the Cold War than that which has followed it especially in the last ten years. This approach, however, showed less success in limited wars in Asia in the 1950s and 1960s, a generalization that applies once more in the present.

There are other cases of Taylor/Huntington pseudoscience of defense institution building and military education and training, to be sure, that have worked less well, as in the case of the South Vietnamese Army in the early 1970s or the expert training given by U.S. forces to Latin American armies since the 1950s which ended in praetorianism and civil war. One could extend this list of less than optimal defense institution building via advanced education on an international scale.

But the central point is the following: namely that a contrast in the application of ideas to the political world by the 21st-century acolytes of Taylor and Huntington in uniform to the descendants of German humanism, von Humboldt's reform of the university, and the attempt by German civilians and soldiers in the wake of the Second World War to restore humanism to the state and to service at arms highlights more the shortcomings of the former rather more than the weaknesses of the latter.

Based on my own contemporary experience of the internationalization of defense and military education far too much of Taylor and Huntington's ideas suffuse this dominant paradigm of internationalized advanced education and training as I have seen much of it in the past 20 years. The ambiguous legacy of these two men, when misapplied in the internationalization of education and training, mutates into an elite codex and self-reflexive civil-military dogma rooted in U.S. society of the mid-20th century, which is seriously out of place in the 21st century. The Taylorite dogma of engineering efficiency in defense and military organization via the rigorous, mechanical reduction of all procedures to a kind of ministerial assembly line based on some false ideal that management is also the Godhead tends to create an aura of certainty and infallibility in defense institution building for its own sake.

This dogma of scientifically rooted industrial and managerial progress (where the ways of the managerial elite of industrialized capitalism stand superior to all other forms of civilization and society) often ignores national traditions, organic structures, and national peculiarities that always bulk large in the evolution of state ministries and general staffs. This issue leads back to Berlin's skeptics of the Enlightenment and the French Revolution, who rejected the pseudoscientific reorganization of society with the rejection of tradition and organic society.

Huntington's exaltations of the prerogatives of the U.S. military elite with contempt for pluralistic society (i.e. the imperative to create a professional military and abolish conscription) and an ambiguous attitude to constitutional principles form the other main features of the pseudoscientific paradigm. His work of 1957 was as much his own critique of liberalism in US society of the Truman and Eisenhower eras, as it was about soldierly ideals in theoretical terms. This feature has undergone a revival in the internationalization of defense education in which Huntington's writings have played a large role. This revival operates because of the connection between the USMA Social Sciences Department, the semi-Praetorian seat of U.S. military professionalism and the doctrine of U.S. civil-military relations at West Point, and other places of advanced education and study in the U.S. military in their number: the US Army War College, the National Defense University, and the other service war colleges as well as the specialized institutions of the study of tactics for intelligence and special operations that have somehow been elevated to the status of an entity that can grant academic degrees. As regards Huntington's canonical text, how do the Iraqis and Afghans read this book? In my experience, the reading of in the Central European and Eastern European context served to reinforce a sentiment of military caste and elite exclusivity that is always at odds with democratic principles.

Let me be more specific. The debased and otherwise watered down amalgam of Taylor and Huntington's ideas also underlies the large education and training bureaucracies in the U.S. armed forces (for instance, in addition to the institutions I outlined above, the U.S. Army Training and Doctrine Command, the U.S. Joint Forces Command, and the headquarters staffs of the the U.S.-specified Combatant Commanders, as well as certain of the U.S. Department of Defense regional centers for security cooperation, also the Defense Security Cooperation Agency) with their own special budgetary and programmatic interests. These institutional interest as well as underlying theoretical flaws in the present lead to an ever more fervent production of texts described as military doctrine.

This doctrine is then to be propagated in the education and training establishments of the armed services, and also be transmitted to NATO, to say nothing of allies and friends of the U.S. forces who receive security assistance. The record of these doctrine organizations in the recent past has been anything but exemplary in either predicting the problems of the present or offering solutions to them via internationalized education and training that corresponds fully with the conditions of policy. In these places one finds the clearest expression of the dogma of the pseudoscientific paradigm in the Taylor/Huntington model in action in the internationalization of defense education that has somehow erected a wall to democratic values and principles with the brick and mortar of dogma and elitism based on a pseudo-academic discipline.

Further examples of problematic attempts at the internationalization of defense education beyond Central Europe, where the record has been more successful, has been the poor showing of Georgian defense decision making and arms in the summer Caucasian war of 2008, despite a decade long effort by U.S. security assistance to establish and reform the defense institutions of the new nation state.

A further, but less dramatic example has been the internal problems in the evolution of the Department of Defense Marshall Center in Bavaria, an institution that collapsed in scandal in the mid-

1990s. I was an expert witness for the U.S. Office of Secretary of Defense in order to reform this institution to a more flexible and more academic model and today my colleagues in Monterey, California, have been giving an oversight function for its programs by the Office of the Secretary of Defense. The case of Iraq and the enterprise of reconstructing national armed and security forces hardly require an explanation by me here, since the problems of theory and practice are manifest. The Afghan campaign and its problems of defense institution building via education and training of Afghan military and security forces have seized the spot light, and, if any thing, only underscore the problem I have highlighted here.

In particular, a case with which I am familiar is the attempt by the United States and NATO to create a military academy for the Afghan National Army undertaken by the staff of the U.S. Military Academy, in which once the plans are taken from the drawing board, the Afghans find that the character of Afghan society precludes the easy and swift duplication of a U.S. military educational institution in the midst of prolonged conflict and the flight of national elites in a three decades diaspora. An absence of qualified personnel makes the extensive wiring diagram in two dimensions into a three-dimensional question mark.

Now a note of caution is in order, despite my harsh analysis of much that surrounds me. I do not wish to damn this pseudoscientific paradigm in all respects. There are specific fields of advanced learning about military affairs that are well suited to an applied engineering approach, and there are features of national defense that require the disciplines taught in business schools for their effective and efficient mastery. In the age of machine warfare, and of total war, as well as the atomic era, classical strategists and military thinkers (even with a humanistic legacy) might well have seemed to be obsolete and useless to many in the face of the mechanization of weapons, the need for industrial mobilization for war materiel on a staggering scale, and for the operations and tactics of war at sea or war in the air, where methods of scientific management of modern industry seemed applicable to the world of 1920 or 1940 or 1960. Or where physicists and others from the natural sciences joined with soldiers in the nuclear age to think the unthinkable and apply physics and engineering to victory in combat, however horrific such an act would have been.

However, this paradigm has mutated in a way made worse by misdirected institutional interest, by false glories in combat since the late 1990s and especially since the mixed fortunes of the protracted Iraqi and Afghan campaigns. There has unfolded a perversion of goals as well as mutation of scale caused by the easy victories in the 1990–1991 Gulf War and in the Second Gulf War that went out of control in 2003–2004, and then required a conflicted, hesitating conceptual and institutional response in the Iraqi and Afghan stalemates. In particular, the strategic idealism of the pseudoscientific approach that failed so awfully in the collapsed Coalition Blitzkrieg in Iraq of 2003–2004 showed the emptiness of the "revolution in military affairs." The full implications of this event have yet to be fully appreciated, not the least because of the following revival of the pseudoscientific paradigm despite its manifest weaknesses.

My censure adheres because the replacement strategy— COIN or counter insurgency—to the revolution in military affairs and *Joint Vision 2010* has emerged more or less from the same military institutions of education and training suffers from serious flaws of context and analysis, all of which derive from the weaknesses of Taylorite/Huntingtonian paradigm. To generalize, military science as evolved in U.S. places of military education in training in the 19th and 20th centuries has been joined with the worst aspects of U.S. applied education for the professions, that is, business schools and vocational training, to aspire to a universality in the internationalization of defense and military education that began in the early 1990s with the end of the Cold War.

The reappearance of irregular warfare/terrorism/guerillas in the past decade has challenged this pseudoscientific paradigm just as revolutionary warfare and small wars in the era of the French Revolution challenged the social system and armies of absolutist Europe; just as irregular warfare challenged European empires and armies from the end of the 19th century through the middle of the 20th century. The pseudo-scientific, Taylorite-Huntingtonian approach has produced a military education realm of ideas and institutions, which well resembles old regime Europe in 1792 in the face of the mobilization of Lazare Carnot or of the British Army unhinged in its mental foundations by the drubbing it received from the Boers in 1899–1900.

Conclusion and Warning

As I conclude, perhaps my humanistic Central European ideal signifies just a caricature, and my depiction of my own experience in the teeth of Taylorite/Huntington false consciousness in more than 30 years in the U.S. system reeks of the *Nestbeschmutzung* of a middling functionary close to his retirement. Surely, such a sin is probable in my case. Perhaps I as much naively romanticize my associates and mentors in the foundation of the Bundeswehr as much as I damn my colleagues embarked on the questionable enterprise of erecting Western style militaries in Iraq and Afghanistan, or in Pakistan based on counterinsurgency doctrine crookedly atop a pseudoscientific basis in education and training. You shall decide whether my theory has any validity at all. Maybe an exact replica of the Bundeswehr University has as little future in Kabul as a lovingly crafted duplicate of the USMA has there, as well.

But there is a more urgent question here, which speaks more directly perhaps to globalization and its consequences for the ideas that are at the basis of how we might internationalize defense and military education that arises from contemporary conflict as well as the state of the popular mind in the midst of the dual crisis of terrorism and economic dislocation on a huge scale. Perhaps al Qaeda terrorism and the Euro-Atlantic stock market crash have ended globalism and globalization, in which case the question is moot. Perhaps Sarah Palin, Rand Paul, Hans-Christian Strache, Thilo Sarrazin, and Gert Willders symbolize the death of globalization as well. I think not, however. In fact, the peril is now more acute than was the case at the beginning of this decade.

The contrast of humanism in advanced defense education versus a pseudoscience of social engineering in uniform, what I have outlined above would be of mere academic interest were the present not confronted with fateful choices in the internationalization of defense and military education caused by the double shocks of the terror assaults and the economic crash.

The pseudoscientific approach visible in the failed revolution in military affairs of the 1990s, which expired in a humiliating set back in the Iraqi insurgency of 2003–2004, has reasserted itself in a new and even more problematic form as so called COIN, an acronym from the 1960s with its intellectual origins in British and French colonial warfare in the 19th and 20th centuries. This idea has latterly been applied to U.S. armed forces for the second time since the 1950s. I hardly need to add that the Habsburgs also engaged in counter insurgency military operations as well as irregular warfare in the Austrian way of war, especially in the 19th and 20th centuries, some of which ended rather poorly, as was also the case for other European powers in Europe, Africa, and Asia. But the Habsburgs had no U.S. Army Training and Doctrine Command, nor does the Theresianum have the same function for the political and strategic culture of your country as the USMA and its ancillary institutions have assumed in my country especially now.

This newly re-minted, yet old pseudoscientific dogma of counterterror and counter-guerilla combat (associated most recently with General David Petraeus and the U.S. Army Training and Doctrine Command and its Australian wing) relies on a mis-reading of history (The British campaign in Malaya in the 1950s as its ahistorical paradigm) as well as a misuse of social sciences (anthropology) for the purposes of victory in small wars and in counter insurgency in the 21st century. The issue here is whether the recent U.S. adaptation of counter insurgency as a grand strategy should become the guiding principle of the internationalization of defense and military education in the present once more on the same Taylorite/Huntingtonian paradigm of elite prerogatives.

The European emphasis on the comprehensive concept, with its center of gravity in non-combatant effort by civilians in the role of security building and state building, as well as the development of civil society and economy either can embrace, adapt, or reject portions of the U.S. strategy based on sound analysis and advanced study. In my experience, however, the propagation of COIN via the large bureaucratic institutions I have described above continues to adhere to the same Taylorite and Huntingtonian paradigm as before. The French and British authors of the original small wars theory and eventual doctrine shared with soldiers in the present the institutional imperative to fashion a single theoretical and practical response to the difficulties of imperial policing as well as the civil-military fusion of irregular conflict in African and Asian empires. Without such a response in professional military writing as theory and then as doctrine, the blowback effect of such irregular combat would unseat the professional, managerial, and institutional claims of expertise, rank, and authority that were as much at risk in the state and society of the 19th century as they are in the 21st century.

The original ideas of the counterinsurgents in the 19th century had a lot to do not only with the resistant native populations, and the lonely, hot, humid, and generally distant and forgotten battle fields on which they fought, but also a vested interest in the position of these same soldiers in a rapidly changing state and society, in which such warfare was never a matter of total public acclaim. That is, the theory also acted to reinforce the claims of the colonial soldiers to their fair place in the metropolitan military hierarchy that existed in both Britain and France of the day.

This phenomenon operates all the more so among the Taylorite-Huntingtonians of the moment. These men include General Petraeus and Dr. Nagel and other 21st-century versions of the small wars and imperial policemen of the past who have stepped to prominence since about 2004 as the revolution in military ground to a halt. The challenge from the men and women who wage irregular war/small wars/insurgencies/guerillas/terrorists poses an elemental test of the military profession in a constitutional state and government amid a pluralistic society. The recent instances of Yemeni ink catridge bombs via UPS and other air freight carriers, as well as the recent sighting of an unknown missile off the southern California coast undermine the pseudoscientific, applied engineering and praetorian claim to power in state and society (see the issue of the repeal of a ban on homosexuals in the U.S. military) that is the political and social outcome of the pseudoscientific, Taylorite-Huntington approach. This paradigm no longer accords with strategic reality in the present.

This flaw grows more serious because our opponents, as Martin van Creveld pointed out two decades ago in his own iconoclastic work on the education of officers, have no need of huge military bureaucracies to formulate strategic doctrines to spread through large, unwieldy operational and tactical organization on a national and international level. As an Israeli scholar, closer to the reality of irregular warfare, guerillas, and terrorists, Van Creveld admired the Viet Cong and the Mujhadeen as being happily free of structure in their flexibility to strike at colonial and imperial regular armies with the very least means to great strategic effect. But is such a thing a model for globalized military education, i.e. that military organizations emulate guerillas and terrorists in their institutions of advanced education?

Such a prescription cannot be the answer to the intellectual shortfalls of counterinsurgency doctrine, which through its misapplication of a willfully chosen historical paradigm, as well as the abuse of anthropology for the needs of strategy, but, which, in reality, is a series of grand tactics and no grand strategy at all.

16. Scholarship and the Soldier in an Age of Austerity: Experiences from the U.S. Forces[*]

In the early days of 2013, a retired rear admiral of the U.S. Navy blogged with vitriol that combat-related research conducted at an American defense university robbed the future officer of his or her prospects and trampled on naval honor—the core of the officer's credo.[1] In this allegation—and in the venom with which it was pronounced—the blogger echoed the Navy Inspector General's October 2012 report on the Naval Postgraduate School,[2] which similarly cast categorical aspersions on the whole idea of advanced study and research in and by the American armed forces. Both critiques imply further that in the heyday of the Global War on Terror, when the coffers of the Department of Defense brimmed with money, Uncle Sam was sold a bad idea that, in turn, was badly executed—this higher education thing, which will bring nothing but ill-discipline and

---

[*] Originally published as Donald Abenheim and Carolyn Halladay, "Scholarship and the Soldier in an Age of Austerity: Experiences From the U.S. Forces," in Uwe Hartmann et al., eds. *Jahrbuch Innere Fuehrung, 2013* (Berlin: Miles Verlag, 2013) pp. 34–54.

[1] RADM Andy Singer's remarks appear in the comments section appended to the online version of an article by Admiral (ret.) Henry Mauz in a publication of the U.S. Naval Institute, in which Mauz, the former Commander in Chief of the U.S. Atlantic Fleet and a graduate of the Naval Postgraduate School's electrical engineering program, gently disputed the broadest allegations in the report of Navy Inspector General Vice Admiral James P. Wisecup, which are also at issue in this chapter. See Henry H. Mauz, Jr., "Clearing the Smoke," in Proceedings Magazine, Vol. 139/2/1,320 (February 2013), available at:
http://www.usni.org/magazines/proceedings/2013-02/clearing-smoke .

[2] Available at the Naval Inspector General's website:
http://www.ig.navy.mil/Documents/ReadingRoom/NAVINSGEN%20NPS%20 Command%20Inspection%2022%20Oct%202012.pdf . The authors of this chapter, both proudly serve—and, obviously, engage in academic research—at the Naval Postgraduate School. We recognize and applaud the ideal of accountability that informs the Inspector General's task but take exception to the aspects of the October 2012 report that would strike at the very heart of the NPS mission to the detriment and discredit of our diligent students in their number.

waste to an officer corps already overburdened with the postwar draw-down and bracing for the pending budgetary collapse.

To an extent, the present war of words about officers and universities represents another manifestation of a long-standing issue. Since the 19th century— when, under pressure in the age of imperialism, the dawn of total war, the example of continental European war academies and the rise of industrial, managerial elites compelled the creation of war colleges and higher technical education first in the U.S. Navy and later the U.S. Army—advanced education, scholarship, and research in the U.S. armed forces have periodically undergone episodes of controversy and reform in the face of crisis, including quite a few postwar budget cuts.[3] Such turning points give rise to the civil-military impetus for institutional reorganization that has advanced and deepened the education of officers to good effect for both the student in uniform and the U.S. national defense—though both sets of benefits may not materialize instantaneously.

The last, most fundamental reform of advanced and professional education at arms unfolded in the late 1980s and the early 1990s with the Goldwater-Nichols Defense Act and the Skelton Commission, the work of noted parliamentarians who have long since disappeared from public life.[4] These efforts sought to lessen

---

[3] Among a large literature, see: Ira Reeves, *Military Education in the United States* (Burlington, VT: Free Press, 1914); John Masland, et al., *Soldiers and Scholars: Military Education and National Policy* (Princeton, N.J.: Princeton University Press, 1957); Gene M. Lyons and Louis Morton, *Schools for Strategy: Education and Research in National Security Affairs* (New York, Washington: Praeger, 1965); John Hattendorf, et al., *Sailors and Scholars: The Centennial History of the U.S. Naval War College* (Newport, RI Naval War College Press, 1984); Carol Reardon, *Soldiers and Scholars: The U.S., Army and the Use of Military History*, 1865–1920 (Lawrence, Kansas UP, 1990); Martin van Creveld, *The Training of Officers: From Military Professionalism to Irrelevance* (New York: Free Press, 1990); Daniel Hughes, "Professors in the Colonels' World," in Douglas Higbee, ed., *Military Culture and Education* (Burlington, VT: Ashgate, 2010); Howard Wiarda, *Military Brass versus Civilian Academics at the National War College: Clash of Cultures* (Lanham, MD: Lexington Books, 2011).
[4] Thomas Bruneau, "Reforms in Professional Military Education: the United States," in .,Bruneau, et al eds., *The Routledge Handbook of Civil-Military Relations* (Mi-

service parochialism through a reform of officer development, especially with changes to education and training in the preparation for joint command and operations at the higher levels of war. The legislation also reflected the post-Vietnam attempt to improve the strategic education of officers as part of the general reform of the forces that had begun with the abolition of conscription and a refocus on Cold-War deterrence on the operational level through improved fighting power.

The present chapter speculates on the fate of advanced study and military professionalism in the year 2012–2013 with the assumption that soldiers and educators stand before another such a parting of the ways on the themes of advanced learning and professional development in uniform. The path away from the university's gates is easier, at least at first, as it goes downhill; ultimately, however, it leads to mediocrity, the diminished horizons of the officer's future, and a degradation of fighting power.

The present stands witness to a winding down of prolonged warfare amid a period of financial stringency, in turn, piled atop the civil-military need to separate fact from fiction in the record of recent combat, security building or counter-terror campaigns that is, to distinguish legend from myth in the record of contemporary warfare and organized violence in the first years of the 21st century. All of this begs the question of how such conflicted forces will affect the professional path of men and women at arms in the decade to come, especially with the pressures of advancement in the face of fewer opportunities for service in careers organized for the perfection of the officer's general as well specialized qualifications for command. In particular, how will austerity in defense budgets, shrinkage in the battle line, and the humdrum return to peacetime garrison normalcy (if

lon Hall: New York, 2013), pp. 193–203; United States House of Representatives, Subcommittee of the Committee on Armed Services, "Another Crossroads? Professional Military Education Twenty Years After the Goldwater-Nichols Act and the Skelton Panel," House Armed Services Committee publication No. 111-67, May 20, 2009.

such is possible in the year 2013) shape the preparation for service of soldiers and sailors? How will advanced study in uniform strengthen the power of the soldierly mind in conflict weigh no less heavily than the imperatives of character at the foundation of the soldierly calling?

This chapter suggests that the accomplishments of the past in higher education and advanced research in the armed forces are at risk from a combination of civil and military perils that endanger the professional essentials of what until now has been the excellence in service and combat effectiveness, even if the strategic effectiveness of military operations since 11 September 2001 is far from a subject of consensus. Thus, the present essay poses these questions in an approach with two dimensions: a.) a summary of recent U.S. literature on military professionalism and higher military education set against the background of turbulence in American higher education beset by globalization as well as financial austerity; and b.) a case study in some depth of how these forces are at work in the authors' own institution, which has become a kind of national battlefield of these issues to the detriment of education, military professionalism, and the creation of knowledge as applied to the needs of security and defense in the present.

+++++

From the modest beginnings of the U.S. system of advanced education arms in the epoch from 1890 until 1910, this system grew and flourished amid downturns (Vietnam, for instance) so that by the 1990s, U.S. higher military education and scholarship had achieved a polish of a remarkable degree in the wake of the Cold War and the victory in the Persian Gulf in 1990–1991. These U.S. defense and military educational institutions became a vital force in the enlargement of NATO and then in the defense institution building undertaken after the 11 September 2001 terror assaults in such places as Iraq and Afghanistan.

The latter engagements, however, unfolded more as tactical unit training improvised atop the earlier setbacks of the Iraqi and

Afghan campaigns that were blind to problems of state building generally. These mixed fortunes of U.S. arms until the late years of the first decade of the new century contrasted to earlier success. Especially the shortcomings of the coalition campaigns in the epoch 2001–2006 drew outside attention to the customs and practices of military command, obedience, morale, and defense governance and management in the U.S. forces as central aspects of how armies organize and fight. There has been plenty to think and to write about in the fields of education and training as a measure of command and the fighting power of armies.

In the years 2011–2013, as the Iraq campaign has ended and the Afghan operation may or may not be in its final stages, this taking of stock has now pushed beyond the barracks square or the staff school to the wider public. Outstanding in this aspect has been a war correspondent long associated with the *Washington Post*, Tom Ricks, who has specialized in defense affairs.[5] Ricks also has written some acclaimed popular accounts of campaigns and soldiering since 11 September 2001, noteworthy for their critical tone amid what often is otherwise a slavish recycling of DoD press releases by journalist-authors who likely had no military experience before finding themselves "embedded."[6] In particular, Ricks' critique of strategic and operational blundering in the first episodes of the Iraqi campaign has made him into a muckraker of the vitals of officership, including professional military education. The health of the inner structure of the armed forces and the future of officers turn on these very issues.

---

[5] Thomas E. Ricks is a senior fellow at the politically liberal Center for a New American Security (CNAS) in Washington, D.C., and was a defense correspondent for the *Wall Street Journal* and the *Washington Post*. See his curriculum vitae at: http://www.cnas.org/ricks

[6] See Ricks' works on the last decade of warfare, including: *Fiasco: the American Military Adventure in Iraq, 2003–2005* (New York: Penguin, 2007); *The Gamble: General David Petraeus and the American Military Adventure in Iraq, 2006–2008* (New York: Penguin, 2009).

In a work titled *Generals,*[7] published in 2012, Ricks suggests that such present-day U.S. Army leaders as General Tommy Franks and others in their number embrace mediocrity because of a system that celebrates averageness at the highest ranks and punishes initiative in subordinates with a zero-defect mentality enshrined in the structure of promotion and advancement. In fact, according to Ricks, well-prepared and intelligent subordinates found tactical and operational means to surmount the varied security-building and combat challenges since 11 September,[8] whereas senior levels of command misconceived operations in their addiction to Blitzkrieg or did next to nothing in the face of frictions after the initial operation—frictions that were caused in no small part by strategic and operational decisions of their own kind.

Ricks reminds his readers that the customs and practices of high command that grew out of the Korean War and the Vietnam War allowed for no termination of officers for incompetence in command under fire. This clubby system of no public humiliation for commanders and of generous excuses made by one general for another's incompetence stands counterpoised to the reforms instituted by George Marshall as Chief of Staff in the Army in 1941.[9] One all too easily forgets the bitter experience of the U.S. Army in the mobilization of 1917, which found it so ill prepared for battle. The phenomenon eventuated again in 1940, when Marshall embarked on a relentless drive somehow to fashion tactical and operational excellence in the ranks of the U.S. Army in the face of overwhelming Axis combat superiority. In the period of mobilization following the

[7] Thomas Ricks, *The Generals: American Military Command from World War II until Today* (New York: Penguin, 2012).

[8] James Russell, *Innovation, Transformation, and War Counterinsurgency Operations in Anbar and Ninewa Provinces, Iraq, 2005–2007* (Stanford, CA: Stanford University Press, 2011).

[9] Forrest C. Pogue, *George C. Marshall,* 4 vols., (New York: Viking, 1963–1987.); Mark Stoler, *George C. Marshall: Soldier-Statesman of the American Century* (New York: Harper Collins, 1989).

French defeat in June 1940 and the outbreak of war in December 1941, Marshall purged the old army of the interwar years, beset with spit-and-polish conservatism and the stuffy, brown-shoed spirit that had reigned for decades before since 1917.

Seized of the "greatest generation" military nostalgia that operates in American political culture and thereby obscures the reality of mid-20th century America and its soldiers, Ricks idolizes select laudable aspects of the officer development and education of the interwar army. Here he somehow neglects the reactionary and blinkered aspects of the same figures, time, and place and thereby deifies Marshall in a manner that is ahistorical. Still, this cultic rendering nonetheless serves Ricks' didactic purpose in the 21st century to highlight chronic deficiencies of command that have their roots in poor preparation for the higher aspects of war and peace and the perennial problem of training dressed up in robes as education. Ricks pillories the bogus cult of elite managerial dicta and the mania of zero defects that he sees as a phenomenon of the 1950s (but which actually arose earlier) that took on pathological dimensions in the Vietnam conflict in the 1960s.

These deformities of command plagued the Iraqi and Afghan campaigns that form the center of Ricks' experience. As a result, the author advocates the rediscovery of past excellence in professional military education, just at the moment when peacetime reductions in the forces have led to alarming and destructive attempts to debase such institutions for reasons of garrison normalcy, austerity, and a barely concealed anti-intellectual agenda.

Ricks wants the professional and academic standards increased, with a regime of research and writing as found in research universities as opposed to the year off, country-club mentality that he finds in the service war colleges, but especially at the Air War College at Maxwell Field, Alabama.[10] The emphasis of such advanced military

---

[10] See the 21 February 2013 response by Ricks on his *Best Defense* blog to a United States Military Academy briefing on the problem of the officer career system and the reappearance of garrison routine, available at:

education, as Ricks writes, should be on rigorous learning in the best sense as a free, creative activity, versus routine training camouflaged as education in a manner that celebrates mediocrity and offers nothing more than a jobs mill to former officers under the motto of "any colonel can... ." He further argues that such advanced professional education should promote critical thinking to master the varied challenges of policy and strategy, and also to grapple with the unknowns of conflict that, in this age as well as in the earlier epochs of warfare, have caused so much confusion.

Ricks also rightly condemns the formalism and rigidity in the education for and experience of command, in which Clausewitz's genius is poorly rewarded in practice, and the gifts of character and intellect that yield flexibility and adaptation in combat tick no boxes on the forms that matter in the metrics of success in command. Ricks embraces the German principle that, in the face of the reality of battle as well as the preparation for conflict, one should act despite the risk of failure, rather than reward ditherers who hold back and do nothing. The author damns the toleration of incompetence enshrined in bureaucratic strictures and wants to drive it out through a renewed excellence in education imbued of the fighting spirit of a generation of young soldiers.

+++++

Ricks' manifesto of reform actually originated with insiders and students of defense education, among whom Dr. Joan Johnson-Freece, a former dean at the U.S. Naval War College in Newport, Rhode Island, stands above the rest in the current melee. [11] While her writing has been confined to a much smaller circle of readers, she

---

http://ricks.foreignpolicy.com/blog/2187?page=3 .

[11] Joan Johnson-Freese is a professor and former Chair of National Security Affairs at the Naval War College, Newport, Rhode Island.
http://www.usnwc.edu/Academics/Faculty/JoanJohnson-Freese.aspx See, among several articles: http://defense.aol.com/2011/07/23/teach-tough-think-tough-three-ways-to-fix-the-war-colleges/ Her most recent work is *Educating America's Military* (Milon Hall/New York: Routledge, 2012).

recently has offered the most trenchant and thoughtful criticism for the need to uphold excellence in advanced defense education and sustain the momentum of reforms embarked on the late 1980s and early 1990s in an era of strategic reorientation, shrinking forces, and austerity.[12]

Johnson-Freece has analyzed the elements of excellence in civilian research universities versus those in advanced professional military education in the services, in answer to the normal catcall from skeptics of service education that the higher aspects of such an undertaking should be civilianized totally. Her reforms, which again are hardly new but which face a wall of resistance wrought by civil-military factors and Colonel Blimp-like stodginess, suggest that the service colleges can emulate key aspects of such excellent universities as Princeton through a series of internal reforms of administration, faculty, curriculum, and student body. These recommendations have profound civil-military implications in a time of reductions in force and austerity.

In the first instance, such advanced education should enable middle and senior officers to be as well educated as their civilian counterparts in the halls of government and beyond. That is, to be as well prepared to serve and work in the higher reaches of strategy and policy, and nowadays, in such varied operations as post-conflict reconstruction. Active-duty officers should instruct in matters of their contemporary expertise and experience in contrast to the echelons of antediluvian former officers, removed from the present by dint of age and time.

The hiring of military retirees into civilian faculty positions, of which the service colleges and other advanced research and education institutions are more richly staffed than say in Germany, or any other leading power, should become the exception rather than the rule, and these positions should be held solely for a person of great profession-

---

[12] Joan Johnson-Freece, "The Reform of Military Education: Twenty-Five Years Later" in *Orbis,* Winter 2012, pp. 135–153.

al promise. The introduction of peer review, a tenure and promotion process, and other customs at civilian universities will work against the accumulation of unproductive faculty. Johnson-Freece also demands that the bloated administrations of defense colleges, filled as they are with former officers, also be radically reduced in force as part of austerity.

The formation and care of the curriculum should rest in the hands of those who teach it, rather than being dictated by an external committee, which often has little or no comprehension of the requirements of advanced study and research. Johnson-Freece also seeks to extirpate the "Gentleman's 'C'" of yesteryear, which often afflicts the attitude and work habits of a student body caught amid the rapid pace of military curricula, the need to feather professional progress reports with accolades and high marks, and the persistence of the view of school as a break from an officer's real work. In this connection, educators must retain sovereignty over intellectual life at their institutions. (At the same time, such curricula should remain relevant and not drift into scholastic isolation at the expense of the needs of the forces and the security of the nation.) Students should not be mollycoddled with an education conceived to reinforce self-esteem rather than to augment fighting power and to apply the means of the mind to national defense.

In many regards, Johnson-Freece's desiderata read like "carry on" to students, faculty, and leaders of the top universities of the U.S. armed forces, which manage this process, typically to the highest standards, on a daily basis—at least for the time being. In other words, making the most of Johnson-Freece's wish list is a matter of refining a well-established system that has taken shape by careful design since the end of World War II, which makes all the more dire the clarion call to dismantle these institutions and the decades of work that has gone into them—and come out of them.

+++++

According to Dr. Johnson-Freece, the fundamental principle of faculty and student life must remain academic freedom so as to ensure that all concerned engage the most bracing ideas and most rigorous search for knowledge without the dead hand of doctrine and dogma. Clearly, she looks out of her office window at a very different Naval War College than did the institution's former president, Vice Admiral James P. Wisecup. Wisecup is now the U.S. Navy's Inspector General (IG) who led the 2012 investigation of the Naval Postgraduate School in Monterey, California, and as his report makes clear, the IG has no use for academic freedom or its purveyors on the campus of a military educational institution.

Wisecup's report on NPS runs 127 pages with annexes and attachments, the conventions of its dense, legal-bureaucratic prose barely able to contain the IG team's vituperation through to the end. The words "academic freedom" come up explicitly in the IG report—as a problematic factor—in the context of intelligence oversight and identifying potential hazards in research procedures.[13] As it happens, intelligence and security, according to the IG's own Overview, were "not specifically tasked as a review area for this inspection."[14] But both areas do offer especially noisome incursions of academic freedom into the black-and-white world of by-the-book procedure and the good order and discipline found in ships of the fleet.

Tellingly, the IG does not go on to explain how, say, security regulations and academic freedom might *not* necessarily be at odds. There is no effort at squaring any circles here. Rather, the findings and recommendations both seem to assume that the two *must* conflict. The resolution that emerges in every point is the systematic diminution of academic freedom in favor of blanket rules and mechanical practices of command and obedience as found in tactical and opera-

---

[13] Navy Inspector General, Command Inspection of the Naval Postgraduate School (report), 5040, Ser. N00/1015, 22 October 2012 (hereinafter "IG Report,") pp. 16, 19–21, available at:
http://www.ig.navy.mil/Documents/ReadingRoom/NAVINSGEN%20NPS%20 Command%20Inspection%2022%20Oct%202012.pdf .
[14] IG Report, p. 3.

tional military and naval organizations focused on preparation for combat or support in the tactical sense. If, as the Observations section of this report posits, "the concept of academic freedom was often cited by NPS leadership and faculty as a reason for the lack of structure in processes and command programs,"[15] then clearly the fig leaf has been stretched far too thinly over far too much of the school's daily business. And if "the NPS leadership and faculty extended valid concerns about academic freedom to the extent that they were justifying lack of compliance with [Navy] processes, procedures, and policies"[16]—by which allegation the IG means to call into question the whole mission and organization of the school—then the obvious next step would be to curtail all this promiscuous academic freedom once and for all.

It is an odd opinion to emerge from the office tasked with upholding the letter and the spirit of the rules in the U.S. Navy. In the United States, academic freedom—which includes the right to teach and the right to learn without undue interference or penalty—represents a special category of Constitutional protections that the U.S. Supreme Court has recognized and upheld with vigor and consistency for decades. As the court wrote more than a half century ago:

The essentiality of freedom in the community of American universities is almost self-evident. No one should underestimate the vital role in a democracy that is played by those who guide and train our youth. To impose any strait jacket upon the intellectual leaders in our colleges and universities would imperil the future of our Nation. No field of education is so thoroughly comprehended by man that new discoveries cannot yet be made. Particularly is that true in the social sciences, where few, if any, principles are accepted as absolutes. Scholarship cannot flourish in an atmosphere of suspicion and distrust. Teachers and students must always remain free to inquire, to study

---

[15] IG Report, p. 4.
[16] IG Report, p. 4.

and to evaluate, to gain new maturity and understanding; otherwise, our civilization will stagnate and die.[17]

As such, academic freedom forms part of those freedoms of expression and association that, for their inherent importance to democracy, are enshrined in the very first item in the Bill of Rights.

Most specifically, a 1967 case, *Keyishian et al. v. Board of Regents of the University of the State of New York et al.*, stands for the proposition that academic freedom represents "a special concern of the First Amendment, which does not tolerate laws that cast a pall of orthodoxy over the classroom."[18] "Orthodoxy" in the *Keyishian* case refers to a loyalty oath—anti-Communist, of course—that was at the center of this case. But academic freedom means rather more, particularly in the contemporary NPS context. As with all First Amendment protections, the concern on campuses is with unnecessarily restrictive policies, unduly "norming" centralization, duplicative reviews, and other tactics that effect an unreflexive orthodoxy or otherwise have a "chilling effect" on the lively and free exchange of ideas.

On the other hand, academic freedom is not absolute. The same sensitivity of the academic mission that makes the ready exchange of ideas indispensible also imparts clear responsibilities to practitioners. This aspect of academic responsibility echoes in the *Keyishian* dissent.[19] It also appears explicitly in the American Association of University Professors "1940 Statement of Principles on Academic Freedom and Tenure":

Academic freedom is essential … and applies to both teaching and research. Freedom in research is fundamental to the advancement of truth. Academic freedom in its teaching aspect is fundamental for the

---

[17] *Sweezy v. New Hampshire*, 354 U.S. 234 (1957) at 250.
[18] 385 U.S. 589 (1967) at 603.
[19] 385 U.S. 589, 695. The majority opinion is binding, but in a 5-4 decision, the other views still carry a certain weight.

protection of the rights of the teacher in teaching and of the student to freedom in learning. *It carries with it duties correlative with rights.*[20]

Thus, the first of the statement's three principles on academic freedom begins with: "Teachers are entitled to full freedom in research and in the publication of the results, ..." a statement qualified only insofar as the research activity may entail commercial gain. Then, the third point reads in its entirety:

College and university teachers are citizens, members of a learned profession, and officers of an educational institution. When they speak or write as citizens, they should be free from institutional censorship or discipline, but their special position in the community imposes special obligations. As scholars and educational officers, they should remember that the public may judge their profession and their institution by their utterances. Hence, they should at all times be accurate, should exercise appropriate restraint, should show respect for the opinions of others, and should make every effort to indicate that they are not speaking for the institution.

If anything, the later "interpretive comments" to the AAUP's statement of principles make even more of academic responsibility, with prominent mention of ethics codes and other self-policing mechanisms. The onus, thus, rests in the first instance with the faculty. And other than its overwhelmingly civilian character, the faculty at NPS gave the IG no particular cause for concern, according to the report.

Importantly, if the law—or official policy—seeks to intervene in this balance of freedom and responsibility, as the *Keyishian* case make clear, the government requires a legitimate interest and a narrowly focused regulation.[21] The protection of classified information

---

[20] The entire 1940 Statement of Principles is available at:
http://www.aaup.org/AAUP/pubsres/policydocs/contents/1940statement.htm ; emphasis added.
[21] 385 U.S. 589, 602, quoting *Shelton v. Tucker,* 364 U.S. 479 (1960), at 488.

represents one such legitimate interest—though even then, the exact limitations require careful explication. Again, the conversation is constant and assumes a good-faith exchange—which is rather the opposite of a mechanical, on-high pronouncement of How All Research Will Proceed Forever.

Various DoD guidance includes paragraphs dedicated by name to academic freedom. The NPS instruction on News Media Release Procedures similarly makes specific mention of academic freedom. In other words, "academic freedom" is not just the alibi of a gaggle of shiftless civilians, sucking up Navy dollars on the left coast; it enjoys pride of place in the Defense Department's ideal for the advanced education of military officers. The Navy itself has embraced this idea since at least 1975; the universally respected independent peer-review institutions that accredit the school as a legitimate university (as they also do for such universities as Stanford and University of California, Berkeley) put academic freedom at the top of their list of requirements. Assuming, of course, that there is any role for university education in the professional and intellectual development of a military officer, academic freedom is indispensible to the entire project.

+++++

A couple of points specific to NPS merit special emphasis here. First, the NPS leadership has often called on faculty and students to make the university competitive with the top-of-the-line civilian schools. Among other things, this agenda, as well as the requirements for advancement for tenure-track professors, oblige faculty to publish like their counterparts in the elite schools—widely and in a diversity of forms and fora. By the same token, faculty of this competitive caliber have high expectations of their intellectual autonomy and academic freedom. From the student side, the thesis requirement of the student officers at NPS states that meaningful original research at the graduate level demands the most open inquiry possible.

But this whole idea rests on the assumption that basic research in such diverse fields as computer science, defense economics, and policy and strategy matters—which proposition the Inspector General wants to refute on behalf of the U.S. Navy. In so many words, the IG's report tells the story of NPS as a couple of senior civilians (no mention of Vice Admiral [ret.] Daniel Oliver's distinguished Navy service before he became President of the university) with malicious intent seizing command of the school and displacing its properly military leadership. These pinstriped pirates steered it away from its planned course of career education for naval officers and heading for the foul waters of corruption on the way to Research, a fabled dark locale that lures an already soft non-uniformed faculty out of the classroom and into perdition with promises of reimbursable funds and professional advancement.

Nothing good comes of this arrangement, of course. Research flouts rules. Research disadvantages student-officers. Research promotes an un-martial ethos of individual advantage-seeking and possibly even profit, but brings nothing to NPS, the Navy, or the national defense. Whatever allegations of fraud, waste, or abuse might have led the IG to campus in 2012, the most egregious transgression, according to the report, was the central role of research in the school. This same charge fuels the blogosphere chorus from disappointed retired midgrade officers who would pile on invective in the name of a research-free NPS.

A little bit of context goes a long way in this case, however—and a rather different plot emerges from a brief examination of the record of how NPS arrived in its current state, which the IG's examiners decry as shambolic and unmilitary. This record unfolds in a series of studies by Navy boards or civilian commissions on the school's role in graduate education for the naval officers, starting at least in 1947, with an American Council of Education report on NPS—the so-called Heald Commission.[22] This effort coincided with

---

[22] The chronology appears in the "Report of the Graduation Education Study Committee," 25 October 1972, pp. 5-6, available at:

the Navy's broader restructuring of its educational function following World War II and in response specifically to the Pye Board of 1944, which addressed this topic. This period at NPS saw a shift away from narrow, technical training imparted largely by uniformed instructors and back to the model of university-style education of officers that had prevailed before the war. The result—a mainly civilian faculty conducting graduate-level courses in curricula specific to BuPers projections and requirements—were also more in line with President Truman's Education for Democracy ideals.[23]

Similarly, in 1973—with the end of the Vietnam War in sight and the dawn of the all-volunteer force breaking over military planning and policy—NPS undertook another comprehensive evaluation of its programs and their suitability for the changing times. The "Report of the Graduate Education Committee" of 20 July 1973 concerns itself most with the needs of unrestricted line officers in the new U.S. Navy and outlines an Operational Systems curriculum, which, indeed, commenced its work on campus as the Operational Research department. Tellingly, the response of the committee was to make even more of the approach that NPS had honed since 1947. The report concludes: "The successful manager ashore who is able to win political and budget battles gains the expertise and knowledge to do this from graduate educational development coupled with broad experience across many disciplines."[24]

Then in April 1975, Secretary of the Navy J. William Middendorf appointed his own committee to "advise the Chief of Naval Education and Training concerning those curricula of the Navy graduate education program.[25] The committee was headed by George Maslach,

---

http://hdl.handle.net/10945/13860 .

[23] See Vol. 1 and excerpts of Vol. 2 of the Truman document at:
http://courses.education.illinois.edu/eol474/sp98/truman.html

[24] Report of the Graduate Education Committee, p. iv.

[25] The charter appears in an appendix of the Report of the Navy Graduate Education Program Select Committee for the Secretary, U.S. Navy, 9 September 1975, Vol. 1 and Appendices A and D of Vol. 2 (hereinafter the "Maslach Report"), p. A-1.

then the Provost of the University of California, Berkeley, and a member of the NPS Academic Advisory Board. The so-called Maslach report prompted several changes at the school that significantly inform the way NPS works even today.

Perhaps the most urgent message in the Maslach report concerned the intrinsic necessity of research to graduate education, especially in the military connection: "Research activities that are relevant to the mission of the institution are an absolute necessity for graduate level programs at any location."[26] The report goes on to commend NPS for its "high-quality research program"[27] and urges the continued development of research at the school, following the particular approach that had eventuated by then: "The research programs at NPS have developed to a relatively high level of productivity as a result of the relationships that exist between program sponsors, between ex-graduates in operational assignments and the NPS institution and a host of other internal naval communication linkages."[28]

"Big George" Maslach was himself an aeronautical engineer, who began his career at Berkeley as a research professor. In his own way, much as Thomas Ricks sets up George Marshall as an ideal of the past, one can say that Maslach, an architect of the rise of the University of California in its glory years of the 1950s and 1960s, embodies the same lost spirit in American public life and the customs of leading institutions. He can be depicted as the measure of the conflicted civil-military relations of the present, which the NPS IG report manifests. His example casts into relief the differing degrees of engagement of the energies of civil society to the needs of an educated officer corps that now are but a faint memory and stuff of twisted legend in the present.

The eight-man panel under Maslach also included representatives from other university engineering departments and industry, as well as the technical director of the Naval Weapons Center at China

---

[26] Maslach Report, p. 27.
[27] Maslach Report, p. 16.
[28] Maslach Report, pp. 14–15.

Lake. As a group, these men all had extensive experience with research in graduate education and its connections with both the private sector and the Defense Department. (Brigadier General [USAF, ret.] Robert A. Duffy joined the committee in his role as president of Draper Laboratory, a not-for-profit R&D undertaking.) They benefitted from all aspects of this relationship, but they also believed that it represented an integral aspect of graduate-level scholarship.

As it happened, Maslach came to the NPS study as a veteran of an earlier battle about research and universities' missions—a chestnut of the U.S. student "revolutions" of the 1960s, at least as regards undergraduate education. From the lofty heights of the University of California at the very moment that uproar of the Vietnam War and social upheaval in the United States began, Maslach weighed in in an interview with Look Magazine that appeared in February 1965, with a cover story on student protests at Berkeley. "Research and teaching are synonymous words," Maslach said by way of refuting the protestors' claim that research and teaching are somehow in opposition. "If you don't do research, you're going to be a trade school."[29]

He and his colleagues brought this same vision to their study of NPS a decade later. "It is important to note that the NPS has a primary orientation to teaching but that research is essential for the vitality of the institution and the educational requirements of the students," the report notes. "The NPS is commended for its development of a viable high quality research program and is urged to continue this development."[30]

The varied and multifaceted influence of research within advanced study shows up in many of the other strong points that the Maslach committee remarked in its study. For example, the report vigorously defended the basic structure of coursework and thesis

---

[29] "The California Uprising: Behind the Campus Revolt," Look Magazine, Vol. 29, No. 4 (23 February 1965), pp. 30–42; the Maslach quote appears on p. 38.
[30] Maslach Report, p. 16.

writing as the hallmark of NPS's educational mission—as opposed to training:

Education can be described as the acquisition of fundamental knowledge and the ability necessary to apply that knowledge to the solution of problems over a wide range of conditions and circumstances. Training, on the other hand, can best be described as the conditioning of thought processes and physical and mental responses to react in a specific way to a specific set of stimuli. Education and training are both important but they should not be confused in the learning process.[31]

Research is not merely of theoretical value in the grand scheme of education, the Maslach report continues. "In some instances the outcome of research findings from student and faculty activities has had an impact on facilities and operations of the Navy. Many examples of this interchange can be cited from the data that was reviewed."[32] The report describes two examples—one engineering/technical and one on costing methods—from the time that had immediate effects on real-world Navy issues.

In the intervening decades, research has blossomed at NPS with meaningful results for the Navy and the U.S. national security to say nothing of the international dimension of the university among dozens of nations that send their student officers to Monterey. NPS faculty and their graduate students embraced and explored little understood aspects of commando operations and other facets of irregular and low-intensity warfare long before U.S. forces required them. Similarly, researchers at NPS spent much of the 1990s developing and refining UAVs—at a time when institutional inertia precluded any such efforts elsewhere in the military. And research at NPS on the institutional change of armed forces, government, and the international system in the 1990s further provided technical expertise to a new generation of soldier-experts in multilateral defense affairs that has been of particular need in the combined, joint operations as well

---

[31] Maslach Report, p. 11.
[32] Maslach Report, p. 15.

as defense institution building of the past ten years. Clearly, such research in service of practice as well as in benefit of knowledge in its most pure form—much of incremental work that built on years of accumulated learning at NPS—continues to the advantage of naval officers at the school and beyond, to say nothing of the national defense.

To be sure, the enduring successes of research owe something to the civil-military interface at NPS. The Maslach report pointed out as much:

The Committee was observant of the fact that there is a strong influence prevalent at the NPS under which the mature naval officers bring their experiences into the classroom. They often challenge the professors and each other to relate fundamentals to actual operational experience. The professors on the other hand challenge the students to relate operational happenings to fundamental knowledge. This is a very desirable educational advantage, which could only happen in an institution like NPS, which has a critical mass of officer trainees and a Navy-oriented faculty. In civilian universities there is also cross-fertilization but on a much different level since students are younger, less experienced and almost totally oriented to the industrialized private sector. The Committee recommends that this value be preserved at NPS.[33]

To Maslach & Co., a Navy-oriented faculty was not a matter of corralling a bunch of egg-headed civilians with chapter and verse from the Bluejacket's Manual. It was a purposeful comingling of worlds and expertise.

It is important to note that achievement of the overall goals of specialty and subspecialty education at NPS is highly dependent upon the "Navy-ization" of the civilian faculty. Only by having a dedicated faculty that is knowledgeable of Navy problems and proce-

---

[33] Maslach Report, p. 14.

dures together with effective school leadership can this be accomplished. This has happened and is continuing to happen at NPS. As a comparison the faculty at civilian universities are "industry-ized" and have an orientation toward the broader scope of industrial and business applications in the private sector.

The 1975 Navy Graduate Education Select Study Commission was full of defense-minded civilians. One of their number—Donald Rice, then president of the RAND Corporation—later became Secretary of the Air Force after a long career in OSD, while another, Sanders, served as an Under Secretary of the Navy after nearly 20 years on the staff of the House Appropriations Committee. Yet a third, William J. Perry, went on to become Secretary of Defense and continues to write and research as a distinguished fellow at the Hoover Institution at Stanford University. Surely their views of how graduate education at NPS should unfold has some relevance even today—beyond the historical curiosity of a bunch of old documents.

The old documents matter here, as well, because they tell a rather different story than the 2012 IG's report on NPS. They show that when Vice Admiral (Ret.) Oliver presided over an expansion of the school's research activity starting in 2008, he was continuing on a course that the school and the Navy had embraced decades earlier. They show that the education of naval officers is not diminished or disadvantaged by research but, in fact, that research is central to the whole undertaking. They show that the incentive of reimbursable funding, which is at the heart of such research, is neither automatically corrupt nor a zero-sum loss for the students, the school, or the Navy. And they show that the Navy and research—specifically research at NPS—get along just fine.

More importantly, in more than 35 years, the Navy has not refuted, rejected, or even seriously questioned the Maslach report or its predecessors. In other words, the findings and the Navy's embrace of them have remained in full effect. The research arrangements on campus have been reviewed several times since by both the civilian university accreditation agencies that certify NPS's academic value, would-be legislative base closers, and successive Navy IGs—the last one in 2009.

Meanwhile, in the face of such threats as cyber warfare, proliferating nuclear weapons, the generalized change in the face of conflict, and the perils of climate change for security and defense, the Navy still requires an educated officer corps at least as urgently now as it did at the dawn of the atomic age in 1946. And the Navy still requires the fruits of far-ranging research, including the projects that only NPS can develop. By the numbers given in the 2012 report, both the Navy and NPS graduates remain overwhelmingly favorable in their estimation of the education—and research opportunities—that NPS provides.

NPS has proven itself amenable to change, and should any of the factors that inform its approach to research and education demand a new approach, the university will rise to the tasks, as it has done for the better part of a century. But so far, the only thing that has changed is the view of a new IG, who seems to have emerged from his own experience with higher education in the military—he headed the Naval War College immediately before assuming his current post—with a desire to norm NPS into a more rigidly Navy-like operation.

The old documents—and the current views on campus and in Washington that they inform—show that such a project would undo decades of careful development. It would deny NPS of the very thing that makes it work for the Navy, and it would deny the students of NPS.

+++++

More noteworthy, however, than this spleen-venting about research and arms by frustrated former officers with an axe to grind about higher education and the challenges of research, a leading admiral of the U.S. Navy in the realm of special operations, Admiral William McCraven, was himself once an NPS graduate student. This man eventually made his way through ever more successful com-

mands to service in the highest reaches of government and then, finally, to command of joint specified U.S. Special Operations Command, which has in the past decade played a pivotal role in the present conflict. His master's thesis of historical case studies of commando raids and clandestine operations (written in the 1990s when he
was a USN commander as special forces were just emerging from
obscurity), later published as a well received book, in fact, can be said
to have been the blue print for the spring 2011 special operations
seizure and assassination of Osama bin Laden in his Pakistani re-
doubt. In this case, research and scholarship carried out at a defense
university apparently influenced policy and military operations in
beneficial manner. This rather famous case represents one of many in
their variety that have failed to make headlines but which have surely
played a role in saving lives and in the strengthening of combat power
in the counter-terror conflict since 11 September 2001.

   This same irregular conflict accelerated the ongoing restructuring of the German armed forces under the motto of
Vom Einsatz her denken, that is, the requirements of security building
operations and outright fighting should guide the present reform and
restructuring of the German armed forces amid budgetary strictures,
which in this case have been too draconian since the end of the Cold
War. The primacy of operations jammed into a narrow horizon, that
is to say, the tactical level of war and garrison routine stand in conflict
with the tradition of the educated officer and the civil-military institutions of the excellence of military professionalism in Germany. This
perennial conflict in its contemporary form poses questions about the
efficacy of research and education in the armed forces in Germany
and elsewhere in the leading democracies and their armies.

   A German readership guided by the theory and practice of *Innere Führung* can surely profit from this personal and willful examination of aspects of scholarship and soldiers in the United States in the
year 2012–2013, even if the political culture and military institutions
of Germany and the United States differ in their character and evolution. In a fundamental sense, German and American institutions of
advanced learning in uniform are joined by a community of fate that

makes this analysis relevant and germane for a readership in continental Europe. The forces of disintegration and the challenges to the educated officer elucidated here hardly are confined to the authors' place of birth and have become generalized in a period of unprecedented crisis in society, culture and economy.

Both the United States and Germany in the course of the latter decades of the 20th century more or less in identical spirit and in close coordination brought their institutions of higher learning associated with armies to a high state of excellence, which today is threatened not only by a collapsing budget, but also by less tangible, but no less pernicious phenomena within the services as well as within society and economy generally. The destructive energy in the services is well encapsulated in the outlandish and wrong-headed assertion in the U.S. Navy IG report damning research in defense as a threat to naval training. Ricks and Johnson-Freece have called rightly for the reinforcement of standards in education, in which Clausewitz's freedom in obedience finds its own particular expression in the officer student's need for excellence in education as a means to achieve the higher aspects of his or her career at arms. Thus is the officer, his or her service, and the national defense strengthened and improved. Hacking at the marrow of the university in the armed forces begets entirely the opposite results.

Carola Hartmann Miles-Verlag

Politik, Gesellschaft, Militär

Uwe Hartmann, *Innere Führung. Erfolge und Defizite der Führungsphilosophie für die Bundeswehr,* Berlin 2007.

Hans-Christian Beck, Christian Singer (Hrsg.), *Entscheiden – Führen – Verantworten. Soldatsein im 21. Jahrhundert,* Berlin 2011.

Reiner Pommerin (ed.), *Clausewitz goes global. Carl von Clausewitz in the 21ˢᵗ Century,* Berlin 2011.

Eberhard Birk, Winfried Heinemann, Sven Lange (Hrsg.), *Tradition für die Bundeswehr. Neue Aspekte einer alten Debatte,* Berlin 2012.

Holger Müller, *Clausewitz' Verständnis von Strategie im Spiegel der Spieltheorie,* Berlin 2012.

Angelika Dörfler-Dierken, *Führung in der Bundeswehr,* Berlin 2013.

Wolf Graf von Baudissin, *Grundwert Frieden in Politik – Strategie – Führung von Streitkräften,* hrsg. von Claus von Rosen, Berlin 2014.

Marcel Bohnert, Lukas J. Reitstetter (Hrsg.), *Armee im Aufbruch. Zur Gedankenwelt junger Offiziere in den Kampftruppen der Bundeswehr,* Berlin 2014.

Arjan Kozica, Kai Prüter, Hannes Wendroth (Hrsg.), *Unternehmen Bundeswehr? Theorie und Praxis (militärischer) Führung,* Berlin 2014.

Angelika Dörfler-Dierken, Robert Kramer, *Innere Führung in Zahlen. Streitkräftebefragung 2013,* Berlin 2014.

Phil C. Langer, Gerhard Kümmel (Hrsg.), *„Wir sind Bundeswehr." Wie viel Vielfalt benötigen/vertragen die Streitkräfte?,* Berlin 2015.

Dirk Freudenberg, *Counterinsurgency. Aufstandsbekämpfung als Phase zur Überwindung schwacher Staatlichkeit und zur Etablierung des Aufbaus einer stabilen Nachkriegsordnung?,* Berlin 2016.

… Bach, Walter Sauer (Hrsg.), *Schützen.Retten.Kämpfen. Dienen für …land,* Berlin 2016.

Dirk Freudenberg, Stephan Maninger, *Neue Kriege. Sicherheitspoliti-sche Rahmenbedingungen, Mentalitäten, Strategien, Methoden und Instrumente,* Berlin 2016.

Alessandro Rappazzo, *Vorsprung durch Leadership. Modernes Lea-dership in der Armee,* Berlin 2017.

Wolfgang Peischel (Hrsg.): *Wiener Strategie-Konferenz 2016 – Strategie neu denken,* Berlin 2017.

Oliver Schmidt, *Deutsche Außenpolitik und die Zukunft der nuklearen Teilhabe in der NATO,* Berlin 2017.

Dirk Freudenberg, *Theorie des Irregulären, 3 Bde.,* Berlin 2017.

Militärgeschichte

Eberhard Kliem, Kathrin Orth, *"Wir wurden wie blödsinnig vom Feind beschossen". Menschen und Schiffe in der Skagerrakschlacht 1916,* Berlin 2016.

Eberhard Birk, *"Auf Euch ruht das Heil meines theuern Württemberg!". Das Gefecht bei Tauberbischofsheim am 24. Juli 1866 im Spiegel der württem-bergischen Heeresgeschichte des 19. Jahrhunderts,* Berlin 2016.

Eckhard Lisec, *Der Unabhängigkeitskrieg und die Gründung der Türkei 1919–1923,* Berlin 2016.

Hans Frank, Norbert Rath, *Kommodore Rudolf Petersen. Führer der Schnellboote 1942–1945. Ein Leben in Licht und Schatten unteilbarer Ver-antwortung,* Berlin 2016.

Eckhard Lisec, *Der Völkermord an den Armeniern im 1. Weltkrieg – Deutsche Offiziere beteiligt?,* Berlin 2017.

Ingo Pfeiffer, *Heinz Neukirchen. Marinekarriere an wechselnden Fronten,* Berlin 2017.

Siegfried Lautsch, *Grundzüge des operativen Denkens in der NATO. Ein zeitgeschichtlicher Rückblick auf die 1980er Jahre,* Berlin 2017.

Viktor Toyka, *Dienst in Zeiten des Wandels. Erinnerungen aus 40 Jahren Dienst als Marineoffizier 1966-2006,* Berlin 2017.

Monterey Studies

Uwe Hartmann, *Carl von Clausewitz and the Making of Modern Strategy,* Potsdam 2002.

Zeljko Cepanec, *Croatia and NATO. The Stony Road to Membership,* Potsdam 2002.

Ekkehard Stemmer, *Demography and European Armed Forces,* Berlin 2006.

Sven Lange, *Revolt against the West. A Comparison of the Current War on Terror with the Boxer Rebellion in 1900-01,* Berlin 2007.

Klaus M. Brust, *Culture and the Transformation of the Bundeswehr,* Berlin 2007.

Donald Abenheim, *Soldier and Politics Transformed,* Berlin 2007.

Michael Stolzke, *The Conflict Aftermath. A Chance for Democracy: Norm Diffusion in Post-Conflict Peace Building,* Berlin 2007.

Frank Reimers, *Security Culture in Times of War. How did the Balkan War affect the Security Cultures in Germany and the United States?,* Berlin 2007.

Michael G. Lux, *Innere Führung – A Superior Concept of Leadership?,* Berlin 2009.

Marc A. Walther, *HAMAS between Violence and Pragmatism,* Berlin 2010.

Frank Hagemann, *Strategy Making in the European Union,* Berlin 2010.

Ralf Hammerstein, *Deliberalization in Jordan: the Roles of Islamists and U.S.-EU Assistance in stalled Democratization,* Berlin 2011.

Jochen Wittmann, *Auftragstaktik,* Berlin 2012.

Michael Hanisch, *On German Foreign und Security Policy. Determinants of German Military Engagement in Africa since 2011,* Berlin 2015.

´égoire Monnet, *The Evolution of Strategic Thought Since September 11,* ´. Berlin 2016.

ttp://www.miles-verlag.jimdo.com

ʕ